THE THEATRE OF DAVID GREIG

Clare Wallace is an associate professor at the Department of Anglophone Literatures and Cultures at Charles University, Prague, and also teaches at the University of New York in Prague. She is author of *Suspect Cultures: Narrative, Identity & Citation in 1990s New Drama*, and has edited various other volumes including *Monologues: Theatre, Performance, Subjectivity*, *Stewart Parker Television Plays* and with Anja Müller *Cosmotopia: Transnational Identities in the Work of David Greig*.

THE THEATRE OF DAVID GREIG

Clare Wallace

Series Editors: Patrick Lonergan and Erin Hurley

B L O O M S B U R Y

LONDON • NEW DELHI • NEW YORK • SYDNEY

Bloomsbury Methuen Drama
An imprint of Bloomsbury Publishing Plc

50 Bedford Square	1385 Broadway
London	New York
WC1B 3DP	NY 10018
UK	USA

www.bloomsbury.com

Bloomsbury is a registered trade mark of Bloomsbury Publishing Plc

First published 2013

© Clare Wallace, 2013

British Library Cataloguing-in-Publication Data
A catalogue record for this book is available from the British Library.

ISBN: HB: 978-1-4081-5732-9
PB: 978-1-4081-5739-8
ePub: 978-1-4081-5951-4
ePDF: 978-1-4081-6060-2

Library of Congress Cataloging-in-Publication Data
A catalog record for this book is available from the Library of Congress.

Typeset by Deanta Global Publishing Services, Chennai, India
Printed and bound in Great Britain

CONTENTS

Contents

ACKNOWLEDGEMENTS

The business of writing books incurs many debts of different sorts but small space to honour them. First and foremost I would like to thank Louis Armand and Hugh who have lived with and through this project while busy with some very important projects of their own. I am ever grateful to David Greig for his good humoured co-operation from the very beginning, offering not only his time and his typescripts, but also his contacts. Likewise, I am enormously indebted to Philip Howard, Vicky Featherstone, Guy Hollands and Wils Wilson who despite many more pressing commitments gave their time to share their unique insights. Marilena Zaroulia and David Pattie were similarly exemplary participants in this project delivering more than expected with welcome punctuality. Thank you all.

The generosity of Graham Eatough, Dan Rebellato and Nadine Holdsworth in sharing some of their hugely useful forthcoming material from *the Suspect Culture Book* and *Modern British Playwriting: 2000-2009*. I hope I have done some justice to their work here. My enthusiasm for Greig's work was encouraged long ago by Aleks Sierz; it developed into a fruitful editorial in collaboration with Anja Müller, and has been enriched by a semester of discussions with Verónica Rodríguez whose research on Greig, globalization and ethics will certainly overtake my efforts, and which I look forward to reading in the near future. Both Verónica and Julia Boll helped me locate materials unavailable in Prague, practical assistance for which I am thankful. Also in the realm of the practical, but vital, Dagmar Lorenz-Meyer helped me with creative childminding co-operations during the summer holidays and lent technological support as well. Finally, the intellectual enthusiasm and collegial spirit of Martin Middeke continue to be a much-valued support and inspiration.

Many thanks to Mark Dudgeon at Methuen Drama for commissioning this book; to Emily Hockley and Kim Muranyi for bringing it to completion and to Patrick Lonergan for patient reviewing and his helpful suggestions.

This book was supported by the 'Programme for the Development of Research Areas at Charles University, P09, Literature and Art in Intercultural Relations,' sub-programme 'Transformations of the Cultural History of the Anglophone Countries: Identities, Periods Canons.'/Tato kniha bylo vydáno v rámci Programu rozvoje vědních oblastí na Univerzitě Karlově č. P09, Literatura a umění v mezikulturních souvislostech, podprogram Proměny kulturních dějin anglofonních zemí identity, periody, kánony.

INTRODUCTION

David Greig: In and Out of Context

It is 2005 and David Greig is doing a play for a group of students and scholars at a theatre conference in Bremen in the north of Germany. The play is *Being Norwegian*, the actors are plastic dolls, Barbie and Action Man, manipulated by Greig as the puppet master, and their playing space is a table. The conference theme is mapping uncertain territories, space and place in contemporary drama. Somehow the incongruity of the performance scenario neatly matches the subject of the play. *Being Norwegian* is a short, bitter-sweet piece about two lonely souls, Lisa and Sean, who find themselves together late at night in Sean's flat after the pub has closed, talking. Both are vulnerable outsiders: Sean reveals how he spent time in prison, messed up his marriage and is estranged from his son; Lisa explains her sense of difference from the society around her by insisting that she is really from Norway. Both survive by withdrawing from reality; Sean isolates himself from the society sitting alone in his flat and the pub, and Lisa becomes a Norwegian. Strange as it may seem it is Lisa's projected identity that creates a space of bizarre potential, a utopian other self-unencumbered by the mundane frustrations of daily existence. And she encourages Sean to share this space by deciding that he too is a Norwegian. The play concludes with the pair swaying quietly in each other's arms and listening to A-ha's 1985 pop hit 'Take on me' – as Lisa puts it: 'Just two Norwegians/ Holding on to each other/In a foreign land' (454). It is typical of Greig's sense of humour that in his hands Barbie and Action Man can manage to take us on a journey through uncertain spaces of self-doubt, failure and fantasy, on the surface of a nondescript table, to the tune of 1980's New Wave pop. Also characteristic is how we are encouraged to recognize, amid the detritus of everyday failures and disappointments, how performative identities can defy the constraints of the everyday and enable some tentative forms of tender human contact.

That subtle blend of comic quirkiness, sadness and contemporary alienation was what first attracted me to Greig's work and leads to many of the core concerns of his theatre that will be explored in this book – questions of identity, belonging and interaction in a world where disjunction and dislocation increasingly seem to dominate. And although the improvised puppet performance of *Being Norwegian* (a piece originally produced as a radio play, but staged in 2007) was perhaps more a product of the conference context than some formal aesthetic programme, the style of presentation accentuated an approach that is far from merely accidental. A tension between comic and serious, distance and proximity, fantasy and reality sits at the heart of Greig's flexible, questing dramaturgy. If the use of mass-produced plastic toys initially produced a distancing humorous effect, the crisis of self-definition that the play gently presents is all too recognizable; so in the end, the comic aspects of the play become entangled with a sense of empathy with the plights of the characters. This method of a loosely epic or neo-Brechtian form of storytelling, at once reflective and engaging, is a primary and wonderfully potent quality of Greig's plays to date.

It is tempting, and to a degree justified to read David Greig's fascination with uncertain territories and peculiar polarities in terms of his own background. Born in Edinburgh in 1969, Greig spent much of his first ten years in Nigeria, where his father worked. The family returned to Edinburgh in 1980, and then in 1987 he went south to study English and Drama at Bristol University. Since the early nineties he has lived in Scotland and has gone on to become a key figure in contemporary Scottish theatre. Yet the question of identity remains open, and is one he has frequently addressed both in his work and in his interviews. Greig attributes his sense of being caught between 'a powerful compulsive desire to be rooted and a powerful awareness that I'm not' (Fisher 2011: 15–16) to his experience of growing up abroad and returning to a home that he still felt detached from. At the same time, when he decided to become a writer, he was convinced that he had to be based in Scotland in order to free himself from being defined primarily by his Scottishness. Oscillating between such 'a powerful pair of extremes' (Fisher 2011: 15) has meant that a sense of belonging is something he never takes entirely for granted, as is plainly illustrated in the interview later in this volume as well as throughout the work surveyed here.

That work now spans over twenty years of activity, and one of the goals of this book is to map its principle trajectories so far. It has become commonplace to remark upon how relentlessly industrious he has been, but what is more compelling in my view is the impressive variety of the theatre he has produced. The chronology at the back of this volume provides a synopsis of that work intended to serve as an orientation guide to its wide-ranging and rapidly expanding territory. Greig's imagination is seldom still and undoubtedly by the time this book appears he will already be involved with a new set of projects and playing with new aesthetic challenges. If the sheer quantity and multiplicity of his work make generalizations daunting, this type of survey provides a valuable opportunity to study its web of connections and to suggest lines of development that deserve further critical appreciation and investigation.

What I hope will emerge clearly is that despite the obvious formal and thematic heterogeneity, there is nonetheless a distinct and powerful artistic voice wedded to a deeply embedded sense of ethical commitment uniting all these works. As we will see a repeated feature of his drama and dramaturgy is the way he tackles complex and contemporary issues not only in imaginatively exciting but also in intellectually stimulating ways. Alan Read in *Theatre and Everyday Life: An Ethics of Performance* (1993) suggests that in the midst of the compromised and compromising circulation of images and consumer experiences, theatre may 'distinguish' itself by 'an ethical stance':

> Theatre after all contributes to an idea of social or public good the best organisation of which should be the central debate of a public politics. Theatre's narratives, however disjunct through aesthetic experiment, always offer alternative realities and insights to the everyday. (Read 1993: 6)

This is fundamentally what I see Greig's theatre over the last two decades attempting – bringing new perspectives to the ethical challenges that

3

inhere in everyday life, placing us face to face with contradictory desires and incommensurable world views, but also with the hope that there is an elusive possibility of change.

Amidst his many ongoing and simultaneous projects it is possible to tease out different strands. There is the work with Suspect Culture, the experimental company formed by Greig and Graham Eatough in the early 1990s for which he produced numerous texts up to 2008. There are the pieces for children and young people that mark a set of co-operations with the TAG and the Citizens Theatre Glasgow as well as with the National Theatre of Scotland. There are adaptation projects that range from classics to new work by authors from the Middle East. There are collaborations and most recent books (or librettos) for musicals: *Glasgow Girls* (2012) and *Charlie and the Chocolate Factory* (2013). Finally, alongside all this is a developing body of dramatic work that will be the main focus of this volume. Beyond writing for theatre, Greig is also involved in development – he has worked extensively with different groups of playwrights from Morocco, Tunisia, Palestine, Egypt, Syria and Lebanon. The 2012 *One Day in Spring* series of short plays from the Arab world staged in Òran Mór in Glasgow is a recent outcome of these contacts. Between 2005 and 2007 he served as the first Dramaturg for the National Theatre of Scotland; since 2006 he has been on the board of the Traverse Theatre in Edinburgh. He continues to be involved in leading writing workshops and has of late been an active voice in debates surrounding Creative Scotland's administration of Scotland's arts funding.

Inevitably then, Greig's theatre straddles multiple concerns that stretch from local to global and that include an assortment of practices from collaboration, through adaptation to playwriting. His plays, too, range from sprawling national histories to mini-dramas that spotlight political issues. Given this variety there are multiple, yet associated, critical contexts that are significant in terms of how the work has been received. Here, I want to briefly sketch four preliminary interpretative directions that open heterogeneous ways of understanding Greig's work and its progress.

The first is a temporal context. Greig began making theatre in the 1990s, a decade now often viewed through the lens of the much vaunted In-Yer-Face aesthetic that informed a great deal, though by no means all, new writing for theatre at that time. As I described in *Suspect Cultures: Narrative, Identity and Citation in 1990s New Drama* (2006), various attempts have been made to describe the impulses coursing through the theatre produced by that new generation of playwrights, the characteristics of the dominant aesthetic and the agendas they espoused or, in many instances, denied. Was the wave of new writing in the mid-1990s energized by the provocations of more established writers (such as Tony Kushner, David Mamet, Caryl Churchill or David Hare) and primarily attuned the problematic subject of postmodern masculinity, as suggested by David Edgar (1999: 26–7)? Was the drama of the 1990s 'collectively characterized by a more widespread emphasis on challenging physical and verbal immediacy, and bleak (arguably nihilistic) observations of social decay, severed isolation and degradation into aimlessness,' as David Ian Rabey contended (2003: 192)? Or was it the case, as Aleks Sierz claimed that what defined the new writing of the 1990s was its visceral tactics of provocation to express (albeit at times in an ambivalent manner) a modern social critique. Sierz's 'new wave' of young playwrights were busy 'questioning moral norms, . . . affronting the ruling ideas of what can or should be shown onstage [and] also tapping into more primitive feelings, smashing taboos, mentioning the forbidden, creating discomfort' (2001: 4). In other words, creating a sensation-driven, experiential type of drama that seemed to disavow established codes of political allegiance and the political correctness of the past. And the fact that so often their work seemed uninterested in 'significant public issues' (Gottlieb 1999: 212) became a bone of contention. The critical energy around new writing and an In-Yer-Face aesthetic in the 1990s, which notably Greig disassociated himself from, has as I have argued elsewhere, been a factor in the comparatively sluggish development of a scholarly response to his work during the period – a situation that is happily altering. Without doubt *In-Yer-Face Theatre: British Drama Today* (2001) provides a remarkable and vibrant account of 1990s new writing; however as with any such label it is necessarily selective. The focus was on London, the determining quality being viscerality coupled with abrasive language. The fact that David Greig's work does not fit the In-Yer-Face rubric points to the limitations of the map of new writing in the 1990s and a plurality that is obscured by a singular label. This in itself is important since it encourages us to consider a more nuanced image of British theatre at the close of the century and the forces that shaped it. And obviously as the 2000s have progressed much has changed, old maps have been redrawn, and new ones created, both theatrically and politically.

This leads me to a second context in which we might position Greig's work, a national one. Yet here too there is a plurality, since Greig is important both as a British and Scottish playwright and theatre-maker. If his role in the former context was initially under-acknowledged, partly because of the prevailing energies of In-Yer-Face theatre and intense interest in some writers associated with it like Sarah Kane and Mark Ravenhill, it was also symptomatic of a blind spot with regard to Scottish theatre more generally in the important surveys of twentieth-century British theatre. Ironically with the impacts of devolution on thinking about Britishness, this state of affairs, too, is changing. So for example, David Ian Rabey's *English Drama Since 1940* (2003) provides an insightful discussion of work by C. P. Taylor, Liz Lochead, Tom McGrath and Jimmy Boyle as an essential ingredient in 1980s British drama. Similarly, *The Cambridge History of British Theatre Volume 3* (2004) includes generous coverage of Scottish theatre, and the *Concise Companion to Contemporary British and Irish Drama* (2008) edited by Nadine Holdsworth and Mary Luckhurst energetically showcases the diversity of its subject. Additionally, there is a lengthy list of works that address Scottish theatre history and dramatic literature as a separate tradition such as Randall Stevenson and Gavin Wallace's *Scottish Theatre Since the Seventies* (1996) and Bill Findlay's *A History of Scottish Theatre* (1998) and Ian Brown's *The Edinburgh Companion to Scottish Drama* (2011) to name just a few of the most readily available.

My purpose here is to make a case for Greig's significance in both contexts (and the importance of those contexts to his work). Rather than get mired in a debate about a hierarchy of national identities and loyalties, it seems more productive to consider Greig's simultaneous roles. His work is obviously a vital element in contemporary Scottish theatre and its debates, but also, perhaps less evidently, in British theatre generally. His initial work in the Middle East after all took place under the auspices of the British Council and the Royal Court Theatre's outreach programmes. Notably, in contrast to *In-Yer-Face Theatre*, in Aleks Sierz's latest book, *Rewriting the Nation: British Theatre Today* (2011), Greig is repeatedly mentioned, signalling an appreciation of his contribution to theatre in the twenty-first century dis-United Kingdom. In fact that book closes with a quote from Greig's *Damascus* as emblematic of a new but hesitant set of attitudes to national identity that characterize British theatre writing in the first decade of the twenty-first century.

As part of a new generation of Scottish writers whose work emerged at the end of the twentieth century, Greig actively participates in the ongoing re-imagining of Scotland in the wake of devolution. That said, critics at times have seemed slightly disgruntled at the apparent lack of familiar Scottish co-ordinates in some of his work. But Greig is not alone in an ambivalence about signposting national specificity in his writing and theatre-making. Nadine Holdsworth notes how relationships between place and identity are prominent features of Scottish playwriting more generally and contends that 'there is a marked trend among many contemporary Scottish playwrights and theatre-makers to theatricalize multifarious sites, geological formations and landscapes as a way of articulating the diversity of Scotland' (2008: 126). Indeed, this discussion about place is reflected, as Holdsworth and others observe, in the founding concept of the National Theatre of Scotland, the 'theatre without walls,' which makes theatre throughout the country as opposed to being anchored in a single building. Greig too explores the imaginative space of Scotland, but the horizons of his work lie beyond any confined or simple sense of national identity – if such a thing could even be said to exist. Consequently it is hardly surprising that in a recent discussion on Scottish theatre as part of the Staging the Nation series of conversations, he argues against a defined idea of a Scottish play and for the capacious notion of a Scottish theatre landscape in which both audiences and writers grow and are mutually sustaining (2011). As he says himself, his 'experience of being Scottish has been one of being intensely and viscerally attached to a place in which [he] is perceived as a stranger' (Svich 2007: 55), largely on the basis of his non-Scottish accent. Yet, it is important to recognize that this sense of being an outsider, as the interview included in this book indicates, is also a moving target.

Co-existent with considerations of Greig's drama in national contexts is the way the work addresses a wider set of economic and cultural conditions catalysed by globalization, and broaches forms of transnational identity within the amorphous context of the contemporary. As Dan Rebellato was to observe in the introduction to *Plays 1* many of his plays stage the dilemmas of citizenship in an apparently borderless world (2002: xii–xiv). Throughout his work as part of Suspect Culture and in his own drama, time and again glimpses of the legacies of modernity and the uncertainties of postmodernity in spatial and temporal terms can been seen in its references to ideology and history, tourism and travel, industrial development and building and technologies of communication. Rebellato also, early on, remarked upon the deep 'imprint of globalisation' on Greig's theatre (2002: xiii). Similarly, we might discover the imprint of postmodernity ingrained in the ways states of alienation and belonging are elliptically portrayed. Here, I think Zygmunt Bauman's explanation of postmodern society as marked by the impossibility of being or feeling at home, of being perpetually 'out of place' (1997: 93), is especially applicable. Characters at odds with their place, whether physically or metaphysically, are everywhere in Greig's work. In the plays from the 1990s particularly the paranoia and racism of those left behind by geopolitical change, the destruction of the modernist architectural dream, or those literally or metaphorically lost in space are all aspects of this dilemma. And since 2000 the paradoxes of power and agency in a globalized environment come to the fore as concerns that animate many of the plays discussed here.

The final context I would like to raise is linked to this set of conditions and the major issue of not merely of how to represent, but of how to creatively respond to the challenges of a world subject to those conditions? Questions of identity, communication and community cannot be severed from those of ethics, agency and responsibility.

Given Greig's early interest the problem of identity within the broader context of the political transformation of Europe after the fall of Communism, his plays have often been discussed as a form of political theatre – a topic that arguably exercises a magnetic effect over British theatre criticism. Certainly not all the work he has produced is political however, if we assume his broad definition of the political as 'dealing overtly with contemporary issues of power' (Rodosthenous 2011: 3), then much of it falls within this ambit. This is especially pertinent since in the 1990s British political theatre, in the shape of the state-of-the-nation play seemed a spent force, and many of the new writers of the decade appeared to have no truck with politics. In hindsight, it is evident that the terms of political theatre had changed rather than atrophied. Amelia Howe Kritzer's *Political Theatre in Post-Thatcher Britain* (2008) – which remarkably makes no mention of Greig's work – charts developments in British political theatre since 1995 foregrounding its rejections of idealism, its use of violence, the growing popularity of verbatim techniques, its staging of the individual alienated in contemporary society, and argues that postmodern and post-structuralist theory has been detrimental to 'issue-based drama' (21). I am uncomfortable with the suggestion that the discourses of postmodernism and post-structuralism are simply synonymous or that we might hold Jean-François Lyotard, Jean Baudrillard and Jacques Derrida somehow directly responsible for the fate of 'issue-based drama' in the United Kingdom, but that is a debate for another day. Perhaps more influential than the alleged toxicity of these modes in contemporary theory and philosophy has been the convergence of the conditions they delineated with the end of the Cold War and the rise of the neo-liberal worldview that underwrites contemporary globalization. That convergence has resulted, as Dan Rebellato has incisively described (2008 and 2009), in a fundamental change in the nature of politics and the exercise of power, which necessitates a shift in cultural response.

What it might mean to produce political theatre now is a question that undoubtedly interests Greig as a writer and he has discussed the topic on several occasions in print. In 1999, when he contributed to David Edgar's *State of Play: Playwrights on Playwriting* endorsed a very general notion of political theatre, one that 'poses questions about society to which it does not already know the answer', it resists stasis; it opens a window to transformation (1999: 66–8). Returning to the question some years later, he explains how he originally

> wanted to get away from theatre that proposed dialectical solutions in the old left-wing tradition and offer a theatre that tore at the fabric of reality and opened up the multiple possibilities of the imagination. Put simply, I was saying that there is no 'political' theatre but that theatre is, by its own nature, political. (D'Monté and Saunders 2008: 212)

Current events and experience had meanwhile reshaped his ideas, and as a result, he felt that he 'was no longer satisfied with letting [his] work simply exist and not questioning whether it was helping or hindering the powers shaping our lives' (213). So in a piece included in *Cool Britannia? British Political Drama of the 1990s* (2008), Greig reworked his earlier attitudes. There he considers the possibilities of what he calls 'Rough Theatre' – an open form able 'to intervene in the management of the imagination' (218–20). Its purpose is to delve beneath the surface of the mundane, and to challenge and transcend our conceptual or imaginative default settings as a means of producing some new experience of reality. Greig's attempts to think through but also to produce a resonant, engaged and complex theatre thus seem to exemplify Rebellato's argument that in its latest form political theatre in Britain is responding to the conditions of globalization where non-realism has displaced realism, ethics rather than politics is at stake and aesthetic experimentalism is used to resist the dominant attitudes of consumer culture (2008: 259). Again, however, we should anticipate that his ideas on the subject will continue to evolve. What is clear, and will emerge throughout this book is that Greig is a theatre-maker who actively and consciously responds to these shifting conditions of the present through his creative work which addresses the complexities of post-Wall European identities, violent conflict, globalization, cross-cultural communication or even climate change.

This set of possible interpretative paths into Greig's work is, of course, not exhaustive, and while each has its merits, none works adequately if relied upon exclusively. For this reason, I have decided upon a topically orientated rather than a simply chronological structure for this study which picks out different currents of interest and focal points in Greig's oeuvre to date. As with the suggested contexts for interpretation already mapped, these are not discrete areas; rather, I see them as interlinked clusters and constellations where each node should present an aspect of Greig the playwright that ultimately contributes to comprehensive picture of his work and its nuanced ethical underpinning.

Chapters 1 and 2 largely treat major formal influences and tendencies in Greig's theatre. I begin with foregrounding Greig's involvement with Suspect Culture and the ways in which his participation in the company channelled ideas around formal experiment as well as the spaces of identity, memory and communication. It won't take long to notice that Chapter 1 is rather brief compared to the extended analysis of its successor. The reason for this imbalance is primarily that to do justice to the full range of Suspect Culture's work is well beyond the scope or objectives of this book. Moreover, I do not want to imply that Suspect Culture's output was somehow merely David Greig's playwriting in another guise. Rather, what I attempt is to identify several of the core aesthetic and thematic concerns explored collaboratively by Suspect Culture in some of their main works that then prove instrumental in Greig's drama. I also highlight the experimental impetus of the company and the ideas that informed their performances and creative practice.

Flowing from this source is an examination in Chapter 2 of the traces of Brechtian dramaturgy across a group of plays stretching from early works that are explicitly modelled on the Lehrstück (Lesson or Learning Play) to recent pieces that combine ethical queries with experiments in form. This chapter considers closely the question of engagement and develops around four main branches to Greig's theatre of political/ethical enquiry. The first deals with the presentation of violence and storytelling in two plays for young audiences – *Petra* (1996) and *Dr Korzcak's Example* (2001); the second with the reverberations of European modernity and the collapse of the ideological constructions of the past – *Stalinland* (1992), *Europe* (1994) and *The Architect* (1996).

The third concerns communities, vulnerabilities and the generation of states of relation – *Yellow Moon* (2006), *Monster in the Hall* (2011) and *Fragile* (2011), while the fourth renovates the Lesson Play format vis à vis contemporary political and ethical issues – *Kyoto* (2009), *The Letter of Last Resort* (2012) and *Dalgety* (2012).

After chapters, these opening chapters, the focus of the book pivots towards Greig's varied explorations of modalities of location. This comprehends the intricacies of belonging and alienation, as well as the privileges and risks of mobility and rootedness already raised in *One Way Street* (1995) and *Europe*. Hence Chapter 3 turns to the plays that use Scotland as setting and some of the many facets of Scottish cultural identity that he has explored since the 1990s. Again, as in Chapter 2 the span of the analysis is broad, progressing through plays that are rooted in specific Scottish environments and use those environments extensively, beginning with Greig's comic devolution piece, *Caledonia Dreaming* (1997) and then moving on to the ambitious scope of *Victoria* (2000) and *Outlying Islands* (2002), the playful romantic musical *Midsummer* (2008), the political allegory and Shakespearean subtexts of *Dunsinane* (2010) and finally the effervescent fusion of ballad and karaoke in *The Strange Undoing of Prudencia Hart* (2011). Throughout Chapter 3 I draw upon David Pattie's understanding of the productively unstable nature of Scottishness in Greig's work to consider his reluctance to subscribe to a one-dimensional sense of national identity.

Counterpointed to this is Chapter 4's focus on the motif of globalization across another cluster of major plays. Here, I gather together *The Speculator* (1999), which raises the tantalizing questions of monetary systems and their impacts on our sense of the world, with the more frequently discussed plays – *The Cosmonaut's Last Message* (1999), *San Diego* (2003) – that present fragmented worlds of miscommunication. These are analysed against *Pyrenees* (2005) and *Brewers Fayre* (2009) both of which tentatively and humorously affirm human connection against the odds. Whereas *The Speculator*, *The Cosmonaut's Last Message* and *San Diego* spin outwards towards worlds of contingency and discontinuity both *Pyrenees* and *Brewers Fayre* conclude with moments of figuratively suggestive homecoming illustrating Greig's evolving approach to the shifting conditions of the contemporary globalized world.

Finally, Chapter 5 dissects Greig's work on and with the Middle East – *Not About Pomegranates* (2001), *Ramallah* (2004), *The American Pilot* (2005), *Damascus* (2007), *The Miniskirts of Kabul* (2009) and *One Day in Spring* (2012). The chapter considers these plays as contact zones and explores the issues they raise about the difficulties, but also the necessity, of cross-cultural communication and the operation of power. That focus evidently returns to the topic of theatre's possible political and ethical role, thus suggesting a looping back to the discussion of the formal properties of theatrical intervention and engagement presented in Chapter 2.

The chorus at the beginning of *Monster in the Hall* (2009) jokingly warn the audience that the play will include 'a small amount of Socialism' but 'You won't notice, honestly it'll be fine' (8); likewise, I found that at each node Greig's work invited some theoretical framing because concepts are so intrinsic to it. This is mostly undertaken at the start of each chapter and is angled towards ideas the plays themselves incorporate and that Greig himself has proposed or discussed at different times. I hope my attempts to do so *are* noticeable and meaningful, but that the intricacies of the theoretical debates are not permitted to derail attention to the works they are applied to.

The second part of the book opens the field to different perspectives that aim to offer resources for further research and criticism, as well as some necessary variety. In the course of researching this book, I have read and listened to many interviews of David Greig and consistent throughout that material is his willingness to openly and thoughtfully discuss his work. That generosity was put to the test in the hours we spent talking about identity, storytelling, writing and his experience in making theatre. The interview here is a distilled version of our lengthy conversation (sadly some of the elaborate anecdotes had to be pruned). Rather than concentrating on the specifics of individual plays or productions, my interest lay primarily in allowing a wide lens image of the work to develop. The result provides many valuable insights not only into his dramaturgy, but also into how he sees himself and his role as a playwright now.

Scholarship on Greig's work shows signs of healthy development since the 2000s. Throughout my analysis I have tried to acknowledge and incorporate the insights of others as much as possible. They contribute to a rich and ongoing exchange around the work that I believe vital to appreciate. The scholarly chapters included here provide two dynamic and contrasting approaches to Greig's work that add to that exchange. Complementing the focus on globalization in Chapter 4, Marilena Zaroulia investigates Greig's 'geography of the imagination.' Zaroulia concentrates on the ways in which 'place and mobility' take on new meanings as a consequence of globalization. She refers David Harvey's 1990 study of the condition of postmodernity (also mentioned in the introduction to Chapter 4) and then goes on to refine his discussion of place with more recent work by Tim Cresswell and Doreen Massey on place, space and movement. *San Diego*, *The Cosmonaut's Last Message*, *One Way Street* and *Europe* are analysed using this framework to emphasize their evocations of the spaces of possibility.

David Pattie by contrast considers the fluidity of Greig's approach to Scottishness in a series of plays and positions this approach in the context of the discourse of Scottish cultural identity more generally. Significantly his chapter brings to this volume a historically nuanced consideration of the instabilities of Scottish identity from the nineteenth century forward through the Scottish literary renaissance to present-day debates. The title of his contribution 'Who's Scotland?' is a quote from a scene *Caledonia Dreaming* where the characters debate who might be a representative symbol of Scotland for the proposed Edinburgh Olympic games. As Pattie concludes Scotland, in Greig's work, is a fluid set of relations rather than any material entity.

Lastly, it is a particular privilege to be able to include practitioners' accounts of their work with David. In sharing their experiences Philip Howard, Vicky Featherstone, Guy Hollands and Wils Wilson illuminate the work from a director's perspective. Their reflections offer a unique opportunity to see how some of the plays studied here evolved and were brought to life in performance and the ways in which creative collaboration in practice has shaped the work.

This book seeks to place Greig as a major contemporary playwright whose drama is worthy of sustained and continuing critical attention. Compared to some of the other playwrights whose careers began in the 1990s, he has rarely been a hub of sensation or controversy and his repertoire of visceral effects is slim, yet here is a body of work that has consistently pushed at the boundaries of some of the most pressing and problematic phenomena of our age. At the same time, the formal range of his writing and theatre-making is unrivalled by his contemporaries. Perhaps the most significant quality of Greig's theatre, and one I will showcase, is its playful enjoyment of ideas coupled with a delight in the potential of narrative complexity, linguistic nuance and the vitality of performance. That imaginative energy, as we will see, above all thrives in the interplay between the ethical, the political, the poetic and the narrative.

CHAPTER 1
SUSPECT CULTURE

'The Possibilities for Alternative Theatre'

Although this book is concentrated upon Greig's work as a playwright, in a crucial sense his path into playwriting is neither direct nor one way. Greig is unusual because he has combined long-term commitment to a collaborative creative group with a steady stream of work outside that group. In the early 1990s Greig and Graham Eatough, both of whom had been students at Bristol University began to make shows together. As Greig describes in an interview with Peter Billingham, at that stage he regarded what he was doing as devising rather than playwriting (2007: 73). Among their first projects were *A Savage Reminiscence* (1991), *The Garden* (mentioned later by Philip Howard), *And the Opera House Remained Unbuilt* and *Stalinland* (all 1992). The company they formed was Suspect Culture. With a collective structure that evolved around a core creative team – actor and later artistic director Graham Eatough, musician Nick Powell, designer Ian Scott and Greig who wrote many of the company's texts – plus a group of international associates, Suspect Culture formally secured funding in 1995 and continued until 2008 producing an impressive body of theatre work.

The aspirations and concerns of the group in the 1990s percolate through Greig's dramaturgy and as will become evident many topics and influences excavated by Suspect Culture continue to be excavated in Greig's other writings. Their starting point, as company's archive website notes, was 'to develop a style of theatre that combined the best of English and European traditions, working with high-quality writing but giving equal weight to visual and musical elements'. Given this objective it would be perverse to try to isolate Greig's texts as if they could exist separately. At the same time it would be neglectful to ignore the obvious fact that this work is intrinsic to his growth as a theatre-maker. Greig describes *Stalinland* as the point at which he realized that his interests lay more in writing rather than in directing. That play is very much bound up with Greig's exploration of Brechtian structures and European identities as opposed to the collaborative journeys undertaken later by Suspect Culture and so is discussed briefly in the following chapter. A more complete picture of the full range of the company's work is presented in *The Suspect Culture Book* edited by Graham Eatough and Dan Rebellato (2013). Here, my purpose is necessarily selective. Primarily, the focus is on the core tendencies and motifs in some of the company's work as embedded aspects of Greig's development, following Greig's own assertion that 'No matter what work we do now it has the ghost of Suspect Culture in its bones' (Eatough and Rebellato 2013: 45).

One of the early influences on Suspect Culture's attitudes cited by both Eatough and Greig is British playwright Howard Barker. As Eatough puts it, that influence appears

> not just on the writing but on what the shows were setting out to achieve, politically and intellectually. What Barker does, whether or not the plays are successful, [is] he scouts out the possibilities for alternative theatre. He neither points towards a mainstream theatre style but nor is he swept up in current avant-garde movements. . . . And for those who didn't want to leave playwriting behind Barker was a model for something that could still be radical, which I think was important for David. (2013: 17)

So maintaining a textual point of reference while exploring the physical resources of performance is the starting point for an aesthetic Suspect Culture began to investigate and develop. This involved the amalgamation of various elements: music, movement, design and text in a manner described by Rebellato as 'intellectual' and 'minimalist' (2003: 62), qualities that have won their work both praise and criticism. While the group's creative methods were diverse, often involving workshops and brainstorming retreats, as Greig admits the writing itself was not collaborative: 'What I found was that I liked to work with the actors in the rehearsal room and then I would go away and write at night – I didn't want their (the actors') words, I wanted them to help me to try to find the right situation' (Billingham 2007: 74). I would like to pursue this notion of situation in several senses. First, in terms of how to situate Suspect Culture's approach, as is evident from Eatough's description of their early stimuli, there is an attempt to explore the possibilities of aesthetically alternative theatre in a British context. Rebellato has described that approach as utopian, finely tracing the influence of German philosopher Theodor Adorno's writings (in particular *Negative Dialectics* [1966]) on Greig and Eatough's thinking (2003). Utopia for Adorno is a necessary potential that can never be realized – art's role is to render that paradox perceptible. Rebellato's evaluation of Suspect Culture up to 2002 concentrates on the political reverberations of the work – an issue I will return to later. Yet since their project bears so many of the formal traces and preoccupations of post-1970s experimental theatre, it may also be understood in relation to the conditions of postmodernity and the aesthetic of the post-dramatic. Both are admittedly contentious, and especially so in the British critical environment as already evident in Amelia Howe Kritzer's perspective on the politics of post-Thatcher theatre mentioned in the introduction, but they nevertheless provide useful vocabularies to portray the situation of Suspect Culture.

Postmodernity is indeed a challenge to succinctly define. However, if we take it to denote an uneven, developed world, phenomenon denoting a matrix of social, political and cultural vectors that includes the impact of electronic media, mass migration, the erosion of traditional forms of politics and attitudes to place, then its relevance to Suspect Culture's projects starts to emerge. It is precisely these epochal resonances of postmodernity as it melds with the intensified advance of globalization that recur throughout Suspect Culture's and David Greig's work – though not consistently in a post-dramatic fashion. Where the term 'postmodern' proves more fruitful than globalization is in the paths it offers for examining the morphing of attitudes to self, spectacle and history in relation to the forces of technology and consumerism. And in a sense this is the era in which members of the company grew up – described with caustic precision by David Pattie later in this volume as 'a particularly harsh mixture of Victorian values and economic determinism'. It is mapped locally in the ambivalent progress of Thatcherism followed by the transition to the amorphous liberalism of the Blair era and after. More generally, as Hans Bertens suggests, a 'common denominator' to the many competing ideas of the postmodern is 'a crisis in representation'. Whether that crisis is perceived as 'debilitating' or 'enabling', it is inexorably political (1995: 11). And Suspect Culture's work emerges from and in reaction to the epicentre of these forces.

Although in *Postdramatic Theatre* (1999, trans. 2006) Hans-Thies Lehmann rejects the 'epochal' character of the term 'postmodern' in favour of 'a concrete problem of theatre aesthetics' (21), the post-dramatic evidently sits within the cluster of conditions just sketched. Post-dramatic theatre for Lehmann cannot be simply defined, but is rather a cluster of tendencies that move beyond or away from the principles of dramatic theatre and the primacy of the play text. He delineates an aesthetic that offers many tools for understanding some contemporary theatre's deconstruction of dramatic conventions, specifically in its attitudes to performance, text, space, time, the body and media. Suspect Culture's work with repetition, fragmentation, sound, gesture and image is richly illustrative of some aspects of the tendencies Lehmann observes (primarily, though not exclusively, in German theatre since the 1970s) and again aligns the company with some continental attitudes to theatre and performance, as well as to experimental theatre in America. Perhaps most critically evocative is the way Lehmann reads this aesthetic in contemporary theatre as engaging with 'a politics of perception' (185), and that assertion I would dovetail with Rebellato's interpretation of Suspect Culture's achievements. The sections that follow hone in on situation in three linked hubs in the company's theatre work – place, self and politics – as a means of unravelling some aspects of their engagement with perception in this context.

Psychogeographies and Utopias: *One Way Street*, *Airport* and *Candide 2000*

A second dimension to the matter of situation in Suspect Culture's projects in the 1990s is how, in addition to their readings of Adorno, both Greig and Eatough found creative stimulus in ideas pertaining to psychogeography and in particular to Walter Benjamin's *One Way Street* (1928) and *A Berlin Chronicle* (1932). Although it garnered some very specific theoretical designations in the 1960s with the development of the Situationist movement, Merlin Coverley's account of its broad currents seem better suited to Suspect Culture's case. In *Psychogeography* (2006), he identifies its defining qualities as 'the act of urban wandering, the spirit of political radicalism, allied to a playful sense of subversion and governed by an inquiry into the methods by which we can transform our relationship to the urban environment. This entire project . . . is one that is as preoccupied with excavating the past as it is with recording the present' (14).

Throughout Suspect Culture's early shows, place is divested of exact specificity or stability yet is seen to impact upon and condition action in diverse ways. Place is repeatedly envisioned as experiential, a blend of layered realities past and present, as opposed to a stable, objectively known setting. Even as early as *Stalinland* an interest in the ways places mutate depending on perspective is ideologically charged. With *One Way Street* (1995) Greig and Eatough created a one-man show that grappled with 'personal history as geography'. Marilena Zaroulia analyses how *One Way Street* layers a reference to Benjamin onto responses to the post-Wall Europe derived in part from Greig's experiences of Inter-railing in the early 1990s, in order to contest notions of place as fixed or stable. Displacement then is pivotal: through citation Benjamin is relocated, the peripatetic protagonist in the show roams through Berlin in search of a lost lover, the guide he is supposed to produce – 'Ten Short Walks in the Former East' – wanders off the expected tourist trail into the messy territory of personal associations. It is, as one of Suspect Culture's long-term artistic associates Mauricio Paroni de Castro so aptly puts it, an exercise in 'emotional cartography' (Eatough and Rebellato

2013: 66). It is also rooted in the renegotiation of identity within a changing Europe. At its heart is the potentially divisive process of European reunification. Indeed, the topicality of such concerns led to British Council funding for the show to tour to the former East and the company's internationalist course was set (Eatough and Rebellato 2013: 21–2). With *One Way Street*, Joyce McMillan felt that the company

> had found the intellectual and emotional content to match [their] style: the political geography of a new Europe that was unifying, converging, removing barriers to movement and communication; and – most importantly – the emerging emotional geography of a world where a new intensity of communication, and similarity of urban experience across the globe, did not seem to deliver love, fulfilment, or a true sense of connection with other people (Eatough and Rebellato 2013: 52).

Although that interest in new Europe waned after the mid-1990s, place and the emotional geography of place continued to be a source of experiment. This is explicit in works such as *Airport* (1997), *Mainstream* (1999) and *Candide (2000)*. If, according to Eatough, globalization was not a term they consciously engaged with at that stage (and it is salutary to remember how these terms enter and then seem to dominate popular discourse), then it was already in the wings as they found themselves 'drawn to the spaces that you'd associate with global economies: retail spaces, entertainment spaces, travel spaces' (2013: 23). These are much more readily understood in terms of postmodern experience; they are, following anthropologist Marc Augé's coinage, the non-places of contemporary life – hotel rooms, motorways, airports and shopping centres. Detached from the usual co-ordinates that endow places with significance, non-places of course are not free of meaning, but as Augé puts it, 'a person entering the space of non-place is relieved of his usual determinants. He becomes no more than what he does or experiences, in the role of passenger, customer or driver' (1995: 103). These are places where personal identity is loosened, but where behaviour is scripted. And it is this tension that animates Suspect

Culture's exploration of the non-place: 'We were very interested in the juxtaposition of the surface of modern life and modern environments with the humanity inside them: what people want to achieve, what they are able to achieve, what isn't permitted in this environment' Eatough explains (2013: 23). This is overtly and provocatively realized in *Candide 2000*, a postmodern version of Voltaire's classic picaresque satire on the philosophy of optimism. Candide's world-ranging adventure is replaced by a shopping mall setting which, as a consumer paradise, contains the world condensed in simulated forms. The passivity of Candide's oft-repeated motto that he exists in 'the best of all possible worlds' becomes the equally docile 'that's what it's like' mouthed by the twenty-first century consumer. The potential sterility of the non-place is signalled by the minimalism of the stage designs for these shows – the baggage carousel of *Airport*, the chrome and plastic furnishings of the hotel in *Mainstream*, even the exhibition space of *Casanova* (2001). Yet, as the exchanges between performers simultaneously suggest, they may also be spaces of possibility where scripts are deconstructed and the default settings of identity are tested. As Eatough describes, 'what these environments give you dramatically is the antagonist, in a sense; they are environments in which it's very difficult to get a meaningful human exchange, or maybe you do in unexpected, slightly perverse . . . or comic ways' (2013: 23). And it is this sense of possibility, indeterminate as it may be that underwrites Rebellato's claim that Suspect Culture's work is characterized by a utopian dimension.

Anti-Narratives of Self: *Timeless*, *Mainstream* and *Casanova*

Augé's primary interest in non-places is, of course, in the patterns of human behaviour they solicit; the ways in which the person in these places

> surrenders himself [. . . to] the passive joys of identity loss, and the more active pleasure of role playing . . . What he is

confronted with, finally, is an image of himself, but in truth it is
a pretty strange image . . . The space of non-place creates neither
singular identity nor relations; only solitude, and similitude.
(1995: 103)

Again this seems particularly well fitted to Suspect Culture repeated
assays on the performance of the identity, while the post-dramatic
tenor of their work comes to the fore with a focus upon what they do
with character, plot and story. In *The Death of Character: Perspectives
on Theatre after Modernism* (1996), Elinor Fuchs has described the
effacement of character in much contemporary theatre as indicative
of 'a dispersed idea of self' (9) that resists singular or coherent
representation. After *One Way Street* Suspect Culture's work moves
away from the conventions of character and towards figures and
scenarios derived from the experiences of the group explored through
devising and workshopping. In his contribution to *The Suspect Culture
Book*, Greig remembers how

each show was built around a nugget of emotional grit that all
four of us shared. 'Are we all the same?' 'What will become of
us?' 'What would happen if we let go?' These questions would
hover until we found a formal question with which they could
marry up – 'are characters and actors the same?' 'Is gesture
possible within a text?' With a question and a form we would
set off into the dark. (2013: 45–6)

These creative journeys result in the collage effects that structure
Airport, Timeless (1997), *Mainstream* and *Lament* (2002). In each of
these, the splintering of narrative and action problematizes the whole
notion of knowing or even establishing a character. *Airport* plays with
the exchange of national stereotypes as a means of safe, but generically
empty, communication of identity while at the same time gesturing
towards types of improbably shared memories. The pairing of solitude
and similitude in the non-place is at the heart of the piece. As Augé
remarks, 'we have learned to distrust absolute, simple and substantive
identities, on the collective as well as the individual level' (1995: 22).

That ambivalence is investigated and tested in Suspect Culture's work through an interrogation of character, story and, arguably, a post-dramatic turn towards a theatre of states rather than action, structured chiefly by what Lehmann calls a 'a scenic dynamic' (2006: 68).

Timeless and *Mainstream* turn to more intimate emotional terrain than *Airport* or *Candide (2000)* and are all conditioned by that 'scenic dynamic'. Described by Neil Cooper as 'a late twentieth-century *fin-de-siècle* epic about friendship and all the littler epiphanies that bind people' (Eatough and Rebellato 2013: 59), *Timeless* melds music and memory. Structured as a performance quartet, that was accompanied by a string quartet with music composed by Nick Powell, with *Timeless* the company consciously attempted to integrate music and action. The piece presents four friends, Ian, Martin, Veronica and Stella, at three moments in their relationship labelled present, past and future. They are drawn together by shared moments in the past that they describe as 'timeless'. Primary among these experiences is one that gradually gathers epiphanic significance for all four – an evening picnic on a beach, which may or may not have happened as they remember it. Their story is a slight one with neither climax nor progress; their characters are elliptical, disturbingly needy, hesitant and incomplete. Echoing the string quartet's role as chamber music, the playing and replaying of versions of this story is contained in three movements, taking on different meanings, acquiring alternate nuances. Thus in each act, each character interacts with the others sometimes as a group, sometimes in pairs but also performs a monologue solo. Throughout, certain verbal motifs – the repetition of the words 'poignant', 'serene', 'inevitable', 'pornographic'; images of birds in flight, lungs contracting, skin shedding; and phrases that signal a shared, personal language – lend a sense of poetic unity and continuity where the usual dramatic signposts are lacking. The question of whether any of this adds up to anything hovers above the exchanges even from the first Act: as Ian says 'Even pictures that don't come out capture something'; by contrast Veronica questions whether framing a failed photo merely results in 'a frame around nothing' (143). In the third act, a projection into the future, each character individually imagines a reunion with the others, and in doing so betraying both their insecurities and their fantasies. A nagging sense of absence and insufficiency curls through these scenarios. The longing to 'say the perfect thing' brings forth a banal substitute 'Blah, blah, blah', vividly suggesting the utopian impossibility of pinning down that ideal communication. It also bizarrely recalls the opening of Heiner Müller's experimental filleting of *Hamlet*, *Hamlet-machine* (1977): 'I was Hamlet. I stood at the waterfront and talked to the surf BLAH BLAH BLAH, behind me the ruins of Europe' (87). The movement of closing scene of *Timeless* comes to orbit a shared imagined perfect moment despite the ruins of fantasy scattered about:

The beach we went to that one time.
We bought pakora from the shop.
Got pissed and watched the sun go down.
And even though it was just some fucking picnic.
Something happened to us all.

This refrain is laced through the characters' speeches, repeated five times in choral unison becoming a stable theme amidst the uncertainties, failures and speculative projections that make up the show. *Timeless* experiments with displacing plot and character in favour of musical movements, along the lines of the allegro, minuet, rondo sequence for classical string quartet compositions, and permeated by the structural use of polyphony and counterpoint. The result is character treated as instrument, plot as musical form, and a set of poetic textual effects that can be seen woven into much of Greig's later solo work.

Mainstream continues in the same experimental spirit but deploys a formally contrasting approach. Indeed, as we will see in the interview later, the process of composing *Mainstream* proved instrumental in Greig's later ideas about narrative and its power. Here that notion of a 'dispersed idea of self', solitude and similitude is again instrumental. The performance involved four actors (two men and two women) who randomly rotated the roles in each scene, while the other two waited up stage, visible to the audience. Greig talks of the play in terms of ghosting and the group's interest in possible worlds theory (2013: 46) which proposes that the actual world may only be one of an undetermined number of possible ones. Such simultaneous possible worlds emerge across fifty-four fragment scenes in which various combinations and recombinations deriving from a core story unfold achronologically. As Eatough recalls, Greig delivered 'a very open text that had no specific settings for the scenes and no characters either' (2013: 28). In place of characters, we have two anonymous figures, designated only by their job titles: Artists and Repertoire (A&R) and Personnel. They meet at a seaside hotel for a 'personal dynamics' interview and may, or may not, have had a sexual encounter after a drunken evening together. The potential exchanges that might develop from this basic premise branch into a tangle of open questions about how we identify and perform ourselves – what constitutes our essential self? A job, a hobby, a favourite drink, a musical preference, a pulse, a resistance to 'the mainstream'?

Repetition and variation – verbal, physical and gestural – are the dynamos of *Mainstream*. Personnel's questions are met with different responses by each A&R ranging from aggressiveness to helpful compliance yet, reminiscent of *Timeless*, the vocabularies used and the fragments of story recur as if intrinsically some experience is shared, undermining a coherent individuality in the very act of self-portrayal. Simultaneously there is an enduring sense of isolation and loneliness to the stories told and the interactions that take place, manifest most intensely in the story told by A&R of being trapped in a car beneath the snow and almost freezing to death. No external, superior perspective is available to order or verify the fragments that swirl together to create the show or to give a sense of narrative or ontological stability. Nor does the prospect that the results of the interview are to be filed provide much sense of purpose. Instead, *Mainstream* offers a multifaceted post-dramatic deconstruction of those assurances through a play of possibilities and broken stories.

Up against these pieces, *Casanova* (2001) is a relatively conventional play complete with a cast of characters, plot and action. Greig's contemporary Casanova is an art collector and sexual adventurer, roaming the world in search of the perfect woman. Committed to the transcendent power of desire, Casanova becomes a victim of his own philosophy, subordinate to his own idiosyncratic habits of consumption. As Trish Reid notes that 'insistence on the never-ending pursuit of pleasure for its own sake constitutes a kind of radical 'nowness' that is in obvious tension with traditional constructions of identity' (Eatough and Rebellato 2013: 73). In *Casanova* that quest can never attain its goal – there is no ultimate satisfaction, merely an accumulation of moments that are eventually cut short by the vengeful machinations of a boring, cuckolded husband. Casanova's reluctance to return home to a retrospective of his life's conquests inevitably stems from an unwillingness to admit the impossibility of finding perfection, of gratifying desire. That reluctance is juxtaposed with the compromises made by the other characters that paradoxically appear more morally suspect than Casanova's honest promiscuity. What links *Casanova* to the other Suspect Culture productions here is the notion of the self as performance, worked out with, before and, even, for others. If reduced to one dimension, that self becomes, as does the character Casanova, a dead exhibit.

Postmodern Politics? *Lament* and *Futurology*

One of the criticisms levelled at Suspect Culture at various points during their existence was that the work was too abstract and insufficiently politically engaged. It is a claim Rebellato's survey of their work up to 2002 vigorously refutes. Certainly Suspect Culture emerged at what is now perceived as a point of transition, away from older modes of bringing theatre and politics into relation that have been touched upon in this book's introduction and will be developed in the ensuing chapters. As Eatough notes, 'We felt a lack of confidence about making seemingly straightforward political statements in theatre and simple political statements in general at that time. They didn't seem to ring true anymore' (2013: 24). It was not that they revelled in their incertitude, but rather that ambivalence rang truer, a motif threaded through a great deal of Greig's other writings as well.

That sense permeates *Lament*, a collage of devised scenes, video recordings and music framed by an elusive sense of loss and regret which resulted from 'a desire to do a political show' (Eatough and Rebellato 2013: 34). A show without a story, it recalls *Mainstream* in its arrangement of fragments of dreamed, projected and remembered selves. Sadness and absurdity are the words used by the company on their website archive to describe the emotions and experiences the show attempts to investigate and communicate, as it 'acknowledges the heartfelt nostalgia we feel today for a world that perhaps never existed'. The space of the exploration is not only 'between the personal and the political', but also between the present and the absent, the existent and non-existent. The method is self-consciously poetic – channelled through images that function literally and figuratively, specifically and generally – it is additionally and perhaps inevitably, an uncomfortable experience. A diffuse focus coupled with a lack of ironic distance saturates the piece. Hovering at the edge of the sensations, the show generates is a vague anxiety that surely all this bemoaning of undefined, amorphous loss threatens to become mawkish, self-indulgent, at worst a sentimental liberal *caoine* or keen.

Suspect Culture explicitly presented *Lament* as 'a poem for the theatre'; this in itself invites reflection upon the nature of the poetics of the performance. It is not insignificant that formally a lament occupies an ancient generic category with written, spoken and musical variants; it comprehends the expression of not only grief, but also complaint, anger and petition. Using music, a chorus of voices and a web of associations charting the process of lamentation from knowingly naive remembrances and melancholy regret to intense anguish, *Lament* references these dimensions of the form deftly throughout, while simultaneously raising the question of the mutation, transformation and disappearance of such cultural patterns in a contemporary context.

Juxtaposition, metaphor, metonymy, synecdoche, cadence and cacophony are among the prominent structuring elements at work here. The opening collage of introductory material presented on video provides the motifs that are played and replayed throughout. In the subsequent 'Maelstrom' section, a rapid juxtaposition of fragmented scenes and images swirls and builds to a crescendo finally halted by a prayerful silence. In the next phase of the performance each motif expands into its own stanza scenario. Repetition intermittently provides a cadence between the sixteen stanzas: a discussion of apricots recurs in different scenarios, mutating from a central part of a humble primitive community's diet to a fad food in a Seinfeld-style comedy, to the focus for bitter nostalgia in a war-ravaged country. Similarly, the scent and the taste of ripe tomatoes recur as a sensory metonym for lost plenitude and communion with nature. Conjoining these image nodes is a multifaceted thematics of loss expressed through a series of contexts that metaphorically point towards a broad critique of contemporary globalized society: primitive communities invaded by Western consumerism, languages on the verge of extinction, endangered species, exploitative tourism and war. These major political issues are interleaved with intensely personal experiences of alienation, ending, grief: the making of a guitar upon which to compose a lament, elliptical senses of political disillusionment, a rather clichéd Irish wake, simple reflections on childhood happiness, a novel finished. The effect is to collapse any neat space of judgement or safe objectivity. The final movement of the performance sharpens these diverse elements to a point of unambiguously politicized rage and reflection.

Intrinsic to the workings of *Lament* is the way in which we are repeatedly reminded of how memory and nostalgia are found wanting. Sentimentality and inarticulacy may ambush the lamenter. The portrayal of a surrogate contemporary pseudo-community of 'Friends' sags beneath the weight of its own absurdity. The performers cannot fully conjure up the idyllic organic communities and stable values of the past. The representation of lost or dying traditions – be they farming, hunting or storytelling – is frequently halted by the absence of sufficient vocabulary, gaps that may be the result of the erosion of memory or the imperfections of fantasy. And as has been remarked by others, even the word catastrophe repeatedly fails to appear coherently in the script, as if the catastrophe itself has failed. Even more than the generalized business of mourning, the lament is an overtly performative form – a fusion of speaking and doing. *Lament* thus works via a consciously flawed expression personal, philosophical and political despair as an act of continuing and necessarily incomplete public validation of that which has been lost and is being lost. In this sense the poetics of *Lament* is ultimately not that of the *caoine*, but a poetics of resistance. The use of mixed media, personal narration seeded in the performers' experiences, fragments of cultural reference and episodic structure make *Lament* a project very much engaged with Lehmann's notion of 'a politics of perception' (2006: 185) in its refusal of dramatic spectacle or resolution. As such it is illustrative of what Nicholas Ridout observes in *Theatre & Ethics* (2009): 'Increasingly, the relationship between theatre and ethics comes to be a question of form rather than content . . . . This focus on process and form goes hand in hand with an openness to the future and the unpredictable rather than a closure around a specific ethical position' (49).

One of Suspect Culture's last theatrical projects embraced politics in a much more direct manner that departed from such a post-dramatic aesthetic, returning to more recognizable issues-driven approach even though the unpredictability of the future was at its centre. Replacing the melancholic and personal dimensions of *Lament*, *Futurology: A Global Revue* (2007) used comedy, agit prop and cabaret to explore the politics of climate change. Despite the prescience of the topic, *Futurology* faltered partly as a result of the scale and diversity of the revue format. Nevertheless, as we will see in the following chapter, prompted by the show's failure Greig went on to write *Kyoto* (2009), a condensed playlet on the same subject.

This is one obvious instance of Greig's assertion that the ghost of Suspect Culture haunts his other work. Another is the way in which the symposia they organized under the title Strange Behaviour provided an open forum for the debate of ideas that make their way into much of his writing. Details of these symposia and some of the proceedings are now available on Suspect Culture's archive website and reveal how the group openly set out to forge connections and explore ideas beyond their theatre work. Greig suggests that 'the Suspect Culture texts are peculiarly disembodied works, uncontained, and inclined, therefore to float' (Eatough and Rebellato 2013: 46). This chapter has suggested some of the conceptual trajectories those works have moved along, namely in relation to place, self and politics. What I hope will come to light in the chapters that follow is how those shared explorations of emotional geography and non-place, text and music, choral effects and poetic structure, body and memory, and the utopian desire to connect filter through his plays in direct and indirect ways, even when far removed from the politics of post-dramatic experimentalism.

CHAPTER 2
LESSON PLAYS

Towards an 'Epic, Presentational, Storytelling Style'

The title of this chapter points in the direction of a playwright whose work and writings about theatre have had a remarkably deep impact on post-war British drama – Bertolt Brecht. As a result, the term 'Brechtian' serves as shorthand for a nexus of attitudes to theatre's political role, to anti-naturalistic techniques of performance, and to narrative structure, to name but the most obvious. It is not my intention to suggest that all the plays discussed in this chapter adhere to some sort of Brechtian template. However, since several of his early works, such as *Petra* or *Europe*, openly draw upon the notion of the Brechtian *Lehrstück* or Lesson/Learning Play, I want to take this reference as a perspective point because it makes visible a legacy of ideas concerning theatre and politics that are especially useful in evaluating Greig's attempts to engage or disengage with particular modes of theatrical representation. So far I have sketched some of his attitudes to the question of politics and theatre and Suspect Culture's oblique politics of perspective. Here the focus will be on some of the influences in the evolution of his dramaturgy and on the analysis of the features of what he described as an 'epic, presentational, storytelling style' that he has gradually been developing (email 8 September 2011). What will underwrite this chapter are the ways Greig's writing has played with and modified Brechtian references, first in a number of metaphorically and symbolically intricate plays that treat points of crisis in modern European identity, then moving towards more minimal, ethically inflected, forms of presentation.

An important contour to Greig's polymorphous dramaturgy has been a rejection of what he describes variously as 'English realism', 'linguistic naturalism' or 'Mamet-style "stage pictures"' (Billingham

2007: 93). Thus in an article for the *Guardian* just after he completed a translation of Albert Camus's *Caligula*, Greig pitted the tradition of English realism against the traditions of continental (and specifically French) non-naturalistic theatre – admittedly an opposition that could be traced back to a debate that was brewing in the 1950s and erupted famously between theatre critic Kenneth Tynan and playwright Eugène Ionesco in 1958. He contends that in British theatre French plays

> are characterised as effete, intellectual and humourless. This is in contrast to English plays which are felt to deal robustly with 'the real world': they 'tell it like it is'. The labelling of the two famous post-war waves of English playwriting as 'the angry young men' and 'in-yer-face' perhaps tells us a little about how the English like to see their theatre writer: drawn from the same stock as the longbowmen of Agincourt, proudly displaying their two-fingered salutes. (Greig 2003)

As a young writer, he strongly felt this to be a 'televisual and dull' tradition that had nothing to offer him, and one of his methods of distancing himself from naturalism and social realism was to reach towards a 'European sensibility' that he found in writers like Brecht and Howard Barker, as well as to the richly diverse heritage of post-war Scottish theatre (Billingham 2007: 79; Fisher 2011: 17–18).

At the same time, as is clear in his contribution to the 1997 Birmingham Theatre Conference and the resulting book *State of Play* (1999) edited by David Edgar, Greig also felt the need to distinguish himself from the dogmas of the leftist artistic discourse of some of his immediate predecessors. As already suggested in Chapter 1, the 1990s presented a much more diffuse and contradictory political field – not just for theatre-makers. The traditionally polarized politics of the recent past had, apparently, dissolved, while political drama of the old school seemed to have peaked long before. The collapse of communism, the acceleration of globalization and the changes wrought by postmodernity, had made questions of identity, the nation-state power, justice and the politics of emancipation increasingly complicated. And the effects of these changes mark both established writers and those just starting out in the 1990s.

In retrospect, it is evident that throughout the decade Greig grappled with how to redefine and transform the political in his work; on the one hand, rejecting the dispiriting 'privatised dissent' (Sierz 2000: 39) of much 1990s new writing, on the other ducking, as he humorously puts it, 'co-opt[ion] . . . into a happy band of 1970s left-wing dinosaurs' (Greig 2008: 212). Hence in 1999, he makes a meticulous distinction between 'writing about politics' and 'political theatre,' describing the latter as making 'interventions into ideology [. . . which has] at its very heart the possibility of change'. At that time Greig saw the contemporary withdrawal from ideology as a logical outcome of the collapse of both the left and the right, and in his view such a disavowal of the political threatened to culminate in a 'culture of stasis' and disempowerment (Greig 66, 68). Yet he was, nonetheless, very reluctant to affiliate himself with 'writing about politics'. Later, influenced by the dynamics of globalization and climate change, the War on Terror and his experiences in the Middle East, he admits that not only had politics changed, but he personally had changed; he 'was no longer satisfied with letting [his] work simply exist and not questioning whether it was helping or hindering the powers shaping our lives'. Instead he found himself explicitly considering how he 'as a theatre-maker, [could] explore, map and advance a progressive agenda' (Greig 2008: 213). It is arguably a risky statement for any writer to make however, as I hope to illustrate, the methods he uses to pursue such an ethical aspiration are rarely as direct as this declaration might suggest.

In an interview with Peter Billingham from 2006, Greig emphasizes the strong influences of Bertolt Brecht and Howard Barker upon his early work. As I have argued elsewhere, Greig's drama cannot be simply mapped onto Brecht's theatre of alienation or distanciation, and this is even less the case with Barker's Theatre of Catastrophe (Wallace 2006). And without a doubt, placing Barker alongside Brecht does little to suggest a harmonious marriage of impulses or dramaturgical perspectives. So, in what follows, I would like to tease out some aspects of each that pertain to Greig's work before moving on to an examination of specific groups of plays that include not only some of his earliest, but also some of his most recent pieces. The span of the analysis will, I believe, strategically reveal the contrasts and contiguities between what Greig was doing in the 1990s and then in the 2000s.

The influence of Brecht's stagecraft in post-war British theatre has, of course, been well documented. Both John Elsom (1976) and Christopher Innes (1992) mention how although several of Brecht's plays were produced in Britain already in the 1930s, it was the 1956 visit of the Berliner Ensemble that proved to be a revelation for many theatre practitioners (despite the fact that the performances were in German). While his Marxism was shunted off to a quiet siding, Brecht's work was welcomed as 'an anti-illusionistic model for theatrical immediacy and directness' that broke with the dominant naturalism of the British stage (Innes 2002: 114). Exploring the issue in greater depth, Janelle Reinelt in *After Brecht: British Epic Theater* (1994) charts the legacy of Brecht's ideas and practice in the British context as one that is varied and hybrid, permeating work by writers as diverse as Howard Brenton, Edward Bond, Caryl Churchill, David Hare, Trevor Griffiths and John McGrath.

Brecht's perception of theatre as a potential 'tool for the reordering of human existence' (Carlson 1993: 392–3) has inevitably been an appealing one for successive generations of British playwrights. And as is well known, his work is structured by an intense consciousness of storytelling as performative and of the effect it may, or should, have on its audience. Memorably in 'A Short Organum for the Theatre', Brecht asserts that what is needed is:

a type of theatre which not only releases the feelings, insights, and impulses possible within the particular historical field of human relations in which the action takes place, but employs and encourages those thoughts and feelings which help to transform the field itself. (in Brandt 1998: 238)

Rejecting both the symbolism of the expressionist stage and the well-worn codes of naturalism, Brecht's Epic theatre was to invert the conventions of dramatic theatre in its attempt to address contemporary political problems and ethical dilemmas.

It is easy enough to recognize many of these qualities in Greig's drama, and several of his earliest plays are plainly modelled on the Brechtian *Lehrstück*. The *Lehrstücke* represent Epic theatre in its most concentrated form. A problem is posed and debated from different, often mutually exclusive, perspectives. Language is unadorned, plot is simple, character is psychologically two dimensional, and the purpose is dialectical, attempting to bypass the division between performer and viewer and to challenge the preconceptions and attitudes to the problem. As Reiner Steinweg elucidates, the learning play, in its various formulations since Brecht, is based on discovery rather than on instruction; it invites the linking of the personal to the political through 'the provocation of associations' (Steinweg).

Beyond the compressions of this form, Greig also inclines towards techniques of storytelling and performance familiar in Epic theatre where the story is to be composed of episodes, each with its own movement or *gest*. As Brecht outlines, these 'parts of the story have to be carefully set off one against another by giving each its own structure as a play within a play' (in Brandt 1998: 245). Such juxtapositional logic is crucial to the shape of much of Greig's drama and the articulated, disjunctive narratives it so often presents. The result is an approach to theme that, as in Brechtian theatre, incorporates multiple perspectives and maintains the tensions between them as a dynamo of interrogative dramatic energy.

Despite the general critical stress upon his didacticism and the Alienation effect, Brecht's best work remains engaging because of the ways it poses questions – not because it attempts to answer them – and as a result of a skilfully crafted 'balance and interplay between . . . sympathy *and* distance, attraction *and* repulsion, tenderness *and* horror' (Bentley 1987: 34). These, to my mind, are pivotal qualities in many of Greig's plays as well, and are crucial to the effects that work produces.

If Brecht furnishes the playwright with an array of tools and devices, then, as was signalled by Graham Eatough with respect to Suspect Culture, Howard Barker provided him with something more ephemeral that, if not directly traced in his work, was nevertheless a catalyst. Greig remarks upon how the attraction of Barker's work for him lay in its fusion of viscerality and intellect. Barker's plays and his cultural manifesto, *Arguments for a Theatre* (1993), provided rhetorically rich rejections of both 'Thatcherite values' and the 'liberal left orthodoxy' that ruptured the limits of political correctness and advocated 'that one could write the unsayable, the unthinkable, and challenge one's audience' (Billingham 2007: 76). That said, it seems vital to observe that Barker makes no secret of his dim view of Brecht, whom he condemns along with G. B. Shaw and most other post-Enlightenment theatre as 'Critical Theatre' (Barker 1993: 119). He denounces political theatre as 'an unacknowledged collaboration with the ruling order' (48) and in opposition proposes a 'Theatre of Catastrophe' that is anti-clarity, anti-realism, anti-narrative, anti-utopian and, above all, tragic. As Heiner Zimmermann points out Barker's criticism of Enlightenment humanism owes much to the works of Friedrich Nietzsche and Theodor Adorno (2012: 66). There seems little enough shared territory between Barker's manifestos and practice, and the work Greig has gone on to produce apart from, tentatively, an espousal of concepts of transcendence through performance. In his assertion of the 'transcendent' quality of theatre though, Greig also draws on Adorno and, in particular, the 'power of contradiction [. . . that] disrupts rationality' with a critical objective. In performance, in this space of contradiction, an experience of transcendence may surface, and that, for Greig, is 'the political foundation of Rough Theatre' (2008: 220).

This chapter is organized around four groups of plays from different phases in Greig's career. Each is associated with a particular set of debates and contexts from war, Europe, community to world politics. Dating from 1992 to 2012, these plays, which have widely divergent target audiences, trace many of the formal contours of Greig's approach to theatre from his adaptation of the Lesson/Learning play, his interest in perspective and contradiction, through to his elaboration of the role of narrative and epic structures.

Stories of War: *Petra* and *Dr Korczak's Example*

One salient feature of Greig's varied output, and one that is perhaps too easily set aside in favour of major topics such as globalization or national identity, is his commitment to and skill in writing for young people. It is a very particular endeavour that is inherently connected to, as David Lane notes, '[t]he ability of drama to expose injustice and present not the problems of society, but the challenges human beings face in making choices within that society' (2010: 136). If theatre for young people is sometimes underestimated, even ghettoized, it is important to note its potential role as space of debate and representation in many respects akin to that of the Lesson/Learning play. Again, the purpose is not to tell audiences what to think but to invite them to engage. Lane goes on to explain how theatre companies and groups in this sector regularly use techniques that attempt to collapse 'aesthetic distance [so that . . .] participation becomes part of the aesthetic itself' drawing on, for instance, Augusto Boal's notion of 'Forum Theatre' (138). Evidently, not all youth theatre shares these goals or techniques, but with regard to Greig's work they are consistently present.

Both *Petra* and *Dr Korczak's Example* are plays written for young audiences about violent conflict. Both were commissioned by the Glasgow theatre company TAG which produces work for children and young people under the auspices of the Citizens Theatre, although *Petra* had existed in an earlier version done in 1994 by Suspect Culture. The revised version, which remains unpublished, was directed by Tony Graham and performed in 1996. It broaches the topic of the civil war and ethnic violence in an unnamed European country. The description of this place which stretches from the mountains to the sea recalls the geography of Bosnia, the site of the most appalling conflict in Europe since World War II. Although the wars fought in the former Yugoslavia continued until 1999 in Kosovo, it was during the war in Bosnia that the most brutal atrocities were committed among them massacres, mass rape, ethnic cleansing and genocide. Notably, it was only at the end of 1995 that the Dayton Peace Agreement was finally signed, bringing the military conflict in Bosnia to a close. Thus *Petra* not only takes an issue that was urgently topical, but also one that is fundamentally traumatic – not a likely subject for a children's play to be performed in schools around Scotland. Indeed, the question of how to artistically respond to such events had already been the subject of aggressive debate in the previous year. At the beginning of 1995, Sarah Kane's surreal and visceral response to the Bosnian War collapsed an apparently naturalistic if sadistic encounter in a Leeds hotel into a nightmarish warzone in which brutal mutilation and cannibalism are defining features. *Blasted* provoked a spectrum of colourfully outraged, indignant and sceptical responses from reviewers. One of the most quotable among them being *Independent* journalist, Paul Taylor's reflection that '*Blasted* is a little like having your face rammed into an overflowing ash tray, just for starters, and then having your whole head held down in a bucket of offal' (1995: 27).

Greig was certainly well aware of Kane's work, they had been friends at university, shared a flat, and Greig went on to pen the introduction to her posthumously published volume of plays. His approach to the topic of the Bosnian War could hardly be more contrasting and indicates their radically different dramaturgical visions. Greig approaches this complicated and bloody history in a minimal, though highly effective way through very simple storytelling. Like the Brechtian *Lehrstück* it is a piece that requires no special facilities or props, and it can reach its audiences in school halls using a cast of four actors and minimal equipment. At the core of the dramatic situation is a form of self-conscious, therapeutic narrative performance that explores the nature of communal identities, and the difficulty of understanding and representing the past. The protagonist, Petra, is a young woman whose child has been killed. In order to allow his spirit to rest, she must tell 'the story of how he came to be dead' (11). The play opens with a tableau – two men in medieval costumes and one with a sword raised. Although the audience cannot yet know it, here is the first image of the child's death. Then Petra explains, in verse, that she has come to the moor at night because she was instructed in a dream to tell her story.

There she meets three ghosts, Ilka a witch, Ivan a tinker and Jakob a soldier, who not only listen, but also enact and critically interact with her tale.

As Petra struggles to formulate the story, she is repeatedly asked 'Why?' by the ghosts. After a first failed attempt, the ghosts offer to act out the scenes in order to help the dead child understand. Petra settles her invisible ghost son on her lap and begins again: 'Listen . . . This is the story of your life. A story about an ordinary boy in and ordinary place. And how he came to be in this ghost field. Far away from home' (13). In a gesture that echoes Brecht's *The Caucasian Chalk Circle* (1948), she draws a circle on the ground to represent the place and begins the fable of a country with a coast, a central plain and mountains where the 'people couldn't stop arguing' (13). After centuries of fighting, the people wanted peace and rather than defining themselves as sea people or mountain people, they 'decided to become Plain people' (15). The ghosts interrupt, urging Petra to get on with the story of the immediate past, so she tells the story of how she met and fell in love with the boy's father. Petra's father, Greck, is a proud mountain man who hates the idea of his daughter marrying a sea man. Greck rises to power, reminding his allies of their difference from the sea people, stirring up old animosities and making absurdly sectarian regulations. Because Petra marries a man from the coast she is ostracized, but they flee to the relative peace of the plain to start their family. Again the ghosts interrupt and exhort her to get to the point. Their new home is ominously named 'the field of blood,' the site of many battles and the place where, incidentally, Jakob was killed. At this point, Jakob commandeers the story insisting that the boy must know his history. The digression leads us back to the distant past to a fabled mountain king called 'Boris,' inspirational hero for the present-day mountain president, Greck. The story of Greck's rise to power and his elimination of all who disagree with his views follows, but once again the ghosts interject and question whether the story is getting any closer to its goal. Petra despairs of ever being able to finish her painful task. Meanwhile, Jakob returns having found the man who killed her son, with another explanation. The man had been acting in a film about King Boris. Afterwards, filled with drunken pride and excitement, they chased the boy's father to his home, when the boy came out to defend him, the actor struck him on the head with his sword. Here, in this 'terrible story' (39) the connection with the opening tableau is forged, but as the narrative so far illustrates, the truth constantly exceeds the explanation:

> **Petra** So that's why you died.
> Because of a moment of madness
> **Jakob and Ivan** But why?
> **Petra** Because they were drunk.
> **Jakob and Ivan** But why?
> **Petra** Because they wanted to show they were the best . . .
> **Jakob and Ivan** But why?
> **Petra** Because the prime minister said they were the best . . .
> **Jakob and Ivan** But why?
> **Petra** Because of hundreds of years of history.
> **Jakob and Ivan** But why?
> **Petra** I don't know.
> I'm sorry.
> I don't understand either. (39)

The play closes with the boy at rest, but Petra faced with lonely survival. Ilka advises her that although the past cannot be undone, the future is open, it all depends on the story she may tell. Petra completes the cairn the ghosts have made to mark the boy's grave with a final stone and ends the play with a song, a hymn to the seasons and to the power of change.

In its use of self-reflexive acting techniques, humour, song and episodic narrative, *Petra* succeeds in exposing the complexities and ambivalences of the human desire for community and sameness. Following Greig's conviction that the mainstream media's presentation, the Balkan conflict as tribal, ancient and somehow inevitably foreclosed a sense of empathy and permitted the West to establish a safe distance from what was happening (Greig 2008: 218), the stress in *Petra* is upon the ordinariness of the characters and the familiarity of their emotions. There is no attempt to naturalistically represent the region or the war, rather what we have here is a 'provocation of associations' (Steinweg). The repetition of the question 'Why?' speaks directly to children's and parents' experience in a vivid and strategic way. This is not some exotic ethnic issue, it is ours too. In the play's 'interrogation of images of difference and prejudice', Adrienne Scullion sees 'Scottish theatre's preoccupation with debates about institutions, organisation and funding . . . about how different groups win a stake in the production and the dissemination of culture, and in the interpretation of representations of the nation' (2004: 477). Certainly, a key element in the play's structure is the fraught issue of who tells the story and how. Nonetheless, overall it seems more plausible to read this narrative performance as a healing ritual, like Peter Nesteruk, as 'a rite of passage for the lead character and for the audience. The exorcism of a ghost becomes the exorcism of communal tension' (2000: 30). Implicit in this process is the recognition that a singular uniform version of events cannot exist, that certain things remain incomprehensible even after a surfeit of explanations have been supplied, but above all, that the story of the future need not be preordained.

At an obvious level, *Dr Korczak's Example* cannot deliver this concluding sense of hopefulness; instead it challenges its audiences to consider the validity and outcomes of diametrically opposed responses to violence. The play is built around the remarkable and tragic history of Polish–Jewish writer, educator and paediatrician, Janusz Korczak, who ran two orphanages in Warsaw. In his introductory note to the play, Greig describes how he had at first been attracted to Korczak's radical ideas about children's rights and education, yet as he read Korczak's diaries, the story of the Warsaw Ghetto and his decision to accompany his orphans to the Treblinka extermination camp soon dominated his interest (2001: 1–2). *Dr Korczak's Example* was written as a companion piece for a stage version of Korczak's children's story, *King Matt*, and was first performed by TAG in 2001 directed by James Brining. The play has had a number of theatre productions in the United Kingdom and in Ireland since its premiere however, as with *Petra*, it was initially developed with an awareness of the TAG Theatre Company's practice of bringing performances to schools and of the resources they had at their disposal.

The resulting work concentrates on Korczak's orphanage in the Ghetto in the summer of 1942, his efforts to save the lives of the children and to maintain normality in the face of the mounting force of Nazi power. Korczak's community of children is joined by Adzio, a feisty street boy who challenges its rules and is finally expelled. At the play's conclusion, Korczak and his charges are on their way to Treblinka, among the many victims of the Grossaktion Warsaw, while Adzio and another orphan Stephanie gain temporary reprieve by hiding in the sewers and later participate in the Warsaw Ghetto Uprising. The performance ends with the cast reading Korczak's Declaration of Children's Rights that was to become the foundation for the United Nations Convention on the Rights of the Child. Without doubt here too is a drama of the unspeakable; the worst depths of murderous extremism are exemplified by the Holocaust. Like *Petra* the play revolves on a double axis: the ethical dilemma treated within the play of how to act in the face of aggression and violence, as well as the ethical question for the author of how to represent such events, without succumbing to melodrama or emotionally opportunistic spectacle, and in such a way as to speak to a young audience.

Once again, Greig resorts to various epic devices and techniques as a means of negotiating these dilemmas, and as Anja Müller observes, to 'establish the framework for communication with the audience' (2011: 95). This framework is created physically by a cast of between three to five performers and numerous dolls. The decision to use dolls to represent characters in the play is both premeditated and meaningful. It is for Greig, 'a stylistic device for the distancing of the actors and audience from the storytelling and as a way of conveying the sense of a larger canvas' (2001: 8). More significantly still, it derives from his desire to respect the suffering of the children involved; 'It felt wrong of me to represent them in an unmediated way' he says (2001: 3).

This mediated communication situation is further enhanced by the alternation between telling and showing, diegesis and mimesis. A heterodiegetic, or external, commentary frames the enacted story, producing a distancing effect that serves to create a space for reflection upon the nature of the story and its protagonists' values. The play begins with an actor providing context and introducing the protagonists using dolls. When Adzio is caught stealing and a policeman intervenes, the actress asks the audience what the policeman would do. Then the Adzio doll is shot. The actor admits:

> That's probably what he would do most probably.
> That's probably the truth of it.
> But if we left it there,
> We'd have no story would we?
> So instead, we're going to lie.
> We're going to make it happen like this . . . (11)

They re-enact the scene and Korczak saves Adzio. This opening serves a twin purpose – the opposed ethical stances of 'violence and humane resistance' are presented, but via a self-conscious narrative that comments on its own truthfulness, suggesting that 'lying in storytelling is not incompatible with truth' (Müller 2011: 96). The sense of narrative instability is reminiscent of *Petra*, but in this play it is the tension between utterly contrary attitudes to resistance that becomes the central focus.

Korczak's pacifism is countered not by the Nazis, who are utterly indifferent to him, but by a child within his own institution. As Müller remarks

> The strength of the play lies in how Greig confronts these two conflicting positions without taking sides. The play on the one hand illustrates the relevance and importance of conversation across cultures without the coercion to consensus. On the other hand, it also asks the question in how far a utopian stance such as Korczak's, can or ought to be maintained in the face of extremely inhumane conditions. (2011: 96)

Korczak's 'blind idealism' (47), his conviction that what is required, is to lead by example in order to defend humanity is aggressively challenged by Adzio's insistence on violent action. Adzio's spirit, his refusal to be cowed by insults, his pragmatic resourcefulness and his survival instinct are undeniably appealing, but his fantasies of revenge and brutal victory over his enemies are themselves closely modelled on Nazi practices of domination and extermination. Against all evidence to the contrary, Korzcak insists upon believing in reason and humanity; responding to the conditions that surround him, Adzio expects the worst of everyone. Adzio's individualism and Korzcak's commitment to community cannot be reconciled. Within the compass of the play's story neither is destined to survive, yet as Müller perceptively notes, their places in history are ironically reversed, Dr Korczak is remembered for his 'individual heroism [. . . whereas] Adzio's death will be remembered in collective form' (2011: 100). *Dr Korczak's Example* draws to a close with heterodiegetic contemplation of the transcendent power of example

> like Korczak,
> like the march of the children, the uprising was an example,
> that has become famous in history.
> Because it showed that people would not accept the world the
> way the Nazis wanted it. (69)

The relevance of example is not just a question of history, but also of the future as play's final declaration of '[t]he right to protest' (70) indicates.

After Idealism: *Stalinland, Europe, The Architect*

At the beginning of this chapter, I mentioned some of the forces at work in the changing attitudes to political theatre in Britain since the 1970s. Perhaps the most vital demonstration of a desire for change occurred at the end of the 1980s when, across Europe and the Soviet Union, cracks in the authority of the Communist regime began to show as people throughout Eastern Europe began to rise up in protest against their governments. 1989 became the year of dramatic, though mostly peaceful revolutions, when Poland, Hungary, East Germany, Czechoslovakia, Bulgaria and Romania successively seceded from the Communist Bloc. The tearing down of the Berlin Wall, the dismantling of Iron Curtain borders and the disbanding of the Warsaw Pact heralded the end of the Cold War and a period of political transformation throughout Europe and in the former Soviet Union. Some of the outcomes of this redrawing of the political map of Europe were as already noted violent, with the eruption of the wars in Yugoslavia as the country broke apart. Yet even without violent conflict the fall of Communism provoked a major renegotiation of identities – political, national and cultural – across Europe at the close of the twentieth century, marking the end of an era and the beginning of another that was both new and undefined. In the light of such a context, it is perhaps unsurprising that much of Greig's early work hovers over these events, including a play I will discuss in a later chapter, *The Cosmonaut's Last Message to the Woman He Once Loved in the Former Soviet Union*. More specifically still, it was in the wake of trip to Central Europe in the early 1990s which as he remembers 'threw up questions wherever I went', that Greig wrote several pieces responding to the emergent 'New Europe'. These, as noted in Chapter 1, included a cluster of works for Suspect Culture as well as *Stalinland*, *Europe* and *The Architect*. As he himself states these plays all 'investigated the theme of the failure of the left and the rise of the globalised, fragmented world' (Billingham 2007: 77).

Like *Petra*, *Stalinland* is unpublished, but I believe it warrants discussion since it marks the point when Greig by his own admission began to see himself as a playwright, rather than as a director. Produced by Suspect Culture, *Stalinland* won a Fringe First in 1992 and was given a production at the Citizens Theatre in Glasgow in 1993. Complimented by a reviewer Robert Butler for its 'spare and effective' images, the play depicts a family reunion just after the fall of Communism in an unnamed town. Using non-linear narrative techniques that juxtapose past and present experiences, dilemmas and decisions, Greig assembles a cast of figures each of which stands in a different relation to the country's communist past. Alex is a glass blower-cum-revolutionary who believes in naming and shaming those who collaborated with the regime. Josef is a sculptor: at the request of his father-in-law he designed an avant garde vase for the German market, then commissioned by the regime he created art to celebrate socialism. Joseph's monumental and unique glass statue, 'The Spirit of the People,' is destroyed by the student revolutionaries as a symbol of the past. His vase, mass-produced and anonymous, survives and is presented as a gift to the new mayor, as a symbol of the country's capitalist future. His ex-wife and model, Helena, is a bourgeois who fled to the West leaving her husband and daughter behind. Lydia their elder daughter is portrayed as a 'quiet dissident'. Karin, their younger daughter born in the West, is now a self-assured entrepreneur. Splicing scenes from the past and the present, Greig opens a wide lens picture of people caught in the torque of ideological change, the confusions and loyalties of the older and younger generations, as well as the East-West resentments and judgements they bear with them. The play's striking central image is of Josef cradling the head of the ruined statue, debating the past with an object that is not only a homage to the socialist ideals he espoused, but also an image of his wife who despised socialism. The family reunion, with all its misunderstandings, compromises and misshapen history, functions as an ironic metaphor for the post-wall political environment and the challenges it presents for the future. *Stalinland* is a notable early example of Greig's use of episodic structure, as well as a device identifiable in several of his subsequent works, that of 'translated' language. One of the reasons he offers for this choice was that he 'wanted that the feel of the language had originally been in some other language – that was partly because that's how I had read Brecht, in translation' (Billingham 2007: 75).

It is an effect prominent in *Europe* which was first performed at the Traverse Theatre Edinburgh in 1994 under the direction of Philip Howard. Sometimes cited as Greig's first play – more accurately it is his first play to appear in print – it is also a work that brings into focus sets of techniques and thematic trajectories tested in *Stalinland, And the Opera House Remained Unbuilt, Stations on the Border* and *Petra's Explanation* (an early version of *Petra*). In *Europe* the question of what being European might involve at the end of the twentieth-century reverberates. This is flagged in the published text which is prefaced by a quotation from Jacques Derrida's *The Other Heading*, intimating the ambivalence of a mutating European identity: 'Something unique is afoot in Europe, in what is still called 'Europe' even if we no longer know very well what or who goes by this name' (1992: 5). Yet, a second, less obvious impetus for the play is raised by Greig himself. Concomitant with the changing face of post-wall Europe was the transformation of Central Scotland as heavy industries were dying, and towns and villages were decimated by the changing economic climate. These semi-deserted locations, at which trains no longer stop, also fed the composition of the play and its exploration of such places as sites of harsh, at times violent, identity politics.

Europe is a striking piece because it showcases so clearly some of the core qualities of Greig's mature work. It marries 'translated language,' Brechtian methods and cinematic narrative splicing with a richly suggestive metaphorical premise in order to unfold a meditation on the conceptual and territorial malleability of contemporary Europe, and how people formulate their senses of self in a period of intense sociopolitical change. Due to its fertile thematic terrain, it has attracted considerable and insightful commentary from scholars. Likening the play to a *Lehrstück*, Peter Nesteruk usefully analyses the 'two opposing poles of identity exchange' in operation. These poles that are destructive and affirmative, exclusive and cosmopolitan delineate the extremes of self-identification and present the problem in dialectical terms (2000: 32). To this Anja Müller adds 'a distinction between residual and migratory characters' (2005: 158) that also facilitates a nuanced reading of displacement and the conceptual heterogeneity of the European continent in the play. By contrast, Nadine Holdsworth argues that plays like *Europe* 'challenge inflexible notions of the Scottish nation and Scottish cultural identity by presenting both in constant states of production' (2003: 25). While Janelle Reinelt's discussion of the play attends to how the 'New Europe' is 'to date an unfilled signifier, an almost-empty term capable of great/little significance and power' (2001: 365). To these interpretations Marilena Zaroulia's emphasis on the relations between conceptualizations of place and transnationalism adds an important dimension. It is in this contemporary territory of shifting meanings that the play's characters negotiate and renegotiate their identities. Perhaps most remarkable is the way *Europe* presents these potentially conflicting elements simultaneously – they are neither temporally nor spatially distinct, but overlap, collide and interpenetrate.

This sense of multiplicity is strategically reinforced by the play's deliberately episodic structure of twenty titled scenes divided across two acts. All but two of these scenes are based on a verbal exchange that unfolds a story. As Peter Billingham observes, the 'generic *gestus*' of each scene makes the Brechtian texture of the play overt (2008: 99). The opening blast of the sound of a train passing at speed, followed by the image of Morocco, a black man with a suitcase in the town square, sets the key for the ensuing variations on the theme of place, belonging and travel. The culminating scene titled simply 'Europe' significantly interleaves two radically different outcomes that cannot be easily reconciled.

The play's setting, a provincial border town in the heart of Europe, might be seen as both a synecdoche and a spatial paradox. It is explicitly described as a place '[h]istory has washed across' (6); the train station's architecture bears the traces of different historical periods and regimes: 'Hapsburg, Nazi and Stalinist' (7). It is at once central and liminal (Müller 2005: 156). The town's importance was as a frontier crossing, but since the border has ceased to be a frontier, trains no longer stop at its station. A sense of being left on the sidelines is accentuated by the fact that fifteen of the play's scenes are concluded by the roar of a train passing, while two others are completed by buses departing or arriving. The soundscape of this play is of enormous importance as we are repeatedly reminded of the thrilling mechanical power of the train and the transport networks that link distant places across the continent, while at the same time we witness exchanges between characters who feel desperately trapped or disconnected.

Thematically *Europe* skilfully engages with the current political complexities of belonging and mobility, as Fiona Wilkie convincingly argues in an essay on transport and travel in the play in *Cosmotopia: Transnational Identities in David Greig's Theatre*. It also works cleverly with a spectrum of modes of presentation mixing aural and visual motifs with choral speeches, conventional dramatic dialogue and direct address. A chorus at the beginning of each of the two acts provides a metacommentary on the situation of the town, creating space for the voice of community. Via the chorus we learn how the co-ordinates of this identity have traditionally been 'our soup, . . . our factory which makes light bulbs and . . . being on the border' (5) – ironic markers of culture reduced to cuisine, illuminating industry and geopolitical location. Yet by act two the comparatively secure, if minor, historical identity of the place and its inhabitants has been eroded; the border no longer exists and the factory has been downsized. It has become unrecognizable; as the chorus states, 'it isn't our place any more' (48).

This process of disenfranchisement is further underscored by the fact that the redefinition of this 'meaning less' place is enacted elsewhere – in the media. Briefly, in a flurry of negative publicity, the town is reinvested with meaning: 'They said the name of our town, politicians and sociologists all across the continent said its name' (89). But even this recognition is unstable as once again semantic slippage occurs: 'it wasn't a name any more but a condition, not a place but an effect' (89). The play concludes with the assertion by its most objectionable character that 'we're also Europe,' a statement that provocatively raises the question of what it means to lay claim to a European identity.

The play's characters comprise two father–daughter couples, Sava and Katia, Fret and Adele; Adele's husband Berlin and his former co-workers at the factory, Billy and Horse; and their childhood friend Morocco. The opening scenes are marked by arrivals – of Morocco, as mentioned above, and of the refugees, Sava and Katia, who are discovered in the waiting room of the now defunct train station. The random movement of apparent outsiders into this space which is both static and in flux provides the main catalyst for the dramatic action – a scenario Greig revisits later with *The American Pilot* (2005) and *Damascus* (2007).

The interlopers' presence solicits a range of responses from the local characters from empathy, sexual attraction to suspicion and hatred, and in this way multiple perspectives on self and place are exposed and juxtaposed. At first the aging stationmaster, Fret, attempts to evict the foreigners from his station. The antagonism of his attitude melts as he discovers a kindred spirit in Sava – they both share a love of railways and a similar ideal of an old and inherently 'civilized' Europe. Adele is fascinated by the strangers because she longs to travel, but has only ever imagined doing so by watching the trains that pass through the station. Morocco, a mysterious entrepreneurial trader, returns in an apparent welter of nostalgia for his homeplace, but later confesses to Katia 'nothing's more of a prison than a home' (71). The traumatized Katia refuses to identify (with) the place she comes from by denying its existence, 'The place I came from isn't there anymore. It disappeared. . . . Its name was taken off the maps and signposts' (41). A comparable sense of surreal erasure is evident when the local factory workers are told by a visiting consultant that they had 'been living in a dreamland' (9). Redundancy forces them to re-position themselves. Billy abandons his hometown as 'a dirty, nothing place . . . a place to die' (23–4). Berlin and Horse stay and, for want of better activities, get involved with the local skinheads. Morocco assists Katia in obtaining papers which enable her to leave in return for sexual favours. He, in turn, is vengefully beaten by his former friends for fraternizing with a foreigner. Adele chooses to go with Katia, while Sava decides to stay with Fret. The play concludes with opposing attitudes expressed through the characters' actions: Adele and Katia are last seen on an international train that carries them to a new set of possibilities, new places and future identities; Berlin and Horse remain rooted in their home soil looking back to the past with nostalgia. They 'defend' this territory by firebombing the train station, killing Fret and Sava and, momentarily, putting their town on the map again.

As is evident from this description, patterns of identity formation are configured in relation to a set of motifs and symbols of connection, movement and stasis. The rail network is a potent image of connectivity, a system that is linked 'to the heart of things' (14) but that demands constant vigilance in order to function correctly. Against this symbolic backdrop characters present a scale experiences. The refugees, Sava and Katia, are vulnerable, dislocated travellers blown about by 'the random chaotic winds of current events' (18); their stopping in the station is interpreted as a threat to the allegedly stable identity and values of the town. Yet ironically, as we have just seen, the town's identity is already destabilized by the severing of its connections with railway network and industry, forcing its inhabitants to decide whether to stay or to go. Feeling utterly powerless, Berlin and Horse are lured by the apparent security of a neo-fascist identity to become 'wolves' preying upon all outsiders. The perils of stasis are weighed against the consequences of mobility. Morocco's status as a trader affords him both privilege and risk. If at first he seems to be a pro-active figure constantly on the move in pursuit of business, then by the play's end his confident self-identification as a business traveller gives way to a more ambivalent image of his situation as both opportunist and victim. Similarly, Adele's romantic belief that 'travel broadens the mind' is countered by Katia with a violent image of its destructive effects on the self:

It doesn't broaden the mind, it stretches it like skin across a tanning rack . . . a pegged skin out to dry. Each thing you see, each thing the continent coughs up for you stretches it tighter until you can't keep all the things you've seen in the same mind and the skin rips down the middle. (53)

In the final scene Katia has become more empowered (even if her scepticism about the joys of tourism remains), her journey with Adele is a matter of her own choosing and her status is ensured by her newly acquired papers. Adele's hunger to roam Europe and her optimistic openness is spliced with Berlin's account of the aftermath of their torching of the station and the deaths of Fret and Sava. In consequence both images, of escape and entrapment are clamped together as the play concludes.

The image of the railway also accentuates the uneasy transition from modern to postmodern, from a cold war to a globalized era. Fret's homage to the glories of the European railway system takes the form of a vivid anthropomorphic metaphor – 'Steel and tracks and trains like blood, muscle and arteries holding the continent together' (53). As Dan Rebellato comments in his introduction to the play, this phrase recalls Fascistic (as well as futuristic) imagery and 'the infamous apologia for Mussolini, that at least he made the trains run on time' (2002: xvi). Yet the intertext appears in a scene entitled 'Points' in which Fret and Sava connect with each other in what Peter Zenzinger describes as 'rhapsodic antiphonic chant' celebrating a common civilization, metonymically represented by the rail network. This positive vision of Europe as a cradle of civilization, a model of progress, where at some fundamental level, 'We speak the same language, we think the same way' (52), is one of modernity's most cherished metanarratives (2005: 270). Its negative underside is, of course, presented by Katia who recalls the brutality of the Yugoslav war from which she and her father are presumably fleeing, and by Horse and Berlin's xenophobia. Indeed, when Sava asks Fret '[w]hat's there to be afraid of in a train?' (85), it is hard to suppress the memory of the train's pivotal role in the transportation of millions of victims of Fascism during World War II. It is precisely the tension between these extremes of possibility that drives the play's ethical challenge.

Throughout *Europe* then the rail system functions as an extended metaphor providing a tantalizingly problematic image of the European body politic. It is no accident that the system is represented as no longer cohesive or comprehensible to even its most faithful adherents; Fret complains that the railway timetables have ceased to be intelligible, 'Four hundred pages and none of it makes sense. Times, stations, trains . . . They've no relation to anything. Meaningless . . . they might just as well be foreign' (11–12). Notably, the younger generation of characters do not share this anxiety or the vision that underwrites it. They are affected by the changes it has produced, but their responses are to specific effects on their individual situations. Their motivations are orientated towards the personal, as opposed to some greater political or social project. Meanwhile, Fret and Sava represent a vision of modern European identity rooted in shared values and a faith in progress – a fundamentally humanist vision, for all its patent flaws. The world they affiliate with was stable, offering fixed itineraries and an assurance of mutual understanding at some level – a (perhaps illusory) ideal that has fissured in the new, postmodern Europe.

Described by Greig as 'a lament for certainty' (Billingham 2008: 85), *The Architect* carries this debate about the value and dangers of ideals back to a British base. Inspired in part by the radical transformation Glasgow in the 1960s and the ways in which the utopian visions behind many grand modern architectural schemes in reality created dysfunctional and dystopian social realities, Greig presents a dark picture of postmodern urban society. Again directed by Philip Howard (who describes the initial production later) and presented first at the Traverse Theatre in 1996, the play excavates, as Billingham puts it 'some of the contradictions that are an inescapable part of the liberal-humanist-Left project: its relative successes but also its fairly significant failures' (2007: 83). If in *Europe* the image of the railway is used as a means to unfold a debate around the politics of identity, then in this play the figure of the architect and his work take on this role as a symbolic hub linking a web of opposed impressions and possibilities.

Like *Europe* the play's cast is small consisting primarily of a middle-class nuclear family; the plot develops as an assemblage of short scenes arranged in two acts. Juxtaposition and contrast are key dramatic elements. The bourgeois nuclear family in ruins is collated with the post-war heritage modernist architecture and the remnants of the ideal of the architect as a god-like designer of social space. The worlds of Leo Black, the eponymous architect, his wife, Paulina, and their adult children, Dorothy and Martin, are offset against each other to reveal an utter lack of coherence or shared emotional territory. Encounters with three external characters Sheena, a woman who lives in an estate designed by Leo, Billy, an unemployed youth, and Joe, a truck driver, again open a plurality of perspectives and catalyse the play's action. Having become a success in the 1960s construction boom, Leo has spent much of his professional life designing cheap housing. In consequence it is bitterly ironic that not only is his own home life collapsing despite his refusal to acknowledge it, but also that one of his award-winning designs is now up for demolition. 'No more big projects' (115) he declares at the play's beginning in a futile bid to keep control. By the end he abandons his attempt to make the illusory centre hold; the family is seen as utterly alienated from each other, occupied with disjointed and aimless activities, while Leo chooses to be destroyed with his doomed architectural creation, rather unfortunately named Eden Court.

The suicidal conclusion to the play was reputedly based on a story Greig had heard in a pub. Later he heard other versions of the story, each concerning a different modern architectural project, but each featuring the death of the remorseful architect of the said monstrosity. Since there seems to be no evidence to prove any such a story, he came to the conclusion that 'The suicidal architect is an urban myth [that] perhaps gives voice to a collective psychic wish for revenge upon the creators of our urban environment' (Greig website). The architect stands as a figure of paternalism, arrogance, a privileged elite whose power and authority are enacted without apparent answerability or concern for those whose lives and environments it shapes. Yet, and it is here that the play's achievement glimmers, at the same time the character Leo is clearly an idealist who, despite his many faults, elicits our sympathy as a figure who experiences the full force of the collapse of all he thought he was working towards.

As in *Europe* the legacy of an earlier age of certainty is brought into conflict with a present age of confusion and change. Perhaps predictably, given the architectural guiding reference, the themes of space/belonging and identity are developed even more explicitly in relation to perspective. The play opens with Leo optimistically attempting to persuade his son to work for him by showing him a model of his latest building project. Although the visual image of the model commands the spectator's and reader's attention, and introduces the play's central spatial metaphor, a less prominent temporal dimension to this exchange is also worth noting. Leo's offer to engage Martin as an apprentice is a bid for continuity, which promises an eventual generational transfer, father to son, of his values, ideals and business. Notably, just as the daughters Katia and Adele in *Europe* refuse their fathers' values, Martin spurns this heritage, severing links with what his father represents.

Greig uses the image of the architectural model twice in the play, once in each act. The effect of the models on stage is to draw attention to space, perspective and scale. The models serve as representations of and designs for (social) space, as well as bringing on stage, in miniature, places that exist or will exist in the world outside. They also allow for a richly ironic and self-reflexive discussion of the role of architecture in creating places and non-places. In the opening scene, Martin's response to his father's homage to the power of the architect, is directed to the model, '[I]t's flat' are his first words in the play. The model is of a car park, with a tower (not yet built either in miniature or reality) and high security walls. The disjuncture between Leo's idealistic vision and the scale model of a typical urban non-place sardonically undermines the former.

The second instance where a scale model appears is in act two where yet again Leo attempts to explain and defend his vision, this time of the Eden Court estate to resident Sheena Mackie. As with the model of the car park, discussion is orientated around the difference between the pristine world of the plan and the constructed space of the final product. Martin's facetious comment that he could make 'the models look real. Cover the walls in graffiti . . . put little models of dossers under the bridges' (102), is echoed by Sheena's remark that the towers should not be surrounded by green but by brown felt as the latter would be realistic (164). The optimistic vision expressed by the architectural plans is deconstructed and debunked by those familiar with the grim social realities of the end product.

The models, and the constructions they represent, suggest parallel realities, a motif developed in particular in the scenes tracking the movements of the Black offspring. Dorothy and Martin are seen seeking arbitrary sexual experiences with strangers – Martin in public toilets, Dorothy hitchhiking on the motorway. Dorothy's and Martin's attempts to escape the space of family might be interpreted as bids to forge other spaces of identity, yet they are highly problematic in two important respects: the places in which they accidentally find themselves, the interior of a truck, a roadside café, the toilet, a gay bar and the roof of a tall building, are anonymous or generic, while the intimacies they seek there are blatantly transitory. The prevailing impression is of disconnection and displacement – each character is adrift ontologically and physically. While Leo identifies with a life project of shaping social space, his children and wife illustrate states of disassociation and various types of refusal to commit. So for instance, Martin indulges a blatantly abstract fantasy of becoming an apprentice to a deaf carpenter in the mountains while he rejects both Leo's practical offer of an apprenticeship in his firm and Billy's offer of a relationship. Dorothy responds to any encounter that suggests a need for emotional commitment with nausea, while Paulina's neurotic fixation with pollution and disease lead her to self-isolation and mental collapse.

The Architect, of course, recalls Henrik Ibsen's *The Master Builder* (1892), despite the fact that Greig claims not to have read the play at the time of its composition. Nevertheless, it uncannily mirrors its predecessor similarly tracing the destiny of the artist/architect from confident self-assertion to doubtful disillusionment and self-destruction. Nevertheless, at closer range and of more immediate import is the way in which Leo Black is the spokesman for a modernist architectural vision that inspired so much urban development. Exemplified by the influential vision of urbanist architect and designer Le Corbusier (1887–1965) in the 1920s and 1930s of mass housing as 'machine[s] for modern living' (Harvey 1990: 39), the ambition was to create rationally ordered space, from which would emerge a rationally ordered society. Greig's character Leo Black is a belated defender of such an ideal, although ironically his award-winning creation is a socially dysfunctional wasteland. Black's modernist monument (modelled, as he proudly declares, on Stonehenge) is demolished at the play's conclusion, its residents having campaigned to be re-housed. Black resents their complaints, obstinately refusing to help because '[he] won't see good ideas blown up just because some people can't see beyond their own misery' (168). Yet, in the end he is forced to accept their will. Refusing to conform to a postmodern context, Leo chooses to stand by the admittedly hubristic certainty of his youthful convictions. The alternative, represented in the play through Pauline, Martin, Dorothy, Billy and Joe, is hardly a more attractive prospect. Leo's masterpiece is an attempt to create a meaningful social space with its conceptual reference to the pre-modern Stonehenge and vision of urban community linked through shared public space, by balconies and walkways, and it is an ostentatious failure. Martin and Dorothy, and their companions Billy and Joe are wary of such grandiose visions of social purpose, but they find no substantial or meaningful replacement. Their wanderings through the metropolis and along the motorways linking urban spaces are fundamentally lonely, fragmented and directionless.

As we will see in Chapter 4, *The Cosmonaut's Last Message* Greig sharpens the images of disconnection and movement so prominent in these three plays, through a continued use of episodic narrative and juxtapositional structure. However what *Stalinland, Europe* and *The Architect* share is the crafting of an overtly dialectical treatment of the transformation of European identities following the collapse of the left and the erosion of the apparent certitudes of modern progress. They share a predilection for concretizing metaphors – the vase and the statue in *Stalinland*, the railway system in *Europe*, the architectural model in *The Architect* – that serve as vehicles for abstract, complex and conceptually dissonant attitudes and ideologies. These parables of contemporary Europe are thus dramaturgically linked by a developing sense of the performative power intrinsic to that Brechtian tension, so keenly described by Eric Bentley earlier, between the co-present forces of sympathy *and* distance, attraction *and* repulsion, tenderness *and* horror' (1987: 34).

Vulnerabilities and Communities: *Yellow Moon, Monster in the Hall, Fragile*

By contrast with these conceptually laden early works *Yellow Moon, Monster in the Hall* and *Fragile* display a lightness of touch and a stripped back attitude to dramatic situation. The techniques of this cluster of plays are in some respects distinct from those just discussed, and yet they also testify to the evolution of Greig's approach to theatre in the intervening years. Although diverse works they are linked not least because they illustrate the development of a style of presentation that is simple, fluid, physical and direct. They also address, and involve, specific communities and audiences. *Yellow Moon* and *Monster in the Hall* were composed with school audiences in mind and commissioned for a particular age group. *Fragile* and *Monster in the Hall* directly deal with experiences of social vulnerability and social services provision. All three works explore potential states of alienation and points of human contact. Each foregrounds the physical presence and resourcefulness of the performers while at the same time anticipating audience response in different ways.

Both *Yellow Moon* and *Monster in the Hall* were written for the TAG Theatre Company, Glasgow. Greig's experience with TAG, as we have already seen, dates back to 1996 with *Petra* and 2001 with *Dr Korczak's Example*, so these plays indicate his continuing interest in writing for young audiences and his success with this genre of work. Guy Hollands directed both shows, a process he vividly describes in his contribution to this book. *Yellow Moon*, the result of one of his first commissions as an artistic director for the theatre, was first performed in 2006 in the studio of the Citizens Theatre before touring around schools. It has been a remarkably successful piece, winning the 2007 Theatrical Management Association's award for Best Show for Children and Young People, as well as being revived in 2007 and 2012, when the Citizens Theatre presented it along with *Monster in the Hall*.

Yellow Moon subtitled *The Ballad of Leila and Lee*, plays with storytelling, mixing an external or heterodiegetic narrative commentary with action and dialogue. Narrative text is unassigned and is divided among the cast of four, there are no props or costumes. Like *Petra* and *Dr Korczak's Example*, the approach to performance is governed by the need for the work to speak to audiences in non-theatre spaces in a fresh, effective manner. Derived, as Greig describes on his website, from a confluence of influences – the tragic ballad of Stagger Lee (there are several popular variants of the title), and reading about depression and alcoholism – the play tells the story of two disaffected teenagers who find themselves on the run in a remote part of Northern Scotland.

Their stories are both simple and complicated – Lee Macalinden comes from a broken home. His mother has suffered from depression since his father left and regularly withdraws to drown her sorrows. His mother's new boyfriend, Billy Logan, would rather he disappeared. Lee steals the engagement ring Billy is about to present to his mother. In the conflict that ensues Lee stabs and kills Billy. Meanwhile, Leila Suleiman, a studious Muslim girl from Damascus who now lives in Scotland, struggles with her fascination with celebrity culture and a sense of her own worthlessness. Her withdrawal from the world around her is expressed in her refusal to speak. In order to feel she is real, she cuts herself. Lee meets Leila in a shop and finds herself caught up in the murder and escape. They head to Blackwaterside to find Lee's father, and are rescued by the estate's alcoholic gamekeeper, Frank, who forces them to work on the estate. After three months a celebrity visitor, Holly Malone, arrives and soon after the police turn up, thus breaking the rough community the three have formed, just at the moment Lee realizes that Frank is his long-lost father. Lee runs away and Frank commits suicide in his mountain hideaway. Finally Leila and Lee surrender to the police, but only after Lee cuts out his father's heart and buries it in the cave hideaway.

The action consists of twenty short scenes each numbered by the storytellers in performance, that present these events from different perspectives combining voiceover narrative with enaction and re-enaction. The ballad form with its multiple verses and repetitions provides the framing concept, just as the play's title references the Stagger Lee ballad. The emphasis placed on these scene changes – in particular the ways they sever a naturalistic progression of action – as well as the speed of the narrative delivery at the beginning of the play generates a possibly ironic, even safe, distance from the story. Strikingly though, this safe distance is then collapsed in moments of physical awkwardness and empathy that are communicated in performance. Lee's ambition to become Inverkeithing's first pimp may be farcical, but his posturing to impress Leila and the discomfort of sexual inexperience are not merely funny, they channel audience response towards a shared experience of embarrassment and desire that anyone who has survived being a teenager should recognize. Similarly, while celebrity culture's superficiality is satirized in the character of Holly, Leila's feelings of abject ugliness and self-harm prompted by this culture are no joke. Meanwhile, Frank's drunkenness may be pathetically comic; his inability to express affection for his son is both brutal and tragic. Greig's approach to each of these issues is markedly unpatronizing, while the deft combination of lyricism, self-reflection, narrative and performative energy ensure that *Yellow Moon* is a work that speaks not only to a teenage audience but beyond, as the recent revivals illustrate.

Monster in the Hall, first performed at Kirkland High School and Community College in Fife in 2010, has similarly overstepped its original remit and has gone on to productions in the Traverse Theatre during the Edinburgh Fringe Festival in 2011, a revival in 2012 at the Citizens Theatre and elsewhere. Alerted to the experiences of young people responsible for looking after ill parents, Greig worked with the Fife Young Carers group and *Monster in the Hall* is a response to that encounter. Again built around a cast of four with minimal equipment (microphones and outsize horn-rimmed spectacles suffice), the play is about a sixteen-year-old girl, Duck Macatarsney, who is struggling to look after her father who suffers from Multiple Sclerosis. Duck panics when the school arranges for an official assessment of their home situation. Their attempts to seem normal are almost derailed when Duck's father goes blind, her school friend turns up to ask for a favour and a cyberspace friend of her father's arrives from Norway, all just moments before the woman from the social services is to appear.

The treatment of this scenario is fast-paced and farcical; mixing many of the same narrative techniques used in *Yellow Moon* with 1960s pop harmonies (Duck is serenaded and interrogated by a group of Duckettes), citations of teen romances and a parallel universe of fairy stories and warrior adventures. As Mark Fisher notes in his review of the play: '[W]here many a writer would have tackled this theme sanctimoniously, Greig treats it with heady irreverence, acknowledging the truth of the dilemma while recognizing that a teenage girl has other matters to deal with – not least the effeminate boy who wants a simulated blow-job outside the chip shop' (2010). Duck or Ducati (her late mother's favourite motorbike) is forced to manoeuvre around a series of increasingly absurd obstacles, beginning with 'the monster in the hall', which as we are told is both 'a metaphor for the things in our lives we can't face' (47) and a real object in their home – her mother's bike. Her fears that her father is busy online every evening watching pornography prove unfounded, but his nightly adventures in 'Otherworld,' a multiplayer game, bring other unwelcome consequences in the shape of Agnetha, the Norwegian anarcho-feminist rocker, his warrior companion in cyber space. Greig raises the comic tension, while simultaneously allowing a painful glimpse of the strain of Duck's daily situation to appear in the midst, in a powerfully moving speech recounting her father's real condition and her attempts to make their life liveable. The play builds to its climax with a fantastically unlikely motorbike chase and an unforeseen resolution. In keeping with the comic generic frame, the representative from the social services delivers, not the threatened rupture of the family, but a creative outlet for Duck's novelistic ambitions and a flutter of leaflets.

Both *Yellow Moon* and *Monster in the Hall* attempt to seize audiences with a particularly physical performance style that is characterized by rapid, multiple narrative moves, coupled with a bid for emotional connection. Greig is quick to credit Guy Hollands's contribution to the shape of this work and how his influence has directed his attitudes to the presentation of story. Also, we may note the ways in which these works refashion the Lesson/Learning play structure for contemporary purposes, in particular in the ways they juggle distance and empathy and use the bodies of the performers to achieve a recognition and re-conception of social (and by implication political) experiences.

Fragile premiered in 2011 for Theatre Uncut also tackles the question of proximity, but clearly has an overt political agenda. Theatre Uncut is a creative initiative that began in protest to the radical governmental cuts in public spending in Britain. As the widespread popularity of the project has revealed, it is an issue that extends well beyond the Cameron/Clegg context. Theatre Uncut aimed to open a debate about important contemporary political issues, to create a space for new work on political themes to be aired and shared and to instigate action. *Fragile* was one of eight short plays performed between 16 and 19 March 2011 by groups across Britain and elsewhere as part of Theatre Uncut's inaugural cultural intervention.

The topic is the impact of the cuts on those who rely upon mental healthcare services. Conceived as a two-hander, the play stages a discussion between Jack a young man who uses the community support centre and Caroline a therapist there, late at night in her home. Jack has just heard the centre is to be closed and has broken into Caroline's place clad in a balaclava. After some discussion Jack proposes immolating himself in protest just like Mohamed Bouazizi (whose suicide catalysed the Tunisian Revolution in 2010). He has come prepared with a flask of diesel – ironically stowed in a recyclable 'supermarket "bag for life"' (53). Caroline, faced with this 'fragile' man doused in diesel, tries to persuade him to hand over his cigarette lighter and that other forms of action would be more feasible.

What makes this scenario potent is its form. Greig assigns the role of Caroline to the audience. The play includes an 'Audience Briefing' to be undertaken at the beginning, explaining that 'in the spirit of big society' the playwright would like the audience to contribute. Using a PowerPoint presentation, the audience are asked to run through a few lines and non-verbal character directions before the play gets underway. Immediately this process eradicates any fourth wall in the theatre space, and casts the audience as a community and as agents in what follows. Here we have participatory theatre in action. The lines spoken by the character Caroline under these circumstances take on new significances. The audience is obliged (if they participate as planned) to explain the very situation they themselves are protesting by their presence at the performance. They become implicated in Caroline's apologetic explanations of the rationale behind the cuts, her resigned attitude to a lost 'dream of Britain' (61) and must face Jack's frustrated response. Still more compellingly is the dramatic turn in this conversation when the audience find themselves desperately trying to persuade Jack that less radical forms of protest that public suicide can truly be effective. Following Caroline's admission of a sense of defeat, her promise that 'We'll use the internet/We'll start a campaign . . . We'll protest' is not particularly convincing. The play concludes with the audience still begging for the lighter. It is an electrifying scenario, ironically generated by an experimental use of one of the most overused and potentially dull presentational interfaces. Yet, in the theatre, in this instance, PowerPoint acutely reorders our attitudes to the performance and positions us at the heart of the dilemma of political engagement it presents.

World Politics in Miniature: *Kyoto* and *Letter of Last Resort*

A remodelled *Lehrstück* format is, I would suggest, also the formal basis for two recent short plays that approach enormous and pressing ethical debates. In fact, the dimensions of both *Kyoto* and *The Letter of Last Resort* seem in wilfully inverse relation to the proportions of the political questions they raise. *Kyoto* was written for David MacLennan's lunchtime play series, A Play, A Pie and A Pint in conjunction with the Traverse Theatre. First performed at Òran Mór in Glasgow directed by Dominic Hill in 2009, it is a piece, as Greig himself explains later, that derives from the Suspect Culture 2007 revue *Futurology*, which also addresses the question of climate change. Here the complicated politics of the environment provide the backdrop to the sexual attraction between two opposed parties in that debate: Lucy a scientist and Dan a civil servant. Having met in Kyoto in 1997 at the United Nations Convention on Climate Change, they have harboured an attraction for each other despite the fact that they are officially opponents. Now, at last, in an anonymous hotel in an undefined post-communist location at yet another conference, they at last have the opportunity to consummate their relationship. After a day of arguing over the abstracted implications of 'Hope or desire' (462), they are alone, but things do not quite pan out as intended. A power cut solicits different responses to crisis that ultimately set them apart. Dan's king-size bed provokes Lucy to comment on the unfairness of the room allocations: 'The sleeping arrangements are a symbol of the underlying power structures' (468) she remarks crossly. Dan counters that she is just paranoid and teases her for wanting to save the world. In the course of this thirty-minute sketch, the characters fight, complain of the cold, reminisce about their attraction for each other, talk about their home relationships. Dan wants room service. Lucy is content to make do with what they have. He is all for heading off to find a hotel porter or to town to buy an extra blanket. She questions his optimism. Their shared memories of conferences and meetings are stifled as Lucy switches topic to the melting polar ice. Efforts to forget about the environment melt away as Lucy admits 'when I looked around me at this new landscape I realized for the first time that I had been wrong at Kyoto' (483). She realizes that although she had somehow identified with Dan's childishness back then, in fact no-one knew what they were doing at all those conferences, despite the dire consequences of inaction. Unsurprisingly sexual congress doesn't happen either – 'it turns out we're freezing and hungry and naked and depressed and guilty and – Anyway there's no future because the world's going to end (484) Dan says grudgingly. Instead, Lucy proposes that they go out and slide on the ice on the lake. Even in this they cannot agree – 'When it gets light' (486) is Dan's response.

Kyoto turns on a personal–political axis where the relationship between Dan and Lucy is metaphorically hinged to huge ethical questions about our responsibility for the environment. The characters' actions and failure to act mirror the greater political debates around how to respond to climate change. That said, it is as Greig claims,

> meant to be funny, it's not meant to preach or teach as a play. The point is this thing, the issue of global warming, has been in the background for ten years in our society. Just like the attraction between these people, it's the elephant in the room, something has been happening for a decade, and we've reached a crisis point where we have to find out what they're willing to do about it. (Cramer 2009)

As the play's conclusion indicates what the next step should be is left undetermined.

The Letter of Last Resort premiered at the Tricycle Theatre in London directed by Nicolas Kent early in 2012 as part of a series of short plays commissioned under the title 'The Bomb: A Partial History'. The play was given a second outing, along with David Harrower's *Good With People*, at the Traverse Theatre during the 2012 Edinburgh Festival. Both productions elicited favourable reviews. As Kent notes in his introduction to the published volume of plays, he had been prompted to revisit the nuclear weapons issue in part by the renewal of the British nuclear weapons programme known as the Trident system – which is incidentally based in Western Scotland (2012: 6). The Tricycle has a well-established reputation as a venue for political theatre, and as I will discuss later, Greig had already contributed to a series of short plays on the theme of Afghanistan in 2009.

The Letter of Last Resort sees Greig use a similar minimalist two-hander structure to elaborate a set of questions on the ethics of nuclear warfare. The core premise is simple: the newly elected British Prime Minister is approached by civil servant John with a task towards the end of her first day in office. She must compose 'the letter of last resort' that should inform the captain of the British Trident submarine of her orders if Britain were destroyed by a nuclear attack. She must decide whether, in the event that London and Britain have been obliterated, she should authorize an attack on the enemy or not. The hypothetical scenario reveals the philosophical paradoxes of the nuclear weapons programme. The Prime Minister struggles with the conceptual rationale of such a task and attempts to humanize it by desiring the names of the individuals who would be involved. Yet within the terms of the problem this seems irrelevant. Attempting to move beyond such an impasse, the Prime Minister and John role play the possible arguments for or against particular courses of action. The result is she realizes, '[t]o write retaliate is monstrous and irrational. To write 'don't retaliate' renders the whole nuclear project valueless' (222). How to envision an ethical response hypothetically after history, after the destruction of one's culture, history, land and self? Faced with the political conundrum that irrationality may be proved by rational behaviour the only conclusion she can draw is that

> We pursue rationality until it creates a logical paradox so extreme that it breaks through the simple binary opposition of rational and irrational and it becomes something else – something beyond – something transcendent. (226)

As we have seen at the beginning of this chapter, transcendence is a notion Greig cites as a means to explain and explore the potentialities of political theatre. The irony of that usage here is knowingly admitted within the dramatic situation with playfully postmodern self-reflection.

The Prime Minister immediately makes an analogy with Pirandello and British comedy, but just as quickly acknowledges that this is no absurd drama. Evidently *The Letter of Last Resort* is absurd and, at the same time, a potent piece of political theatre that transcends simplistic binary oppositions, leaving the audience, like the character of the Prime Minister at the play's close, in an unscripted, undecided place.

Naked Rambling: *Dalgety* and Beyond

To close this chapter's tour through the evolution of Greig's dramaturgy and its survey of the qualities and resonances of its 'epic, presentational, storytelling style,' I want to turn to a notion that recurs in some of Greig's most recent comments about writing for theatre. I began by citing his attempt to describe what 'Rough Theatre' might involve, in particular the 'power of contradiction' to upset presumptions, even rationality (2008: 220). Throughout the plays analysed in this book, regardless of their political or apolitical ambitions, this tactic can be identified and is, I believe, key to comprehending the ethical aspect of Greig's work as a whole. Yet it is also a more elliptical force in how he sees the theatre-making process. In a 2011 interview with Jennifer Williams at the Traverse Theatre, Greig likens writing to stripping. As self-exposure, theatre channels the fearful, the embarrassing, the taboo and the author must somehow deceive himself into bypassing his own sense of repression or conscious restraint. The writer's task, he suggests, is to bring exteriority (the perceivable) into contact with interiority (the intangible). But the process does not conclude there. The writer, the director, designer and performers can only attend to the concrete, the tangibles that in performance can elicit the intangible. Alongside this scheme of oscillation runs an ongoing impetus – that a play must always begin with an unanswered question, 'a question about what it is to be human' (Williams 2011).

Greig's short play *Dalgety*, presented at the 2012 Edinburgh Fringe Festival and then as part of Theatre Uncut later in the year, comically unites this idea of metaphorical self-exposure with something literal, current and political. Stephen Gough, popularly known as 'The Naked

Rambler', is a nudist activist who has since 2005 been repeatedly arrested and imprisoned for public nudity. His only crime is a refusal to wear clothes, for which he has now spent over six years in prison. His case uncomfortably exposes the legal mechanisms of social control and state policing and maintenance of the bounds of normality and, quite obviously, illustrates the exercise of state power over the individual in tragic and absurd ways. Greig's play approaches the topic obliquely but is quick to exploit the bizarre dimension to the whole debate. Again, it queries what it is that fundamentally makes us what we are, while at the same time eschewing the ponderousness of such an enquiry.

Set in a sleepy police station in Dalgety, not far from where Gough was last arrested in 2012, Greig humorously unpacks the provocation presented by the Naked Rambler's rejection of social norms, not to some abstract system of authority but to individuals who represent that authority – two humble local police officers who are looking forward to the end of their shift. The scene opens with the Sergeant and Constable discussing bodies – the Sergeant is busy ogling the physical perfections of the Olympic sports people on television, while the Constable is concerned with getting home on time to complete her calorie-burning exercise routine. But normality is overthrown when the Naked Rambler knocks on their door forcing them into a discussion of nudity and the law. Meanwhile, beyond the safety of the station, the world has inexplicably and incomprehensibly changed. The 'civilized' world has disappeared, the Tesco carpark has vanished and a tribe of naked people light a fire and sing beneath a tree. Illogically, the only remnant of the twenty-first century is a continued access to Google, for what it's worth. The responses of the Sergeant and Constable could not be more contrasting. She decides to join the naked, primitive community outside, while he locks himself within the now meaningless stronghold of the police station armed with a gun. The play is, of course, a joke but an incisive one on our notions of what guarantees civilization, the ways we protect it, and how fragile its basis might actually be. The comic situation juxtaposes the acceptable titillation and voyeurism encouraged by the media's coverage of the Olympic spectacle, with the unacceptable provocation of the lone nudist. It asks what defines us – our bodies, our ability to run, our sense of community?

This chapter has charted Greig's inclination to transform models of non-naturalistic theatrical presentation to transcend the expected as a means of addressing questions of power and engaging audiences. Formally, a development can be traced from an early interest in the Lesson play through to intricate explorations of the politics of identity in post-Wall Europe to a style of writing that is generously open to performance, conscious of its audience as participants and ethical in its bearing. Thematically the movement from Europe, to the United Kingdom, to world politics is significant too as it leads to considerations of communities and their co-ordinates. In the chapters that follow, the place, space and forms of community serve to connect their assorted concerns, first within the frame of the nation, then the global and transnational, and finally in the contact zones between cultures.

CHAPTER 3
SCOTLAND

Of, About, Despite – Imagining Scotland

'I rarely write directly or recognizably about Scotland . . . But I am always writing from Scotland: Of it? About it? Despite it?'. This was how Greig presented his artistic relationship with his homeland in an interview with Caridad Svich in 2007. Despite the apparent evasiveness of the statement, it is a subject he has often talked about and that regularly features in discussions of his work. That said, Scotland is a topic Greig approaches with palpable circumspection, perhaps justifiably. Looming large here are questions of national identity, the politics of place and representation. And they are magnified by the progress of devolution in the United Kingdom and the new horizons, this political process has opened up. Bertold Schoene in his introduction to *The Edinburgh Companion to Contemporary Scottish Literature* (2007) notes how 'Scotland's transition from subnational status to devolved home-rule' has generated healthy, and sometimes heated, debate around notions of national authenticity and cultural specificity in the face of the everyday realities of social heterogeneity and cross-cultural interconnectedness (Schoene 2007: 1). How does one write Scotland? What are the defining characteristics of contemporary Scottish culture and literature? What does it mean to be a Scottish writer or playwright? Should one even worry about such questions?

Some of these issues were flagged by Dan Rebellato in his introduction to *Plays 1* (2002), and as Greig's career has developed, his comments have remained apt. Rebellato points to the varied nature of Scotland, its historically 'permeable border' and its vantage point from the margins of power: 'Scotland is both itself and not quite itself; there are rich and vivid alternative maps to be drawn of Scotland's imaginary geography, depicting the thick concentrations of historical memory and the flowing urban landscapes of cultural internationalism' (2002: xii, xi). Adrienne Scullion similarly reads this double focus in the work of contemporary Scottish dramatists who, since independence, have responded 'by telling stories . . . that are *both* international and outward-looking *and* essentially and immediately committed to work within and about Scottish society' (2001: 388). That dual vision is one increasing noticeable in Greig's work since 2000.

At an obvious level, Scotland is home for Greig; it is the place in which he deliberately stationed himself as an author with a view to interacting with an audience, and he is deeply committed to working in Scottish theatre. In discussion with Mark Fisher, he describes how when he first envisioned himself as a playwright, it was a Scottish audience he had in mind – 'It was to do with that particular audience. I knew that what I wanted to say was for those people. It was a conversation with them' (Fisher 2011: 23). It is a conversation that has, over the years, spun in a few different directions with hiatuses and diversions. As Maggie Inchley observes, in the 1990s and early 2000s, characters in his plays are rarely depicted primarily in terms of national identity, while personal or transnational identities are more prominent (2012: 80). But equivocating comments notwithstanding, upon closer inspection references to Scotland can be found in almost all his plays, sometimes as minor and sometimes as major keys. What becomes evident is that Scottishness for Greig is a field of debate, enquiry and at times resistance, a space that remains, as David Pattie analyses later in this book as, 'usefully unfixed'. With this in mind, I have chosen as the basis of this Chapter 6 plays that use Scottish settings – they chart how Greig has explored Scotland as a creative and polymorphous space from some of his earliest work to some of the most recent.

Olympian Heights: *Caledonia Dreaming*

Caledonia Dreaming subtitled *An Edinburgh Fantasy* is an as yet unpublished play that was written for and produced by 7.84 Theatre Company and directed by Iain Reekie. In a sequence of short sketches, we are introduced to a group of characters as they move between various locations in the city. Gradually they are all drawn to the Caledonian Hotel, where as rumour has it Sean Connery is staying. Each character carries a dream, an ambition or a fantasy. Stuart, a Member of the European Parliament, wants to bring the Olympic Games to Edinburgh. Lauren, an English sauna/sex worker, dreams of settling down in her own home. Eppie, a bored middle-class housewife, fantasizes about when she met Sean Connery as a young girl. Darren, a working-class young man, dreams of becoming Sean Connery's personal assistant. Jerry, a doorman at the Caledonia Hotel, longs to make it as a singer. David Pattie elaborates on the elusive figure of Sean Connery who comically serves as an ideal of Scottish achievements for the characters throughout the play, despite their class, racial and national diversity. As the apotheosis of Scottishness, Connery's arrival at the hotel gathers almost messianic import. He never materializes at the Caledonian; instead, at the Heart of Midlothian on the High street, the characters, now all a little worse for wear, experience an epiphany when a black limousine allegedly bearing Connery pauses and they catch a glimpse of the latter-day Scottish messiah through the open car window. What I would like to foreground are some of the aspects of the play's structure and politics less prominent in Pattie's chapter later.

First performed at the Traverse Theatre in Edinburgh in 1997, and reprised in 1999 at the Edinburgh Fringe, the play's action takes place on the eve of devolution. The combination of such a politically momentous context, comic irony, aspiration and Greig's description of the play on his website as a response to *The Cheviot, the Stag and the Black, Black Oil* (1973) mark this piece as a playful and provocative engagement with Scottish identity on various levels.

An overtly political, leftist and didactic theatre company, 7.84 was founded by playwright John McGrath in 1971. The title of the company, a statistic – 7 per cent of the world's population control and 84 per cent of its wealth – indicates the spirit of the project that aimed to bring theatre to places and people left off the map of middleclass culture. The Scottish branch of the company developed *The Cheviot, the Stag and the Black, Black Oil* written by McGrath, using Highland ceilidh as its basis. The play, now a canonical work of political theatre, combines Gaelic songs, sketches, interviews and filmed reconstructions of events to 'chronicle[s] the exploitation of the Highlands of Scotland' from the clearances to the discovery of oil in the North Sea (Shellard 2000: 152). But rather than a lament for all that ordinary Scots have lost, *The Cheviot* winningly combined variety entertainment with polemic, encouraging audiences to celebrate working-class resistance and to question the motivations of those in power be they landlords or oil company executives (Nelson 2002). So, when Greig writes a play for this company and describes it as a response to *The Cheviot*, expectations are bound to run high.

Like *The Cheviot*, *Caledonia Dreaming* is structured episodically and performers multitask. Temporally and spatially it is more unified – summer 1997, Edinburgh – yet its reflections on Scotland are more diffuse. Plainly, rather than charting a history of exploitation or raising a call to action, *Caledonia Dreaming* develops a multifaceted image of contemporary Scottish identity that ranges from burgeoning patriotism to cultural cringe. It is also an image inflected by sardonic humour and urban points of reference. Greig's approach to politics is markedly elliptical. Major political questions appear only tangentially in six titled sketches described by Greig on his website as 'wound 'choruses' which reflect on the devolutionary issues at the time the play was written'. The first of these set in Edinburgh's Camera Obscura provides a panorama of the city with choral commentary. Here we have a tourist gaze, guided to observe the beauties of the city, but also counterproductively distracted by more dubious details, a student sunbathing topless, a soldier secretly smoking, a violent robbery and how Princes Street Gardens 'used to be a lake of sewage' (8). The next, entitled 'The Yes Yes Campaign,' points towards set of positive, can-do attitudes for the future, but like 'Camera Obscura,' is leavened by details that undermine the positivism of the chorus. 'Scottish Conservatives' drolly presents a collage of personal and Hibernian FC defeats. 'The West Lothian Question' reroutes this controversial, but tedious, debate begun in 1977 over whether MPs from Scotland, Wales and Northern Ireland should have the right to vote on affairs that concern England only. The question goes to the heart of the tenability of the Union. One of the solutions to the inequality of the situation would be the dissolution of the Union altogether – obviously an inconceivable option until recently. Instead Greig's chorus jokingly asks another 'unanswerable' question: 'Why's it always raining in Harthill?' (47), thus bypassing the political conundrum altogether. 'Self Determination' is a riff on mixed Scottish, Irish, English and Italian family origins and affiliations. 'The Heart of Midlothian' unfolds the story of why it is a tradition to spit on the heart – not for good luck as the tourist guide in 'Camera Obscura' suggests – but rather to commemorate the Edinburgh Mob riot against the bankers in 1736. Now in place of civil unrest, 'Every gobbet of saliva. That lands on this sacred heart. Is a little personal riot' (72).

Tourism, new-found positivism, self-deprecation and pessimism, parliamentary dilemmas, mixed identities and historically embedded acts of resistance – each gesture towards political realities of 1997— also have continued to be a feature of Scottish national politics and culture post-devolution. Throughout the play these issues are treated with Greig's characteristic dialectical, irony infused, method bringing opposing impressions together to create a complex and unstable picture that concludes with the visionary, if histrionic, fantasy of the grand opening of the Edinburgh Olympics complete with Sean Connery reciting Robert Burns' 'A Man's a Man For A' That'. For some, *Caledonia Dreaming* many seem too self-reflexive and tongue-in-cheek to taken as a serious rejoinder to its predecessor. As Greig mentions on his website, John McGrath was, apparently, none too impressed. But I would agree with Dan Rebellato in reading the play's resistance to simplistic or unified resolution as politically strategic and meaningful – 'By insisting on this paradoxical doubled and undefinable Scotland,' says Rebellato, 'Greig's work is trying to preserve a radical space in the simplifications of a politics based on national identity' (2002: xxii). As such it is clearly contagious with his other 1990s work. *Caledonia Dreaming*'s light, anti-agit-prop approach is without doubt radically different from the aesthetics of *The Cheviot*, but ultimately they share a particular sense of resilient optimism.

'Just History': *Victoria*

It is difficult to imagine a work in greater contrast to the comic, ironic, urban qualities of *Caledonia Dreaming* than Greig's next Scottish project, *Victoria*. Commissioned by the Royal Shakespeare Company, directed by Ian Brown and presented at the Barbican in London in 2000, *Victoria* is a large cast history play structured in three interconnected movements. Contrary to what we might expect, the RSC were apparently not looking for 'a big statement about Scottish identity' (Billingham 2007: 88), but what Greig delivered was his most Scottish of works to date, a play that delves deep into cultural and national identity. As Nadine Holdsworth describes, *Victoria* generally drew positive responses from London theatre critics who 'admired [its] ambition and scope' (2008: 134) and who noted how it contrasted strongly with much work on the British stage at the time. That said it is a piece that, due to the resources it requires, has not been revived. Originally intended as a trilogy, in the end compressed into three-act piece that ran for three hours, the very scale of the project invites reflection upon the changing cultural climate in the wake of devolution.

The resulting work is composed of numerous short scenes; a compendious seventy two in all, that trace the impacts of modernity upon a remote part of the West Highlands. Set in an unnamed 'rural place on coast of Scotland,' the play takes three specific periods – 1936, 1974 and 1996 – over three seasons, autumn, spring and summer, and across three generations of characters, to form an intricately structured epic triptych of twentieth century Scotland, that as Pattie also notes, 'captures a country in flux'.

In each play, identities and world views are delineated by attitudes to place. In the first, entitled 'The Bride,' class distinctions filter responses to the Highland environment. The characters are clearly divided into three socio-economic groups – the aristocratic residents of the estate (Lord Allan, his son David), their guests (an assortment of 'invaders' composed of a group of prosperous, pretentious lowlanders and David's English fiancée, Margaret) and locals (farmers and servants of the estate). David, the laird of the estate, has returned from Europe brimming with the fervour of Nazism and a sense of his own degeneracy. The rugged grandeur of the landscape, to which he lays claim, stands in sharp contrast to David's sense of himself as an effete and 'damaged specimen' (26). The guests, who are little more than caricatures, come to enjoy the Highlands as a playground, to profit from the mountain air and some inept deer stalking. Margaret opposes their romantic appropriations of the place with dreams of modernization projects that would, in her view, bring the community up to date and out of isolation. Finally, in the third group, Victoria, the minister's daughter, longs to escape the mountains, sea, forest and 'a weight of oldness' (20), to emigrate with her lover Oscar to Argentina, while farm worker Euan prepares to fight in the Spanish Civil War.

In the second section, 'The Crash,' only fragments of the old social strata remain and these are further eroded as the prospect of oil wealth hoves into view. Margaret and her son Jimmy still reside in the Red House, though Jimmy cares little for the heritage it represents. Disruption occurs when a helicopter of American oil speculators crashes into the mountain. Vicky, a geologist from Illinois, is the only survivor. She responds to the place with a curious sense of déjà vu, claiming to have 'recognised it straightaway' (81). The crash brings together an unlikely couple, Euan (brash entrepreneur and son of Oscar and Shona) and Vicky, a relationship that enables the capitalist-minded Euan to shape the future of the community and its environment. Significantly, by the end of the play, the Red House is sold to the highest bidder, Euan, on the basis of his plans to develop the loch in anticipation of the impending oil industry.

Finally, in 'The Mountain,' the landscape has become a site of contestation. Euan, now the owner of a vast aggregate quarry, wishes to mine the mountain for his granite business. Euan's views on the utility of the environment and his right to exploit it are opposed by a camp of protestors represented by Annie. Oscar has died, though his ghost haunts his son. The record of his experiences during the Spanish Civil War is pored over by his granddaughter, Victoria. In a direct echo of the original Victoria's desires in 'The Bride,' young Victoria wishes to shake off 'the weight of oldness,' to escape the mountain and 'all that made [her]' (172). This rejection of home and its heritage is mirrored by Old Victoria's return after decades in Argentina, and her recognition that despite her flight she has remained bound to home like 'a stone half in the ground' (180). The play concludes with the voices of three generations of Victorias, performed by a single actress, against the backdrop of a determining landscape from which they can never wholly detach themselves.

Throughout the three parts, it is evident that Highlands environment provides a complex but unifying frame. So in addition to providing a historical panorama, *Victoria* is also, I would stress, an ecologically calibrated epic. Repeatedly characters remark upon the air, the sea, the forest and the mountains, and their sense of being in relation to them. Oscillation between acceptance and rejection of the environment is maintained throughout Greig's exploration of its imperative role in shaping their identities. This remote spot in Scotland's Western Highlands seems to exercise a gravitational pull on its inhabitants (Inan 2010: 116). Place is defining, but also imprisoning; those who attempt to escape, to 'walk into some new life' (172), find that they are held by what they wish to leave behind, a predicament illustrated by the recurring image of a stone protruding from the earth.

In each period, the mountain is the critical space, facilitating a sense of perspective as an apparently fixed point of reference. The stalking party of part one and the collection of the corpses of deer from the mountainside are echoed in part two when the locals are employed recovering the remnants of the helicopter and its passengers from the same territory, and in part three when young Victoria and Billy burn Oscar's remains up on the mountain. Yet, as is clear from these examples, the meanings ascribed to the landscape are shaped by the political and social conditions. Nature may seem to dwarf human endeavour, outliving the shifting human perspectives of the Highlands, indifferent to their movements, but it is also transformed by human action as the final episode in the triptych most brutally depicts.

Understandings of environment, therefore, are enmeshed with a consideration of the imprint of the past on the present in a Scottish context. As Greig says in the introductory note to the play, his interest lay in how 'in smaller places . . . history is refracted and revealed in a different way [to how it is in urban centres], its effects inscribed more subtly on the landscape, and in sharper relief on the lives of the people' (6). In the unnamed coastal village, the lynchpin characters are depicted coming to terms with history in different ways. Victoria of part one flees the confines of rural Scotland for the supposed freedom of the new world, but is seen in part three accepting the trauma of self-exile. Vicky's fascination with regression and reincarnation marks an attempt to recover a distant point of origin as a means of making sense of the present. In contrast, young Victoria in part three attempts to reject the weight of the past, in the shape of her grandfather's diary, which is thrown on his makeshift funeral pyre. Suggestively her words echo those uttered by the oldest Victoria sixty years ago, perhaps pointing to the futility of such a rejection and a discreetly recursive view of history.

Despite their geographical isolation, *Victoria*'s characters do not stand outside world events, but are implicated in the fierce ideological battles of early twentieth century, and in the modern era, capitalism brings those conflicts home. Greig harnesses the tensions intrinsic to modern progress between creation and destruction, celebration and condemnation, and binds them to the present, using various devices, most strikingly the recurring motif of fire as both destructive and cleansing. Testifying to the literary qualities of Greig's writing here, the three quotations that preface the play set the tone for each of its movements. The verse by John Cornford suggests an attitude that interlocks with the opinions expressed by a number of characters in part one – the sense of the present moment as a swift moving, devastating force, but simultaneously brimming with potential just as history like 'roaring sands' must be mastered and 'sw[ung]' to its final course'. A feeling of expectation and excitement is voiced by Victoria who is bent on leaving Scotland and tries to persuade Oscar to come away with her:

World's moving. People moving, we've only to cross the sea. Same sea we're looking at. The world's waiting for us, we've only to take our places in it. You and me. Just to see ourselves in a place that isn't here. The thought of it's like breathing again. Like waking up. (20)

Similarly, the sense of being on the cusp of momentous change is evident in David's fascination with Nazi ideology, and which he allies to the natural purity of the Scottish landscape:

I am a national socialist. I believe in the nation. In the aristocracy of working men. Mountains, sea and forest] The forces are gathering . . . The forces of the north, the pure, against the forces of the degenerate, the civilised, the carriers of disease. There will be a fire. A magnificent fire. (29)

Margaret, David's fiancée, only partially grasps the implications of David's 'modernist' assertions – for her simply, '[i]f being a modernist means wanting things to become more modern then I'm a modernist too' (48). Her progressive and unsentimental vision of a modern future entails a causeway to connect the village with the outer world and a society in which everything is taken care of by civil servants. Ironically, the social transformation envisioned by Margaret also ultimately involves her own obsolescence. By contrast, Euan, having listened to David's apocalyptic vision, and having been rejected by Victoria, is motivated to sacrifice himself to fight Fascism in the Spanish Civil War.

These dramatic modern dichotomies and violently animating convictions seem redundant in part two of the play, set thirty-six years later. A nostalgic note is struck by the second prefacing citation, an excerpt of a poem by Sorley Maclean mourning the lost generations of rural Scotland:

. . . I will go down to Hallaig
to the Sabbath of the dead,
where the people are frequenting,
every single generation gone.

Victoria, Euan and Gavin are among those who are gone; Shona, Callum, Margaret and Oscar have remained. Margaret's progressive modernism has paled into aristocratic conservativism. She resents Oscar's proposal to buy the Red House in order to transform it into a community college, and wonders if the work of the Allan family over the centuries 'carr[ies] any weight' (71). It seems not; the dilapidated state of the property and her son Jimmy's libertarian attitude signal the end of such an era and its values. The energies of part one have dissipated – individualism and confusion are now the key notes. Vicky survives the helicopter crash but leaves her colleague to die. Oscar, once feckless and carefree, has become a cantankerous socialist haunted by his past deeds. But the socialist metanarrative he has espoused, summed up in his story of his first day in Madrid (which later is revealed to be borrowed; it's Euan's memory, not his), no longer presents any clear purpose or justification for his past actions. Shona can only advise him to regard the past as a dream (122). Their son Euan, in rejection of his father's politics, is individualist and capitalist, and is motivated solely by a desire to exploit a profit margin. The determining destiny of the pre-war period is replaced with a sense of the accidental. As Oscar says to Vicky, '[s]ome people survive for no reason. Chance. We do our best for each other in the face of chance' (106). And chances, for Euan at least, are there to be exploited in the new Scotland.

In part three, while the legacy of modernity may seem a distant and abstract notion, its consequences are expressed through a pervasive sense of disjunction and misunderstanding. Euan grumbles to his PR advisor that the Green protestors, who want to stop him from taking a whole mountain for gravel, fail to appreciate 'the beauty of the obvious' (134). Young Victoria's response to Oscar's diary is one of incomprehension, 'I can't get it to mean anything' (158). Her boyfriend David, in contrast, is only excited by the story's potential as a profitable publication. Victoria feels nothing at her grandfather's funeral. Her father, Euan, critically remarks: 'I see no – forward movement in your life,' to which she answers 'Forward to what?' (144). If the quotation from Henrik Ibsen – 'There really are times when the entire history of the world seems to me like one great shipwreck from which the only imperative is to rescue oneself' – is regarded as the motif in this final section of the play, it best describes young Victoria's ambivalent and postmodern attitude to the past. She attempts to exorcize it by partially fulfilling Oscar's wish to be cremated and for his ashes to be scattered in Spain. However, during the improvised cremation on the mountainside she burns not only Oscar's remains, and her money, but also his diary. 'I read it. Just history' (180) she says as it is tossed in the flames. Like the tension throughout the play between conflicting positions, this too is a gesture at once thwarted and liberating.

Victoria is an ambitious piece of theatre, an unabashedly epic state-of-the-nation play. Greig deftly uses a microcosm, as Holdsworth puts it, to 'trace[s] the various political agents that defined the landscape throughout the twentieth century, from the landed gentry to multinational corporations' (2008: 134). In his own words it is a piece about utopias, and the problems of ideology moving from Fascism and Communism in the first play to embryonic Thatcherism in the second, to the clash between Green thinking and postmodern capitalist logic in the third (Billingham 2007: 86). Crammed with ideas about history, politics and responsibility, *Victoria* is also remarkable for its intricate structure and poetic symmetry, and the concentration of these qualities has also perhaps contributed to the fact that it is not one of Greig's most produced works. The patterning of roles, images, motifs and language reinforce a sense of the present ghosted by the past in complex and ambivalent ways. Above all, *Victoria*, like his next play, *Outlying Islands*, is fascinating as an ecological drama; its conflict revolves around man and environment, culture and nature, and the ways in which place holds people and people shape their place.

Bird Watching: *Outlying Islands*

Greig's following work continued to explore these relationships, but with more emphasis on the force of isolation upon its characters. *Outlying Islands* as its title suggests is set on the periphery, on a tiny island in the North Atlantic in the summer of 1939, where two young

Cambridge ornithologists have been sent by a government ministry to produce 'an inventory – of the natural contents of the island' (155).

The play, directed by Philip Howard opened at the Traverse Theatre in Edinburgh in 2002 and later transferred to the Royal Court in London, won a Fringe First, a Herald Angel and a Critics' Award for Best New Play, as well as many enthusiastic reviews. Greig has described how the project was partly inspired by Robert Atkinson's 1949 book *Island Going*, in which Atkinson describes a decade-long ornithological study of rare bird species in the Outer Hebrides in the 1930s and 1940s. In addition to wildlife, he also studied the lives and traditions of the islanders. Clearly Greig uses the book as a foundation, to the extent that even the elusive Leach's Fork-tailed Petrel gets a mention. But this is a play that goes beyond the esoteric thrills of birdwatching, tackling questions of environmental ethics, desire, social convention and Darwinism, peppered with a few rather improbable, comic references to Laurel and Hardy.

Compared to *Victoria*, *Outlying Islands* is a model of structural simplicity and this was certainly one aspect to its success and popular appeal. Forty miles from the mainland, four contrasting characters face a month of isolation in a harsh but pristine natural world that transforms them all. Robert and John typify two complete different attitudes. As Robert tells John, like the species of birds on the island, they are fundamentally different: 'Nature divides us into the gambler and the saver. I'm a gambler. You're a saver' (149). They are accompanied by the island's leaseholder, Kirk, and his niece Ellen. The aptly named Kirk is a puritanical old man whose fixation on financial compensation reveals a mercenary and pragmatic attitude to his world. Ellen, despite his severe control, has managed to develop an enthusiasm for cinema, and Stan Laurel in particular. Their dwelling for the month is an abandoned chapel, caustically dismissed by Kirk as 'a pagan place' (136). Robert and John are under the impression that their task is to study the island's bird population. When the true nature of the project is accidentally revealed by Kirk – the Ministry of Defence is interested in using the island for anthrax testing – they are appalled. During an altercation following this discovery, Kirk dies of a heart attack. In the ensuing days Ellen mourns her uncle; they bury him and continue with the survey. Meanwhile, sexual tension mounts as the three interact and observe each other. Finally, Ellen seduces John in the chapel. Robert comes back and watches them before plunging into the storm outside to throw himself from a cliff. At the end of the month, the boat from the mainland collects John and Ellen to return them to civilization.

The four characters are the compass points of the play at the centre of which is the centrifugal force of the island. On one axis, we find Kirk and Ellen. Kirk embodies an older generation – his views and his identity are rigid, and he is suspicious of the outsiders as representatives of a world he sees as corrupt and decadent. He is characterized by two main concerns: the demise of traditional Christian beliefs and morals, and his right to financial recompense for the use of his property. Through Kirk a particular Puritan Protestant world view is expressed, which holds firmly to the view of human nature tends to degeneracy, and that God has ordained the natural world is for human use. In accordance with these tenets, he has no respect for the non-Christian history of the island. The people of the past fell into 'blasphemous practices' and when forced by hunger to the mainland have sewn their godlessness there as well (161). He finds further proof of his beliefs in the pernicious effects of modernity, rife in London, of course, and that have even begun to encroach upon Edinburgh: 'it's coming. Chaos and filth. Women have begun to uncover their heads. Cinemas have arisen. We are becoming a pagan people' (158). He vehemently denounces both the pagan desire for novelty (160) and for any romantic appreciation of nature.

Ellen, as Dilek Inan also comments, is representative of a new generation, one that is less fettered by the bonds of convention and open to change (2010: 119). Her forthright ways and sense of humour offset the self-importance of the others. Ellen remains conscious of her duties, feeding the guests, tending the fire, waking the corpse, but in the course of the month she becomes self-aware and assertive. Following his death, she describes her feeling for Kirk honestly as 'warm hate' (180); nonetheless, she dutifully sits with his corpse for three nights before the burial and, at the play's close, goes to bid him farewell. His death frees her, not only from this hatred but also to choose her own life's path. Weighing her emotions she admits her lack of sadness, what she feels is 'Awake. Is all. After winter, spring (196). As many commentators have observed, Robert is overtly cast as a force of nature, yet so too is Ellen, though in less extreme terms, through images that align her with the wildlife on the island. She likens her eczema ravaged hands to bird's claws at the play's beginning, she mothers the chick abandoned in the chapel, along with the island's bird life, she is the subject of both young men's intense gaze and, as Robert predicts at the outset, she selects a lover. Counterbalancing this natural imagery is Ellen's love of cinema. She also describes her awakening as the beginning of a film in which she and the boys now play a role. And countering their objectifying and desirous gaze is hers, in which John and Robert are pictured in terms of her fondness for Stan Laurel: 'Laurel and Laurel you are' (196).

On the other axis are Robert and John. Robert is an aggressive, elemental force. Intellectually questing and contemptuous of social restrictions, he like Ellen is determined to be free. An adherent of social Darwinism, Robert is supremely confident in the laws of nature and survival of the fittest, making him an absolutist not entirely dissimilar to Kirk. His veneration of nature and the cold scientific language he applies to every situation leave little space for sensitivity, mercy or affection; indeed, ultimately, as Joyce McMillan asserts, 'Robert's ruthless and amoral nature-worship seems frightening and inhuman' (2008) Robert sums up human relations bluntly within this frame of reference, for him Ellen is first and foremost a 'sexually ready' female 'on the lookout for potential mates' (151), Kirk is but 'a parasite' (169) and he feels no remorse for provoking his death. He secretly photographs Ellen as she bathes and relentlessly pursues her with his gaze. He ridicules John for being sexually repressed. Passionate and visionary Robert may be, but he also emerges as an unlovable figure, alienated and alienating simultaneously.

John, by contrast, is convention-bound and is perpetually anxious to preserve the codes of behaviour from the mainland. Illustrative of their fundamentally differing attitudes, Robert's desire to fly with the petrels is balanced against John's admission that he is thinking of applying to the Air Force. He has come to the island in Robert's academic wake, excited by the prospect of their potential discoveries yet also deeply fearful of the unknown and unfamiliar. He soon finds himself sandwiched between Robert's thoughtlessness and downright irresponsibility and Kirk's dour pragmatism. Being from Edinburgh, he is also sandwiched between the Englishman and the Highlanders and is chafed by both. Throughout the play, John is constantly apologizing for his use of mild swear words, for transgressing social codes, but he seems quite helpless in the face of Robert's superior force and ambivalent charisma. He appreciates the island as a unique natural environment, but he attempts to rationalize Kirk's desire to profit from its destruction. He is attracted to Ellen but is terrified of his feelings. It is she who finally initiates a consummation of their relationship. To quote Joyce McMillan again, 'John's hyper-conventional morality' may appear 'feeble [even] irritating', yet despite all this he is the one to survive.

Once again in *Outlying Islands* landscape provides a vital space for contending ideals, and these are unfolded through dialogue, reflective monologues and a narrative shared by Ellen. The romantic prospect of landfall is no inert backdrop. Rather, as Holdsworth comments, the island has a character that is 'compelling yet remote and inhospitable' (2008: 139) acting, as I have mentioned above, as a centrifugal force. Each responds to this territory in his or her own way. For Kirk it is 'a useless lump of rock' (167), once inhabited by pagan people who were deservedly punished by God through famine. He would happily allow the Ministry of Defence to use it as they like as long as he is well paid. Although he hopes to claim for the lost income, ironically his life is claimed by the island first. In death he becomes part of the environment he so scorned in life.

For the others, being on the edge of the world catalyses a reassessment of their values and their existence. If both Robert and John initially respond to the island as a sanctuary, soon their attitudes become more evidently divergent. For Robert this sanctuary is a space beyond the distortions and dishonesties of civilization, where nature may have full rein, where he may realize his intellectual ambitions. As his monologue at the play's opening suggests, he is inexorably drawn to this space where the island 'claims' him: 'The more outlying the island – The further out it is in the remote ocean – The stronger the force that pulls us towards it' (131). Here is a zone of absolute and existential honesty, as well as of mortal struggle for survival – a zone where, for Robert, nature is all and where he feels at home. In a sense Robert 'goes native,' his immersion in the environment is so compelling, that he has no desire to leave. Observation drives him beyond scientific curiosity to an intense sense of empathy and transcendental oneness from which there is no return. Inspired by the petrels, he longs for liberation, to 'live unweighted by the mainland, tethered only to an outlier. . . . Living without time. . . . No beginnings and no endings. Limitless. Imagine departing from the land' (227). The erotically atmospheric scene, in which Ellen makes love to John while Robert watches, arguably has a different meaning for each character. For Robert it is a moment of realization more than of jealousy, a moment of absolute freedom that he aligns with the birds' flight in the storm. Glimpsing this liberty and its impossibility on land motivates Robert to end his life.

John is deeply threatened by such ideas and clings with increasing difficulty to his mainland securities. His continuous complaints about immediate physical realities: the cold, the wet, the wind, and the broken door serve to earth Robert's flights of fancy. In his monologue, he confesses a sense of disorientation as 'time has begun to evaporate' (201). Destabilized by his rising sexual desire and the absence of social control to guarantee decency, he feels as if he is falling. In contrast to Robert's abandonment of the outside world, John struggles to remind himself of the returning boat, the imminent war and people on the mainland. Increasingly the island becomes a negative force that he must withstand, and although he succumbs to Ellen, his interaction with the Captain of the ship in final scene indicates how readily he will return to mainland life. It is pertinent that as John leaves the island, he does so with a physical (if symbolically charged) souvenir, the table at which he has dined, worked and lost his virginity, and, above all, the only recognizable domestic object on the island. It is also striking that his description of the suitability of the island for the ministry's uses combines both Robert's and Kirk's earlier vocabulary: 'Pristine. A diamond' (230).

In a manner akin to Robert, isolation on the outlier sparks in Ellen an acute awareness of her own existence and determination to live as she wants. Ellen is not frightened of nature as is John, nor does she worship it as does Robert. Notably she does not participate in the nature–civilization debates that delineate the boys' attitudes, but develops a confidence in asserting what she finds natural and right. She actively rejects John's prudishness and quietly counters Robert's cruelties. Her uncle's death permits her to assume her role as owner of the island, a place in which she is entitled to act as she pleases. Part of her act of laying claim to it is to tell the boys the story of how the island was created. Ellen's narrative contradicts the scientific explanation with a folk legend of performative force and with a feminist dimension. The islands, she tells them, are not the result of volcanic activity but the stones and pebbles dropped by a giantess as she crossed the sea between Ireland and Scotland as she was building her house. The farthest island is a stone the giantess hurled at a bird, but missed. 'And that,' says Ellen with finality, 'is the true story of this island. This island which is mine' (198).

Although initially she seems merely an object of desire, the focus of an imperial the male gaze (Blandford 2007: 154) this tendency is mitigated as she imposes her own perspective. Similar to the natural environment, the boys have come to study. Ellen does not acquiesce to being an object, but radically affects them, inevitably drawing them into a relationship of transformation. Besides the folk legend, Ellen's is a perspective permeated by cinema. In her monologue, she describes watching Robert run down to the sea shore strip, masturbate and swim. Rather than reacting with shame, she compares this experience of watching and feeling with her response to Stan Laurel's performance in *Way Out West* (1937), a film she has watched thirty-seven times. When she seduces John before Robert, she is fascinated at how they are 'caught in his gaze . . . Like film stars' (225). She converts his voyeurism into something that empowers her, depicting him as a bird watching them in the dark. As Ellen is about to leave the island, she again becomes circumscribed by the men's language; she is referred to as a 'lady', 'a brick', and a 'girl'. Yet, her version of events stands in vivid opposition to the official account – for John, Robert fell, and for Ellen, he flew.

In *Outlying Islands*, Greig presents a spectrum of responses to the environment and attitudes to the ethical dilemmas this environment provokes. Whereas Robert is possessed by the island, absorbed and destroyed by nature; John resists, compromises and survives. But it is in Ellen that affirmative change takes place. As she takes possession of her inheritance, she also takes possession of her own nature and desires in a spirited and healthy way, counteracting the extremes of the two young men.

Rightly a number of critics have linked this notion of change to broader concerns within contemporary Scottish theatre and identity politics. Holdsworth groups *Victoria* with *Outlying Islands* to argue that 'the occupation of the periphery is suggestive of other possibilities, other priorities, other modes of being and living that are indicative of a wider national agenda of self-reflection and change' (2008: 142–3). Both Aleks Sierz (2011) and Steve Blandford (2007) highlight the ways history in these plays is a space in which a complex debate about national identity is enacted following devolution. Perhaps this is unsurprising given the fact that the Highlands in particular have so long been contested territory. They certainly provide the writer with rich resources.

'Change is Possible': *Midsummer*
(A Play with Songs)

It takes some time before Greig returns to Scotland as a setting for a full play, and when he does the result is a frothy idiosyncratic experiment. *Midsummer* is a mixed genre piece – a quirky romantic two-hander with songs written by Gordon McIntyre. First performed at the Traverse in the autumn of 2008 and directed by Greig himself, *Midsummer* quickly became a hit, was revived in 2009 and has toured extensively since. In interview with the *Sydney Morning Herald* where it travelled in early 2012, Greig describes the play as a kind of 'reverse musical'; 'We wanted it to be home-made and acoustic and about ordinary people and not set anywhere glamorous' (Blake 2012). Yet the minimalism of the production – two actors, a bed and a couple of guitars or ukuleles – exists in inverse proportion to its exuberant theatricality. Performers Cora Bissett and Matthew Pidgeon delivered a blend of competitive yarn spinning, contemplative monologue, dialogue, song and guitar playing. Besides guitars and ukuleles, the main prop was a bed that served for the Friday night drunken sex scene (performed fully clothed), as well as being later on pressed into use as an IKEA car park and even a film screen. And despite its simplicity and comedy, as Philip Fisher noted in his review of the 2010 Soho production, it is a piece that 'works on a number of levels, as a love story, Edinburgh guide, drama and beneath-the-surface philosophical treatise considering the middle-class, thirty-something experience today'.

A tale of mid-life crisis, a drinking binge and a very wet summer weekend, *Midsummer* archly winks at *A Midsummer Night's Dream*. In place of the Forest of Arden with its cast of virginal couples and mischievous fairies, we have Edinburgh's wine bars, pubs, clubs, parks and streets and a pair of misguided, far from chaste, adults grappling with what it means to be thirty-five. Copious amounts of alcohol, instead of a magic potion, propel them into Bacchanalian excess, some grisly mishaps, mortification, remorse and, as the weekend draws to a close, against all the odds, some new beginnings.

Midsummer is also, without doubt, an Edinburgh odyssey. Greig has described it as a hymn to his home town. Playfully mingling place and emotion, it succeeds in delivering a quirky psychogeography of the city. The Sydney production underscored the importance of the play's location by including a map with the paths followed by the characters. That map of contemporary Edinburgh is ever-present in the references to the places the characters roam over the course of the weekend, from the Castle Terrace car park to the Conan Doyle pub to a bench under Salisbury Crags. Consequently in addition to the obvious reference to *A Midsummer Night's Dream*, is a faint, incidental, trace of Joyce's *Ulysses* channelled in the repeated phrase 'Yes, I say yes' that echoes the final words of Molly Bloom's famous life-affirming monologue: 'yes I said yes I will Yes'.

Discussions of *Midsummer* in the British media often hovered over the musical status of the play, though it is questionable whether there is much to debate. Greig is at pains to distinguish the work from any conventional generic idea of musical theatre. What interested him was the possibility of working with Gordon McIntyre of the group, Ballboy, on a 'lo-fi, indie musical', rather than some serious attempt to overhaul the musical genre in general. Discussing the project, which was at that point still developing, with Mark Fisher in 2008, Greig and McIntyre described how they wanted the songs to 'deal in emotions and amplify the mood of the moment' rather than as a means of 'mov[ing] the story forward'. The result was a cluster of six songs and two pieces to be spoken to music laced through the narrative that serve to slow its manic pace and allow for a poignant effect.

Starting from the premise that it was to be a love story narrated from two perspectives, a man's and a woman's, *Midsummer* introduces two characters: Helena and Bob both of whom have reached a point of stark self-examination and existential stocktaking. Helena is a divorce lawyer with a luxury apartment in an affluent part of the town. Bob is a small time crook with 'no apparent defining features' (7) who lives in a basement flat off Leith Walk. Helena is having an affair with a married man and thinks she might be pregnant; Bob is divorced and is estranged from his teenage son. They meet in a wine bar where Helena has just been stood up by her lover and Bob is waiting for the keys to a stolen car. She has a bottle of 'forty-pound New Zealand Sauvignon blanc' (6) to finish, and he has a 'damp paperback copy of *Notes from the Underground* by Dostoevsky' (7).

The scene is set for a storytelling performance in which Bob and Helena vie for their version of events. In Bob's, Helena invites him home for '*some extremely wild, uninhibited sex*' (7, 10); Helena asserts that what she really said was '*Would you like to get drunk with me tonight?*' (13). They kick off their evening with a 'Song of Oblivion' and inevitably, if inadvisably, end up in bed together. The wild and uninhibited antics are almost derailed by a cringeworthy, but hilarious, interruption. Elmo, her nephew's talking soft toy, buried in the bed is activated and starts asking for 'a cuddle' (16).

The narrative twists and turns through the events of the next two days, beginning with their hangovers and a sense of reality crashing in. By midday disaster looms for both: Bob has managed to sell the stolen car but hasn't made it to the bank in time to deposit the money; Helena has arrived at the church too late and is standing outside with vomit on her bridesmaid's dress being interrogated by her autistic nephew. The wedding is wrecked, and Helena flees to join Bob in a pub for the breakfast. After walking through Princes Street Gardens in the rain and finding that they agree on everything, Bob accompanies Helena to her car where she learns that the plastic bag he is carrying contains fifteen thousand pounds of Big Tiny Tam's money. Feeling reckless and depressed at the thought of turning thirty-five, Bob invites Helena to help him spend it. The remainder of the play follows the stories of Bob and Helena's spree, from champagne in the park, to Japanese rope bondage in a club. On Sunday, reality again drags the characters to earth. Bob is pursued by a furious Big Tiny Tam who, after a chase on foot through the city, drops dead. In Bob's first version of events, this part of the story finishes with a witty punch line; later a more sober conclusion is admitted. Traumatized by mortality, Bob seeks out his son, who is at football training, but fails to communicate with him. Meanwhile, Helena unsuccessfully attempts to meet her lover in the vast expanse of a foggy IKEA parking lot. Following these emotional failures, the pair meet again to talk and walk. Helena finally takes her pregnancy test, the result is negative. On Monday as she is about to go to work, a second encounter with the ticket machine prompts a change of heart and, on the spur of the moment, decides to join Bob on his busking trip in Europe. As we are reminded by the performers, for each character, this 'legendary' story serves a somewhat different function. For Bob what is most important is to 'capture the feeling' (48), while for Helena she wants to remember 'every detail' (48). However, for both it is a space to recover the past and to revel in a moment that changes their lives.

The business of coming to terms with the past and a sense of diminishing opportunities coupled with the blossoming of a romantic optimism is one part what makes *Midsummer*'s tale of excess so winning. The other is the self-conscious use of genre references that frame the tale's delivery in a playfully postmodern fashion. Despite the comic silliness, there is a poignant and affecting honesty in the characters' creeping self-awareness. Helena's career success is balanced against a feeling of gut-wrenching loneliness. Bob's bravado is comically undercut early in the play with 'The Song of Bob's Cock' (21) in which he is reproached by his penis for being so promiscuous and advised that it might be time to settle down with a single pair of hands to 'guide [him] through the years' (22). Bob's thirty-fifth birthday brings little to celebrate and is remembered only by the Health Clinic which offers him a mid-life check-up and his boss who threatens to kill him. The effects of age are humorously amplified in the play's references to running. Time running out, running for your life and running out of control are all aspects in the narrative mix. Greig himself is a keen runner who started only in his mid-thirties, so the comedy here is clearly autobiographical. As Bob and Helena sprint through the rain for their Saturday appointments, the fact that neither is very fit is all too obvious. The narrative detours into a contemplation of why people take up running. Is it a running away from death or is it rather a running towards one's childhood? Greig plumps for the latter interpretation, but leavens the optimism with images of the beleaguered protagonists realizing that, despite their best efforts, they have run out of time.

'Aging and the future are' also the subject of Bob's filmic interior monologue in the Conan Doyle pub. Bob's annual conference with himself in the 'Department of Philosophical Underpinnings' is a grim set of observations about himself and that '[b]asically' all that lies ahead is 'a long slow haul towards death' (41). Although with less overt pessimism, Helena and Bob concur as they walk through Princes Street Gardens that at thirty-five 'this is it' and all one can do is accept it (44). A philosophical challenge to their sense of resignation comes from an unlikely source. 'CHANGE IS POSSIBLE' (46) is the message delivered by the ticket machine at the Castle Terrace car park. It is a message they both initially dismiss, but later come to appreciate. Envisioning the possibility of change is at the heart of what Greig sees as the task of political theatre. Here politics has little purchase, but *Midsummer*'s delightful celebration of the possibility of personal transformation is not entirely divorced from that more serious agenda within Greig's work.

Out of the Woods? *Dunsinane*

Dunsinane was commissioned by the Royal Shakespeare Company, opened at the Hampstead Theatre, London, early in 2010 under the direction of Roxana Silbert. Once again history and place are at the forefront of Greig's theatrical project. The play begins as the English army camouflage themselves in preparation for the final attack on Dunsinane. It goes on to envisage what happens after Macbeth is deposed and the new king, Malcolm, is installed. Action is centred on the English general Siward, his youthful soldiers and their fateful interaction with the Scots, as they find themselves in the midst of alien territory on an impossible peacekeeping mission.

In an interview for the BBC, Greig describes *Dunsinane* as an act of speculation. As a sequel to *Macbeth*, the play's title explicitly hails its predecessor and the location of its concluding action. This citation is noteworthy in the way it alters the focus of the source text, directing us away from Shakespeare's tyrant to the site of his demise, suggesting the precedence of place over personage. It also recalls the displacement involved in the tradition of superstitiously referring to *Macbeth* as 'The Scottish Play'. As Greig mentions in the interview: 'to some degree for Scottish writers, it's always felt a little bit cheeky that unquestionably the greatest Scottish play was written by the great English playwright' (Wrench 2010). *Dunsinane*, then, is also an act of repossession.

A sense of Scottish difference and marginalization inevitably is a feature of the cultural terrain of Scottish-English relations with a long history. Taking such a context into account, *Dunsinane* unravels zones of incomprehension and misunderstanding between Scottishness and Englishness, while simultaneously alluding to contemporary zones of conflict in the Middle East. Greig's *Macbeth* sequel is both intertextual and subversive; as he says it is an 'answering back . . . . Playing with some of those concepts and characters, and claiming just a little bit of history from another point of view' (Wrench 2010).

Greig repositions *Macbeth* in relation to topical questions of sovereignty and national identity, but also to broader issues of truth and justice. One of his motivations was to question the 'truth' of Shakespeare's *Macbeth*:

> there's also something that most Scots know about the real King Macbeth, which is that he probably wasn't a tyrant, he was probably quite a good king. He ruled for about 15 years at a time in Scottish history when the turnover in kings was something like one in every six months, so he must have been doing something right. He also embarked on what, at that time, was an epic six-month journey to Rome; if you had been an unpopular tyrant that would have been insane – you'd have lost your kingdom. So he must have been very confident that his kingdom would be there when he got back. So the cheeky bit of me thought, 'What if the stories of Macbeth being a tyrant turned out to be propaganda, a bit like the weapons of mass destruction?' (Whitney 2010)

This is the point of departure for the play which opens with the English army removing the tyrant king and taking the castle at Dunsinane. But far from being simply historical, it is loaded with contemporary resonances. The apparent success of the military operation is soon mitigated by the discovery that Gruach – Lady Macbeth – is alive and that her son, and heir to the throne, has escaped. Macduff and Malcolm, it transpires, have fed the English with misinformation so as to win control. This presents Siward with the undesirable task of administering justice and peace brokering in Scotland. The play is divided into four sections that chart the seasons and Siward's growing disillusionment and brutalization in an environment that becomes more, rather than less, alien as time proceeds. The otherness of Scotland is woven of three main strands: language, politics and place.

Although it is partially suppressed since the play is performed in English, one subtle and important aspect of the encounter between English and Scot is the language barrier. As is indicated in the prefacing stage directions, the Scottish characters speak Gaelic, while the educated or privileged Scots are bilingual. The monolingualism of the English places them at a disadvantage in their chosen role as mediators and arbiters of justice. In a very real sense, the limits of Siward's language competence are the limits of his understanding of the world.

Gruach is especially disparaging about the shortcomings of English (and by implication, the English). As she sets about seducing Siward, she comments that 'it's like dancing in wooden shoes' (69). Later, she expands upon the woodenness of English expression: 'Your English is a woodworker's tool. Siward. Hello, goodbye, that tree is green, Simple matters. A soldier's language sent out to capture the world in words. Always trying to describe' (76). By contrast, Gaelic is apparently detached from a simple denotative function, 'We long gave up believing in descriptions. Our language is the forest' (76) says Gruach. The texture of the imagery here echoes the play's opening scene, where the soldiers disguise themselves as Birnham Wood. And just as the military force is allegedly 'impenetrable' (12) so too, it seems is the Gaelic tongue.

Another aspect to the literal language barrier that Greig craftily elaborates is, of course, that all utterances in Scotland are characterized by semantic slipperiness that appears to foreclose the possibility of mutual understanding, or the establishment of the facts of the situation. While Macduff resists simple stereotypes of the Scots by insisting to Siward that they are 'not a mysterious people', they are 'just lost' (120), there are times when deliberate mystification is deployed. Throughout the play irony is among the Scots' favoured tools for resisting or challenging English preconceptions, as is comically illustrated when a young soldier asks Gruach if she eats babies:

Gruach   Don't you eat baby meat in England?

Boy Soldier   No – not in Kent, anyway.

Gruach   You should try it.

Boy Soldier   I don't think so.

Gruach   It's delicious. Very tender. (59)

Gruach's ironic teasing reveals the boy's vulnerability and his insecurity about what norms might pertain in this hostile and unfamiliar land.

Although Siward enters the political arena in Dunsinane convinced of the rightfulness of his mission, once the Queen is discovered the truth is increasingly elusive. Repeatedly he seeks transparency and is repeatedly refused. When he confronts Malcolm, he is chastened for being so literal-minded in a wonderfully circuitous speech:

> **Siward** You lied to me.
>
> **Malcolm** Siward – there's a small thing I ought to say if you don't mind – and I'm not trying to avoid your general point, but there's an important clarification I must make before we go any further. In Scotland to call me a liar is really unacceptable – if – here in the great hall for example – a man were to call me a liar that would – essentially – demand a violent response – a statement like that being – as it would be – a matter of honour – and so usually the way we manage this sort of thing in Scotland is by being careful not only not to tell lies – but also to be very very careful about the way we hear and understand words. So for example – if a person in Scotland says 'It seems a person has died' we tend to hear that word 'seems' – 'seems' – and of course that word makes a difference . . .
>
> **Siward** I thought you said the chiefs were simply waiting for you to arrive and establish yourself before they would pledge their allegiance and crown you king.
>
> **Malcolm** Siward – do you mind if I ask – are you going to continue with this insistent literalness? 'You said' – 'He said' – you sound like a child. (28–9)

Political truth in Scotland is neither comparable with that in England, nor is it compatible with the account of the conflict that brought the English to Scotland in the first place. Again alluding to *Macbeth* to illustrate this point, Greig has Gruach display her hands to Siward – not a bloodstain in sight.

Malcolm is artful in his management and distortion of information. When the parliament is finally gathered, semantic indeterminacy and linguistic difference are mobilized. Siward is appalled at Malcolm's insults to his fellow countrymen, and his promise to rule in his own interests. Although Macduff reassures him that 'Most of the chiefs don't speak English. The ones that do know he's joking' (81) Siward fails to understand the purpose of such jesting and wants to know whether Malcolm's speech is 'a joke or the truth?' (81). Both, Macduff replies. A similar tactic surfaces later in the play when Malcolm argues that 'weakness is his strength' and that '[T]he best way to maintain the appearance of something being true is for it to be actually true' (110).

If this equivocality confounds Siward, it is remarkably consistent throughout the political situation portrayed in the play. In logical terms the difference between Siward's and the Scots' understanding of the truth value of statements can be identified as the difference between the logic of either/or versus the logic of and/and. Politically, neither excludes violence. Yet whereas Malcolm's brutality is strategic, Siward's is absolutist. The former results in the death of a farmer and his family who failed to demonstrate sufficient loyalty to the King, the latter results in the wanton immolation of villagers 'in the pursuit of peace' (94). Paradoxically, Malcolm's political goal is comparatively well defined when juxtaposed with Siward's campaign for justice, even though audience sympathies may lie more with Siward.

A final dimension to the otherness of Scotland is the strangeness and harshness of the environment, which we have seen used in a number of Greig's works already. This was emphasized in the stage design featuring rocks, open space and a cross. Each section of the play opens with a monologue spoken from the perspective of an inexperienced English soldier. The effect is to foreground the voice of the ingénue, for whom Scotland is an alien land 'a wild place compared to Kent' (10), where nothing is as it seems and 'whichever way you walk you hurt yourself' (40). In the land of bog, rock and forest, the invading army finds instability at every turn: 'Where everything that in England was normal – Summer, land, beer, a house, a bed – for example – In Scotland – that thing would turn out to be made of water – This is what you learn here – nothing is solid' (39). Ironically, the nature of the climate is the only point of consensus. As Malcolm declares, '. . . I'm King of this country and even I don't understand it. Sometimes I think you could be born in this country. Live in it all your life. Study it. Travel the length and breadth of it. And still – if someone asked you – to describe it – all you'd be able to say about it without fear of contradiction is – 'It's cold" (29). Siward fails in his attempt to bring peace to Scotland; his efforts lead him to lose his bearings. The final scene of the play fuses the ultimate aimlessness of Siward's moral quest with the striking image of the General and a single boy soldier disappearing into the snow.

Siward's fate illustrates the hazards of intervening in a political and social environment that he fails to comprehend. Speaking of the play's inception, Greig describes how he 'had this image of a soldier standing on the edge of a very Scottish landscape, a bog. And the emotional feeling is that he has to conquer this land somehow but it's a bog. His desire is to do good, to be a good commander, but he knows he's about to step into this big horrible morass' (Whitney 2010). Indeed, one of the chief strengths of *Dunsinane* is the way in which Greig invests Siward with ambivalent sympathy despite his flaws.

Throughout the play Greig achieves a precarious balance working with the three strands of otherness just described and by continuously undermining the conventions that inform them. The claims made for the subtleties of Gaelic are juxtaposed with the poetic, yet humorous, soldier monologues anchoring each section of the play. Racial stereotypes are undercut by the Scots' political acuity and sophistication, Siward's simultaneous sensitivity and intransigence, and his soldiers' naive superstitions. Simple binary oppositions between centre and periphery, known and unknown, self and other, right and wrong are thus destabilized, forcing an experience of intense contradiction to the fore.

Concurrent with all this, *Dunsinane* also works as a complex political allegory. In an interview with Peter Billingham in 2006, Greig comments how 'engagement and certainty . . . remain the major questions' in his work generally, and mentions that his next play 'is very consciously about Iraq, although through the prism of . . . *Macbeth*' (2007: 91). At the time of the play's opening production few reviewers omitted a mention of the work's resonances with contemporary politics in Afghanistan and Iraq. Just as Greig invites his audience to reconsider the sources beyond the text of *Macbeth* through intertextual play, he equally invites this audience to recognize correspondences with the War on Terror in Afghanistan and Iraq in the first decade of the twenty-first century. Numerous elements in the play reinforce this. On a general level the politics of invasion, cultural ignorance, local complexity in terms of language and allegiance are all familiar to a British audience with even minimal interest in the subject. Additionally, semantic equivocality and ambiguity are issues that have arguably reached a new level in the realm of public (mis)information concerning events and policies in the Middle East. Above all, a central motif in *Dunsinane* that directs an audience's attention to the present-day politics is the question of (dis)engagement. Early in the play, Gruach advises Siward, 'There is a dance of leaving . . . Try to learn the steps' (78). At the play's conclusion Siward appeals to Gruach to 'take the first steps' (133) but she refuses, warning that he will 'go home in the end. Beaten and humiliated' and that she will continue to attack him even in his homeland (136). Debates concerning the withdrawal of British and American troops from Afghanistan were at their height at the time *Dunsinane* was first staged, while American military presence in Iraq was being restructured, making this question of 'a dance of leaving' acutely topical.

Karaoke Ceilidh: *The Strange Undoing of Prudencia Hart*

The Strange Undoing of Prudencia Hart shares a good deal of the dramaturgical spirit of *Midsummer*. Like the former play, here too we have a celebration of storytelling as performance, where music plays an integral role. Similar also is the textual structure where dialogue, narrative monologue and song are blended. Finally, for both Georgia McGuinness worked as designer. Greig traces the idea for *The Strange Undoing of Prudencia Hart* back to 2006 and a conversation with Wils Wilson which she recalls in her contribution to this volume. Encouraged by Vicky Featherstone at the National Theatre of Scotland, they went to Kelso to research the project and then in 2010 Wilson, McGuinness and Greig finally worked the idea up into a story (Greig 2011: v–vi). Without doubt the play is indicative of one of the paths taken by the National Theatre of Scotland in supporting and developing forms of theatre that are collaborative, may travel widely and are inclusive. In addition, *Prudencia Hart* opens a few slippery questions about the status of folk/popular culture today and sees Greig tackle a new and again contested terrain, that of the Scottish Borders/Lowlands.

As the stage directions indicate, the play requires only a communal space: '*a pub or a bar, a ceilidh place, a community hall, anywhere that people are gathered, warm and have enough drink*' (2), and as the audience gathers folk music is played. The opening song is a wistful traditional ballad 'The Twa Corbies' – the two crows – an atmosphere immediately interrupted by a debate, in rhyming couplets, about where to begin Prudencia's story. The audience is bombarded with possible narrative points of departure that in fact undo any later suspense. Her story may begin '*in medias res*' at the moment she knows she has been trapped by the Devil, or when time stands still, or when she is transformed, or even *ab ovum* at the moment of her birth (3–4). But, no, declare the narrators, 'In storytelling – that most misused of all arts – Horses must absolutely not go ahead of carts' (5), despite the fact that this is precisely what has just occurred. Prudencia's tale begins with snow, snow that would in ballads augur an adventure, our self-conscious heroine reflects, snow represented by the team of performers by bar napkins torn up by the audience at the beginning of the evening. What follows draws together a contemporary story with elements of the Tam Lin ballad in which Tam is captured by the Queen of the Fairies and is rescued by an heroic young woman who outwits the fairies; and Robert Burns's 1790 poem 'Tam o' Shanter,' about a man who after a night of raucous drinking encounters the devil with a party of witches on the way home and just barely escapes.

A fusion of forms, *The Strange Undoing of Prudencia Hart*, obviously combines ceilidh, ghost story, ballad, a self-reflexive narrative along with a spoof on academic foibles. Mark Fisher in his review of the play contends, the setting of the play is 'a world of academic pedants, a place of memes, signifiers and post-post-structuralists, where the head triumphs over the heart every time,' where Greig 'satirises the empty dichotomies of the career academic' (2011). Certainly, the play begins with a comic dissection of some painfully familiar vagaries of academic politics. But the opening scholarly tussles over the status of the Border Ballad are cleverly embedded within a telescoped narrative structure of story within story, Ceilidh within Ceilidh, pub within pub that soon transcends satire.

The heroine of the innermost story, Prudencia Hart, is a member of the Edinburgh School of Scottish Studies, at work on a PhD thesis on 'the topography of Hell'. She is on her way through a heavy snowstorm to Kelso where she is to participate in a conference plenary entitled 'Border Ballads: Neither Border nor Ballad?' An earnest young scholar swimming against the tide of contemporary theory, Prudencia believes that heritage should be collected, protected and appreciated, and is of infinitely more value than anything contemporary popular culture can offer. Her approach is regarded by her peers as, at best, outdated and, at worst, risible. Her nemesis, Dr Colin Syme, a colleague from Edinburgh belittles her attachment to narrative ballads as 'Middle class and reactionary', 'romantic tosh' (9). Somewhat inevitably the focus of his well-funded research is 'Working-class performativity,' football chants and celebrity culture (9).

During the plenary, her colleagues from Edinburgh, Aberdeen and Perth vex her with their deconstructive readings of Border Ballads. Each has his or her own axe to grind. Professor Macintosh applies a 'negative reading technique' to 'The Border Widow's Lament' explaining that it is 'neither a ballad nor about a widow nor a lament either' (10). Token Gaelicist Siolaigha Smith presents a 'post-post structuralist' (10) feminist interpretation. Colin Syme argues that rap, karaoke and reality TV are just as relevant as folk culture as the ballads collected by Walter Scott. But Prudencia cannot bring herself to equate the folk art of the past with pop culture that

> songs, and stories and all the great
> Examples of the BASIC HUMAN URGE TO CREATE
> Were of no more importance than
> A schoolgirl's Facebook status update (12).

She vainly attempts to present her 'traditional perspective' to convince her indifferent audience of the value of beauty. Adding physical humiliation to intellectual defeat, as she sits down her chair slips off the stage and she falls head over heels to the ground.

Unable to escape Kelso because of the snow, Prudencia finds herself stuck with her loathsome colleagues at the local pub where the local folk Club is singing Bob Dylan songs very badly. She struggles to give the session the benefit of the doubt, but the proceedings are almost derailed by Colin's noisy iPhone Kylie Minogue ringtone. The sleepy session is then abruptly halted by the barman to make way for the Midwinter's Eve party, to celebrate the night 'when past and future kiss' (24). The Kelso Folk Club cedes to Karaoke, pints are exchanged for flaming sambuccas and a chorus of corbies who open a second level of storytelling, sharing with the audience a graphic account of a wild and strange midwinter's party. As they explain to Prudencia, in a mock academic footnote, it is the night of the 'Devil's Ceilidh' when 'a gap or gate opens up in time. The Devil roams abroad and human souls can be taken down to Hell before their time. The Devil hosts the Ceilidh with the intention of luring souls, usually a maiden, into his trap' (35).

Prudencia, traumatized by the drunken, karaoke bacchanal, and reluctant to be locked into the pub after closing time, ignores their warning, heads out into the snow to find accommodation and soon gets lost in a weird suburban wasteland. She is rescued by Nick from the B&B which turns out to be a haven of Scottish kitsch. Nick flatters her with his interest in folk studies and tempts her with his vast library of antique texts. All at once she finds herself trapped by the Devil himself.

Eventually Prudencia discovers a means of freeing herself from the Devil's grasp: using rhyme to loosen the bonds of possibility, she seduces him. But true to ballad form she needs a knight to escape. Here the language of Prudencia's flight wittily ballad straddles archaic and contemporary: Salvation can only be achieved if she can leap through the 'pale slash in the fabric of the universe/Not unlike the graphic in the Silk Cut adverts' (69) and her knight errant takes the shape of Colin Syme 'a beer-bellied ninja' (74) striding across town to the tune of a football chant. Like Tam Lin, the devil transforms Prudencia into various forms in order to force Colin to release her, but he holds fast. After some time unconscious in the snow, they return to the pub where, at last, a proper Ceilidh is in session.

Reviewing the play in the Edinburgh Festival in 2011, Dominic Cavendish tentatively suggested that *The Strange Undoing of Prudencia Hart* 'maybe . . . a metaphor for Scotland today, torn between crashing modernity and the lulling comforts of nostalgia'. It is an interesting point, yet it is also vital to observe that the play concludes with transformation and the dismantling of assumptions about value – a point Greig underscores when he talks about the play in an interview later. Both Colin and Prudencia are altered by acquaintance with the 'topography of Hell' in Kelso. Colin, despite his apparent postmodern superficiality, finds in himself a conventional romantic hero. Prudencia has come to recognize the limits of her superior scholarly detachment and finally agrees to actually participate in the Ceilidh. Conspicuously, her contribution is a playful postmodern fusion that transforms the Devil's Ceilidh into the 'Devil's Kylie' with a sense of triumphant irreverence. The face-off between traditional and postmodern, folk and pop, serious and frivolous is thus wittily collapsed in the course of the action and is disarmed in this final moment of song.

National Costumes

As we can see, Greig's Scottish setting plays span the poetic and serious to the light and humorous. Compared to the plays discussed in Chapter 2 they are, with the exceptions of *Caledonia Dreaming* and *Dunsinane*, less determined by a concern with politics. More relevant to their diverse operations is an ethics of storytelling that does not permit one-dimensional identities room to settle. The characters in *Victoria* and *Outlying Islands* find themselves challenged and transformed as they interact with their environments. In *Midsummer* and *The Strange Undoing of Prudencia*, congealed ideas of personal identity are playfully overturned. These plays' unfolding of the politics of place, cultural memory, the dynamics of cliché and stereotype presents a complex theatrical investigation of the significance of locality and belonging that is always in relation to and entwined with places beyond. Most strikingly, however, in *Prudencia* the collapse of the distinction between local and international goes so far as to suggest the impossibility of cordoning off cultural localities from global influences, and their threads cannot be disentangled. As David Pattie argues, Scottishness is 'a complex, ever-changing network of interactions'. Identities are always plural, shifting and, in some sense, performative. Greig himself articulates his keen awareness of this in his introduction to a collection of essays on England by Scottish writers, *Lovesongs to the Auld Enemy* (2007): 'In the end national identity is something we can put on or take off like a costume. Sometimes it's uncomfortable. Sometimes we feel proud of it. But it's nice to have one' (2–3). That sense of national identity as costume is one we will see carried forward in the plays discussed in the next two chapters where sometimes characters wear parts of numerous national costumes at once.

CHAPTER 4
GLOBALIZATION

States of Ambivalence

Running parallel with Greig's diverse creative journeys through Scotland is a body of work that explores experiences of a contemporary world where place and identity defined in terms of national or cultural specificity are deconstructed. All through his work with Suspect Culture and in many of the plays written from the 1990s to the mid-2000s, Greig seems intent upon developing a theatre that orbited questions of the self, agency and communication in the current changing scenario. Rebellato perceives in this work an attempt to 'come to terms with the immense changes being wrought across the world by globalization' (2002: xii). Throughout this chapter, I would like to consider in more detail what such a 'coming to terms' has involved – how an assemblage of conditions produced by the confluence of postmodernity and globalization are represented and challenged by Greig in his plays since the late 1990s.

The reason I place postmodernity and globalization alongside each other here is that though not synonymous, they are intertwined discourses. By the second decade of the twenty-first-century globalization is both a ubiquitous and a hotly-contested phenomenon, whereas postmodernity as a key term seems to have receded. In an insightful overview of the changing dynamics of this debate, Omar Lízardo and Michael Strand note how the buzzword globalization has come to take precedence in the ways we now see the world. If postmodernism hardly stirred people to angry public demonstration as globalization regularly does, at the same time some core areas of concern – the social, the political, the economic and the aesthetic – are to some degree shared (2009: 62). Their impacts are numerous, but one of the most radical and far-reaching effect is a radical change in the conceptual space of the world. As the significance and authority of the nation-state shrinks and transnational corporate power grows, we are increasingly confronted with forms of displacement and deterritorialization. So for instance, Arjun Appadurai in *Modernity at Large: The Cultural Dimensions of Globalization* (1996) highlights the way these processes bring people from different classes, regions and countries into contact with each other as never before (37). Paradoxically, postmodern globalization yields both sameness and diversity: the spatial homogenization of franchised fast-food restaurants, multinational chains of clothing shops, supermarkets and hotels as well as fragmented heterogeneity with the production of new senses of locality, both material and virtual. Anthropologist Marc Augé, already mentioned in relation to Suspect Culture's work with place, analyses how our experience of our space and place in the world is shaped by 'the proliferation of imaged and imaginary references, and in the spectacular acceleration of means of transport' as well as, perhaps most importantly, the production 'non-places.' Non-places may be removed from traditional notions of 'culture localised in time and space' (1995: 40, 33–4), yet increasing portions of our lives are spent in or passing through them. This leads us to a second major aspect of postmodern globalization – its effect on our perceptions of time. A fascination with acceleration, simultaneity and technological progress can certainly be traced throughout the modern era; nevertheless by the late twentieth century, as David Harvey argues, there has been an intensification of time–space compression (1990: 240) that is now perhaps most vividly expressed in the virtual worlds created by computer technology and the internet.

Clearly, it is easy to point to an abundance of apparently diametrically opposed tendencies: homogenization and diversification, global connectedness and disjuncture, contraction and proliferation, empowerment and disempowerment. The co-ordinates of these conditions, and the problems and possibilities they inscribe, are the subject of urgent debate that ranges from the intensely specialized to the popular. Illustrative of this, and of relevance to the subject in hand, are two recent books on the question of globalization and theatre: In *Theatre & Globalization* (2009) Dan Rebellato focusing on its neoliberal foundations contends that 'globalization is a specifically *economic* phenomenon' (4) that must be countered by cosmopolitanism. Cosmopolitanism returns us to a contemplation of communities and ethics, and 'entails', Rebellato argues, 'a commitment to enriching and deepening th[e] global ethical community' (2009: 60). By contrast in *Irish Theatre and Globalization* (2009) Patrick Lonergan prioritizes a notion of 'globalization as a meme – as a self-replicating cultural motif that survives because individuals choose to believe in it'. Consequently, in recognizing one's participation in globalization, one might also recognize the need to be proactive (20).

Central, however, to all attempts to grapple with this issue is the admission that it is a far from unified or monolithic system, and its diverse processes have wide-ranging effects on the world and our perceptions of ourselves in it. These effects are intrinsically political in the broadest sense of the word. As I discussed at the beginning of this volume, Greig's ideas about how theatre can or should engage with politics are not static, nor should we expect them to be. What is most obvious in his essay 'Rough Theatre' is an awareness of postmodern globalization as a constellation of processes and possibilities to which it is imperative to respond. Specifically, he zones in on the ways in which '[t]he institutions of global capital manage the imagination' (2008: 214) through the media so that particular values, assumptions and views become normalized. This observation chimes with Appadurai's assertion that, in order to understand the 'cultural dynamics' of globalization, we must address 'the fact that the imagination has now acquired a singular new power in social life'. Across the globe as never before, people are encouraged to 'see their lives through the prisms of possible lives offered by mass media in all their forms'. The disjunctions between these imagined possible lives and the realities of power and privilege give rise to new tensions, 'new kinds of politics, new kinds of collective expression, and new need for social discipline and surveillance on the part of elites' (1996: 49, 53–4).

Greig's views on theatre's role in this context are somewhat mixed. In a presentation called 'Theatre and Prostitution' delivered at the 2004 Strange Behaviour symposium, he is doubtful as to whether theatre is really 'resistant' or if 'it's just as possible to build it into the commodification process of global capital'. He seems to come to a more positive conclusion in 'Rough Theatre'. 'Theatre doesn't change the world' he argues, but 'if the battlefield is the imagination, then the theatre is a very appropriate weapon in the armoury of resistance' because it cannot be 'globally commodified,' it is founded on possibility, contingency, changeability and finally, it is 'accessible to everybody' (2008: 219). Looking at Greig's 1990s plays through the lens of postmodernity's compressing effects on time and space, I highlighted three repeated elements: 'space and places of belonging, or of alienation; point of view, . . .; and a structural logic of juxtaposition and accidental encounter' (2006: 288). These nodes of place, perspective and encounter remain prominent with a growing emphasis on the contours of transnational identities and the 'geography of the imagination' discussed by Marilena Zaroulia. As the plays analysed in this and the following chapter testify, Greig's works attempt to intervene in this arena using various destabilizing and oppositional strategies in their treatments of economy, migration and displacement physical and metaphysical. If postmodern globalization is often seen to offer a plethora of potentially detrimental or dislocating effects, Greig turns to the ethical resources of human communication and contingent communities as a means of suggesting, however partially, utopian possibilities of transcending those negative conditions.

'The Veins and Arteries of Commerce': *The Speculator*

The Speculator was developed in conjunction with the Traverse Theatre directed by Philip Howard. The play, twinned with one by Lluïsa Cunillé, was performed in Catalan Barcelona's Grec Festival and then in English at the Edinburgh International Festival in the summer of 1999. Intended as part of a project, headed Caledonia/Catalonia, about political and cultural identity, the co-operation marked the opening of the Scottish Parliament. Given the context, it might seem peculiar that Greig takes Enlightenment era Paris as a setting and economics as a topic. Yet, it is a work that attempts to bring the past into contact with the present through an act of imagination. Echoing the motif of time–space compression just mentioned, *The Speculator* is a ludic historical drama that plays with anachrony and is remarkably prescient in its treatment of embryonic economic theory and a world just opening to the possibilities and risks of globalization.

The play revolves around three principal characters: a Scottish speculator, a naive Scottish lord and a French playwright. It is 1720 and each is on the cusp of a life-altering change of personal destiny as their orbits intersect. At the same time, as Michael Billington was to note in his positive review of the 1999 production, the play is 'a sprawling epic on public themes' brimming with 'the hazards and excitements of financial, sexual and creative speculation'. *The Speculator* is at times reminiscent of Caryl Churchill's *Serious Money* (1987) with its use of chorus and its attention to the exhilarating force of venture capitalism, but it also unfolds the largely unknown story of one of Scotland's most infamously ambivalent Enlightenment figures, John Law.

Historically Law was an influential Scottish economist who advanced the notion that money valuable not in itself as gold or silver, but as exchange value. After unsuccessfully attempting to promote his economic schemes in Scotland, Law became Controller General of Finances for France under Louis XIV, where he was instrumental in the establishment of banknotes as recognized currency and in 1716 he founded what was one of the first central banks, the Banque Générale. Law then pioneered the Mississippi Company, a monopoly that controlled trade and development in the French territories in Louisiana and Canada. Sale of stocks in the company was intended to offset France's burgeoning debts following the War of Spanish Succession. On the basis of grossly inflated future profits, the value of shares in the company soared astronomically, making Law one of the world's richest and most powerful men. The scheme spectacularly collapsed under pressure from Law's opponents who wanted to cash in their stocks and from counter-speculation. The crash of the Mississippi Scheme, along with the South Sea Bubble, was Europe's first major stock booms and catastrophes. Law, held responsible for the former, was forced to flee France and died a poor man in 1729. The dramatic arc of his career makes him a fascinating subject. For some, Law was a visionary, but the disastrous collapse of his scheme, accompanied by the fact that he was a compulsive gambler, a murderer and a womaniser, has meant that until recently he has been sidelined in the accounts of Scottish Enlightenment thought (Murphy 1997; 2009). Greig presents Law at the turning point in his fortunes. He is a man who believes he is 'limitless' (29) but who is clearly also on the edge. The play sustains a tension between two possibilities: that Law is a genius, so far ahead of his time that his ideas are incomprehensible to his contemporaries, or that he is an eccentric and misguided extremist who is increasingly detached from any reality outside the borders of his speculative financial scheme. He is temporarily protected, physically and emotionally by two acolytes – his bodyguard, Phillipe, and his lover, Catherine. Fleetingly Law toys with a nostalgia for Scotland that is sparked by an accidental encounter with the teenage Lord of Islay whom he discovers in the palace gardens with a set of bagpipes under his arm. He invites Islay to come to play for him, and to tell him stories of home, but his affinity with his fellow countryman does not prevent him fleecing him in a game of dice. For Law all relations are governed by a system of exchange, so even the company of a fellow Scot is a commodity, as is illustrated when he dismisses Islay: 'You've been a temporary refuge. A pleasure. How much money do you want?' (30).

The second historical figure Greig works with is the writer Pierre Marivaux. 1720 is also a turning point for Marivaux's career when he lost his inheritance in the Mississippi scheme, but also when he began to write the comedies that made him a success. Greig's Marivaux is torn between his marriage to Colombe who is rich but plain, and his passion for Silvia, an actress in the Italian Company. Here too economy plays a role. Colombe reminds Marivaux that he is 'contracted' to her (40) that she owns him. Meanwhile, Silvia withholds herself from him, forcing him instead to tell her stories of their love, thus exacerbating his desire to possess her. The monetary motif is further developed in cultural terms. In collaboration with the popular playwright Dufresny, Marivaux agrees to write 'a play in praise of credit (84) for their new patron, John Law. They are handsomely paid, in banknotes, for their promised product. For a brief period they luxuriate in their superior financial status and the power it affords them. The reception of their creation is satirically incorporated by Greig, as we witness the curtain call on the first night. The play entitled *L'Amour et la vérité* – a play Marivaux actually did produce at this time, but which is now lost – is received with 'desultory applause' (90) since their patron has fallen from favour with the regent and everything associated with him has been devalued.

The third figure is the ingénu traveller in Paris, Lord Islay. As Greig describes, Lord Islay did in fact visit Law in Paris and did discuss the gardens at Law's family home in Scotland, Lauriston Castle, but in 1719 (1999: i). He went on to become one of the founders of the Royal Bank of Scotland in 1727. Greig's fictional version has been sent to the continent to get an education; as he wryly tells Phillipe, 'the advantage of being Scottish is there's always somewhere better to go' (13). Despite his national insecurities, Islay is bursting with youthful optimism and ardour. By the time he meets Law, he has already fallen in love with a tavern waitress, Adelaide, a woman thirteen years his senior with a troubled past. It is patently not a match made in heaven, nor indeed is it a love story that might find its way into a play by Marivaux. Instead of acquiring an education to equip him for his role as a Scottish aristocrat, Islay gambles everything on Adelaide and commits to an unknown, unscripted future in America. Their story is threaded through the play in five scenes in a witty mirroring of the play planned by Dufresny and Marivaux for Law – 'Marriage and money. A satire. With a happy ending. Five acts' (34).

Unsurprisingly, the theme of speculation is writ large across the play. Speculation is the heart of Law's concept of the economy, enabling currency to circulate. Without it, 'The veins and arteries of commerce become sluggish. Without speculation . . . We freeze. We die' (44). Greig's re-imagining of history exploits this space of the 'what if' and its hazards. Speculation, then, is a dynamic force that animates the play and also underwrites the various economies of desire at work within it: the desire for profits in America, the desire for a lover, and the desire for success. And each economy is subject to the impulses of supply and demand.

Some of the play's characters expect that they can manage these impulses. Law is utterly convinced of the validity of his system and believes the manipulation of the masses will stem opposition. His patronization of the arts is pragmatic – he wants to popularize the idea of America as a land of infinite promise and paper money as more valuable than gold. 'Gamblers stake blind. Speculators imagine a possibility/And have the courage to force it into existence' (85) says Marivaux confidently in Act two. However, the distinction is hardly as stable as Marivaux would like to pretend. The futures each of the main characters banks on, literally and figuratively, cannot be guaranteed by sheer force of will; there is always an element of blind gambling, of the absolutely unknown or unforeseen.

The ebb and flow of desire throughout the play responds to fluctuating levels availability, familiarity and faith. Law argues that dreams are of far greater value than the dividends: 'Proof is our enemy. The more real America becomes the less they will desire it. The less they desire it the less they will speculate, the less the currency circulates' (44). This is illustrated by various scenarios within the play. Colombe is willing to pay an outrageous sum for a mirror in a gold frame, because it reflects a fantasy. Phillipe's loyalty to his master is at its height when Law is a mythical figure whom he has never properly seen. By forcing Marivaux to narrate his desire for her, Silvia keeps their relationship in the realm of the imagination, where it is boundless. When, encouraged by Colombe in disguise, she finally consummates the relationship, her power over Marivaux is dwindles and he returns to his wife.

Faith and a necessary suspension of disbelief are thus tested throughout *The Speculator*. If Law's utopian scheme is drowned in an 'ocean of disbelief' (116), the potential of the new world resonates throughout the play and overflows the historical frame. As Philip Howard remarks in his contribution to this book, the play was conceived as 'a "rambunctious" postmodern costume drama' and this is reflected in its non-linear form and distortions of chronology. America not only opens new markets for commodities as passing references to chocolate, tobacco and labour suggest, it actually ruptures temporal and physical unities in the play. The faltering steps of the early modern world economy are depicted as an expansion of consciousness, an act of imagination that hails a contemporary globalized world in bizarre ways.

The transition between old world and new is embodied by St Antoine, a Frenchman who has become an American, a disciple of Law who appears in group scenes in the course of the play selling a dream-like future. St Antoine's story is introduced amid the choric swirl of share dealers and brokers in Act one. Notably, he is the only one without a stall; what he offers is the intangible, 'Infinite America' (16). As St Antoine narrates how he walked away from his life and the past, the time frame buckles and he is reborn in the new world in the future: 'in New Orleans I saw myself/In mirrored towers rising from the swamp. I heard my voice in wires above me' (18) Here is a parallel universe, 'a world of possibility' (19), of freedom in which the past is weightless, a universe that can only be imperfectly grasped by the eighteenth-century characters, but inevitably are immediately recognizable to audiences immersed in contemporary consumer society. Greig uses anachronism not only to dramatize the incomprehensibility of the world St Antoine portrays, but to establish an eerie sense of connection with the present. Commodities from the future open a gate to the past. The ethical dilemmas of the eighteenth form a palimpsest with those of the late twentieth. The cigarettes St Antoine offers and the Harley Davidson he invites Islay and Adelaide to try transport them to a visionary other world where '[b]uildings rise thousands of feet high. . . . silence is not allowed to exist. Words circulate and flock like sparrows at dusk. Cities crumble to dust behind you. Your memory becomes powder and scatters in the wind' (81). It is at once a terrifying and mesmeric prospect. The alignment of the early modern with the postmodern in this speech points towards the America in the play as a metonym for globalization. This America is clearly not a geographically fixed space, but rather like globalization it is an idea, with a strong economic impetus, that conceptually alters the world. In *The Speculator* the potential of Law's ambivalent vision is halted; however, as the recurring image of the mudfish in the play suggests, it merely awaits a more propitious time.

On his website, Greig describes how *The Speculator* was inspired by James Buchanan's *Frozen Desire: The Meaning of Money* (1997) and notes how it 'seems to explore and pre-empt the dot.com bubble' which happened in 2000. *The Speculator* explores the potential of imagined worlds, and this is the connection with the Caledonia/Catalonia project to celebrate the inauguration of the Scottish Parliament. Yet, the note it strikes is not wholly celebratory; it is mixed with a considerable ambivalence. As Catherine warns Marivaux towards the end of the play, 'Ordinary life – there are failures and successes. Gentle curves. Dreams explode. Chaos' (111). In this respect, it is a play that echoes the anthropological analysis, described at the beginning of this chapter, of the expanding power of the imagination in social life as globalization develops. *The Speculator* has certainly not been among Greig's most successful works – it was rather sarcastically dismissed by Paul Taylor in a review as 'Not a play . . . that is ever going to be a licence to print money' (1999). Arguably, given developments in the globalized economy since 2000 with its parade of high-profile investment scandals and barrage of ongoing financial crises that resound through contemporary neoliberal ideology, it is nevertheless a play that remains uncannily ahead of its time.

Satellite Signals: *The Cosmonaut's Last Message to the Woman He Once Loved in the Former Soviet Union*

The Cosmonaut's Last Message premiered in the same year as *The Speculator*. Directed by Vicky Featherstone, it was first performed by Paines Plough Theatre Company in the Ustinov Studio, Theatre Royal in Bath in the spring of 1999. There is much to connect the two works, in particular a shared notion of weightless systems. Whereas John Law's proto-globalized scheme envisions a world of transactions untrammelled by a stable gold standard, *The Cosmonaut's Last Message*, as Peter Billingham notes, 'reflects a prevailing atmosphere of our time', 'one of breathtaking disorientation and emotional and ideological weightlessness' (2007: 109). Here we have a work of theatre that portrays a 'global ethnoscape' – to borrow a term from Arjun Appadurai – that is deterritorialized, self-conscious, culturally heterogeneous and 'profoundly interactive' (1996: 48). It is a play that consciously and creatively presents a world in which ideologically defined identities are absent, where characters struggle to find themselves amid a proliferation of cosmopolitan possibilities and where the lines of communication are perhaps impossibly tangled. Even its unusually lengthy title, which is habitually truncated by commentators, indicates a communication situation in which something is always lost.

In conversation with Mark Fisher, Greig explains how he structured the play according to a 'central image' – 'everything had to bounce between Earth and space like a satellite signal' (Fisher 2011: 25). The result is a set of juxtaposed micronarratives which though initially seem disconnected are gradually revealed as nodal points in a loosely networked plot structure. The play's opening scene is in space. The Soviet cosmonauts, Oleg and Casimir, orbit the earth on a mission that seems to have been forgotten. It is a scenario with a tantalizing historical counterpoint. In 1991 cosmonaut Sergei Krikalev was on a five-month project at the Soviet space station MIR. While he was in space the Soviet Union dissolved and his tour of duty was extended for another five months until finally he returned to Earth, landing in the newly independent Kazakhstan. As a result, Krikalev was nicknamed 'the Last Citizen of the USSR'. In Russian, MIR has several meanings, 'world' and 'peace' being the primary ones; clearly in *The Cosmonaut's Last Message* the name of the space module, Harmony 114, ironically echoes the name of its historical predecessor.

Below on Earth the play's other characters wander randomly, similarly bereft of purpose. Various trajectories are traced, motivated by accidental encounters. Casimir's daughter, Nastasja who works as an erotic dancer in London and dreams of being a film star, is having an affair with Scottish civil servant, Keith. Keith is on the verge of a life crisis. He bumps into Eric, a World Bank official, in Heathrow while waiting for a plane. After several whiskies, Keith gives Eric Nastasja's address and, inspired by Eric's advice, he leaves his life behind by staging his own suicide. Keith's wife, Vivienne, is a speech therapist. Following his disappearance, she is interviewed by a young policewoman, Claire, who is incidentally also one of their neighbours. Suspecting Keith's new tie, which has a Cezanne painting as a pattern, might be a clue to his whereabouts, Vivienne sets off to Provence to find him. Eric, likewise, sets off to find Nastasja, rescues her from her job, and installs her as his mistress (along with her friend Sylvia from whom she refuses to be parted) in a flat in Oslo, near his workplace. Vivienne does not find Keith, but meets Bernard a former space scientist who suffered a stroke and is now UFO spotter. He speaks little English and she speaks little French, but somehow they communicate. Bernard has intercepted Casimir's attempt to communicate on his monitoring system, but believes it is a message from another life form. Casimir dies while trying to repair the ship's communication system. Oleg, finding the prospect of continuing alone too unbearable, destroys the ship. Bernard sees the explosion and suffers a second stoke. Vivienne rushes to his aid, but he can no longer speak. Eric sends Sylvia to find Keith to retrieve a cassette Keith had made of Nastasja breathing as she slept. The play concludes with Sylvia entering a bar in the West Highlands where Keith is hiding and inviting him to talk.

The Cosmonaut's Last Message develops around various character pairings, and a doubling effect is achieved by actors performing more than one role. In this way metaphorical affinities are suggested between the identities of Keith and Bernard, Vivienne and Sylvia, Nastasja and Claire, Eric and the various proprietors of an airport café, a bar in Provence and a pub in the Scottish Highlands. Consequently, despite the disjunctions in communication and failures of understanding throughout, as Rebellato explains, '[t]hese ghostly doublings, [and] corporeal puns, emphasize, beyond the power of the narrative, the connections between people that exceed the social wedges that consumerism has driven between us' (2002: xxi).

The play's settings also map out various senses of distance and proximity. On one hand *The Cosmonaut's Last Message* showcases the cosmopolitan, with scenes located in Scotland, London, Oslo, Provence and outer space, while other geographical locations are mentioned as characters attempt in vain to express themselves. On the other, on stage all these far-flung locations are imaginatively drawn into a single performance space. The motif of spatial and temporal (dis)locatedness is unfolded in and between the play's many short scenes. Casimir and Oleg meticulously record their position in the ship's log, but they are severed from Earth not only by distance but also temporally; as Oleg resignedly notes '[t]he time lines have diverged' (253). These timelines, as Billingham argues, must be seen in terms of the transformation of world politics following Perestroika. The end of the political and ideological metanarrative of Communism and the advance of global consumerism and mediatization results in fragmentation, disorientation and confusion, as well as new opportunities and new mobilities. The astronauts themselves become 'redundant', they no longer have a place in the world they orbit (2007: 107). Simultaneously, below in a café in Provence, Bernard and the Proprietor argue violently over whether Americanization is a boon or a curse, and the likelihood of Pepsi advertising in space.

Closed within their 'comfortable middle-class home in Edinburgh' (209), Keith and Vivienne may be specifically located but fear the world beyond their living room, which they imagine as hostile and violent. Like the cosmonauts, their communication lines (in this case the television reception) are not working and to venture outside their capsule (in their view) might be fatal. More of a threat, however, is their obvious emotional alienation from each other. Vivienne's accidental meeting with Claire ironically illustrates completely different attitudes to place and identity. Although the land around the house is owned by Vivienne, she has little sense of proprietorship; Claire in contrast has planted a garden though she has no claim to the land. Claire's loathing of waste, a word repeated throughout the scene, extends to Scotland more generally. She and her husband go camping on Skye because 'it's the most beautiful place in the world. And it's in Scotland . . . It's a shame to waste it' (233). Claire is studying Gaelic for a similar reason, 'it would be a waste not to learn another language. And it's Scottish too. So it'd be a waste if nobody speaks it. A waste of all those place names. A waste of all that poetry' (233). Claire's uninvited cultivation of Vivienne's garden is discreetly juxtaposed with this other laying claim to a space of a unified and unproblematic national identity. Such a prospect is later undermined when Keith attempts to speak Gaelic in a pub in the West Highlands and is told by the proprietor 'Mountains we can share. Place names we can share' (298), but to leave his language alone.

In *The Cosmonaut's Last Message* no character, then, is rooted or at home. Peter Zenzinger remarks how a 'sense of "metaphysical homelessness"' percolates through the play (2005: 276). This brings me back to Zygmunt Bauman's point, mentioned in the introductory chapter of this book, about postmodern society being characterized by the impossibility of being or feeling at home, of being perpetually 'out of place', always 'on the move' (1997: 93). As the cosmonauts observe the earth from space, repeatedly the earthbound characters either discuss the heavens or look up, as if scanning for some stable co-ordinates. Nastasja scales the roof of the Oslo flat to better see the sky, while the more subtle oppositions of Highlands, Lowlands, North and South intersect with the ever-present theme of perspective in a world of shifting views and affiliations. One notable effect of the peripatetic dynamic at work is that different places are rendered equal since they have little effect on, or meaning for, the identities of the characters. It is deeply ironic that it is a typical non-place, the transitional space of a Heathrow airport terminal, in which soul-searching conversations and gems of wisdom are exchanged, despite the play's other more meaningful locations. If Oleg and Casimir's mission originally might be seen as a heroic modern destiny, it no longer signifies in the postmodern, post-cold war world below. Their years in orbit in the non-space of their ship leave them with nothing more than nostalgia and fantasy, and eventually these retreats become just as confining as the spaceship itself. The remaining characters in the play pursue personal journeys or are launched on seemingly accidental paths; some of these are blatantly illusory and fanciful, others are a means to deny or evade realities.

The enduring impression is of identities divorced from a coherent singular sense of vocation or belonging, governed by chance and co-incidence. So for instance, Nastasja, though convinced she could be a film star, finds herself working as an erotic dancer in a basement in London. The chance of her realizing her fantasy is slim as she is obviously a vulnerable economic migrant, at a linguistic disadvantage and with little but her body to sell. Her destiny is determined by the actions of others, her astronaut father, Keith, and finally Eric. Indeed her cinematic ambitions are quickly discarded when Eric offers to take her away from the club to Oslo. Less superficially Keith, following Eric's suggestion that 'the chaos of . . . li[fe] can be simply left behind'

(239) abandons his marriage, the affair and the rest of his established middle-class existence for the unknown. Eric seems closest to having a vocation, as he tells Keith they are both,

> Species – servant, genus – civil. We are the people who maintain order, . . . We serve. We civilise. It's not a job people admire, it's boring, maybe even despicable but people like us . . . are the bulwark against the flood. (238)

Despite the analogy, Eric and Keith have little in common. Eric, as a representative of the World Bank, evidently also represents the force of global capitalism. Eric's success in this world is guaranteed by a ruthless understanding of human desire as an economic system and his superior purchasing power. As he tells Nastasja, 'the only way to get rid of desire. Is to possess the thing you want. When you have it, you no longer want it. Then you're truly free' (270). Implicitly such a consumerist modus operandi applies not only to Nastasja herself, whom Eric wishes to own, but similarly to his involvement in peace negotiations in the Middle East and work on a landmine treaty. He is, in an important sense, Natasja's opposite number, empowered in inverse proportion to her disempowerment. Considering such sliding scales of agency, Zygmunt Bauman proposes the figures of tourist and vagabond as 'the metaphors of contemporary life', hinging mobility to the freedom to choose one's 'life itiner[ary]' (1997: 93). Through the characters of Eric and Natasja, Greig deftly reveals the disparity between being a 'tourist' and a 'vagabond'. That said, Eric's greater freedom is portrayed negatively, as vacuous. Beyond the impulse to sate a desire there is no grander ideological rationale to his actions, no fund of idealism to draw upon. Thus, the character's wealth and power is offset by a troubling impression of moral bankruptcy.

The Cosmonaut's Last Message concludes with an invitation to communication, and if Greig's work is to be regarded as engaging with contemporary conditions of existence in a globalized world, then communication is a vital part of its political import. As the play illustrates in a world of time–space compressions, meaningful interaction is often the first casualty. The sheer ephemerality of human interaction here leads Zenzinger to remark upon the 'Beckettian influence' in this play (2005: 274). Certainly the existential dilemma faced by Casimir and Oleg in outer space to some degree recalls Beckett's drama, *Krapp's Last Tape* (1958) and like Krapp, Oleg's attempt to record his 'last message' implies the insufficiency of language to express his feelings, underscored by the doubt that the message will ever reach its destination. Greig's opening citation, a part of 'Thoughts of a Module' by Edwin Morgan with its clipped and grammatically jumbled sentences, spoken by a machine, however, dramatically points to the new complexities of communication in a technological age. Technology, while seeming to connect characters, more often is just another barrier – the spaceship's communication system, televisions and radios regularly produce nothing but static. Vivienne's profession as a speech therapist is ironically undermined by her inability to talk with her husband. Their stilted and equivocal dialogue is finely wrought by Greig, as is Nastasja's flawed and idiosyncratic English. Bernard and Vivienne's parallel conversation in different languages, the stroke victim's inarticulacy, Claire's fatal lack of interpersonal skills, and Eric's peace negotiations, serve to keep a flock of open questions about communication and its purposes in the foreground of the play, making it an intricately metaphorical engagement with alienation and loss at the end of the millennium.

Global Village – *San Diego*

If *The Cosmonaut's Last Message* originates in the motif of the satellite signal, then *San Diego* is more akin to a sprawling hypertextual network of disturbing associations and contingent links. Many of the same themes are apparent – communication, migration and mobility, states of homelessness and alienation – however, the sense of millennial fragmentation precipitated by the fall of Communism is replaced by an assemblage of meditations on globalization inflected by the attacks of the 11 September 2001. Described by Greig on his website as 'an epic, disconnected dream narrative or fantasia which takes place inside the playwright's head twenty or so minutes between the announcement that the plane he is on is due to land in San Diego and the plane actually touching down', the play experiments with authorial intervention, multiple interwoven narratives and juxtaposed tableaux in assorted locations. Prompted by various experiences – his first visit to the United States, reading about globalization, re-reading Thorton Wilder's *Our Town* and a writers' retreat where he attempted to surrender to his 'subconscious' – *San Diego* presented audiences and reviewers with an abrupt dramaturgical change of direction following the lyricism and intense locality of *Outlying Islands*. First staged at the Edinburgh International Festival in 2003 by the Tron Theatre Company, directed by Marisa Zanotti and Greig himself, its conceptual and self-reflexive qualities incited mixed reactions with one reviewer dismissing it as 'a huge, postmodern ego-trip' (Cavendish 2003) while others were more receptive to its theatrical experimentalism and elliptical treatment of globalized identities (Good 2003). Like *The Speculator* it is a formally ambitious project, distinguished partially as Aleks Sierz aptly notes by its oblique references to the work of several of other British playwrights including Sarah Kane, Martin Crimp and Joe Penhall (2011: 9).

The allusion to Thornton Wilder's *Our Town* (1938) is the one I want to pursue here because it provides not only a self-reflexive template, but also a springboard to the swirl present-day issues the play plunges into. Greig mentions how he was interested in the way this play 'combines a radical form with a very conservative message' (McMillan 2003). Well before the vagaries of postmodern self-reflexivity, Wilder memorably subverted naturalistic representation by using the device of a Stage Manager who introduces the characters, fields a discussion about the play and its setting with (actors planted in) the audience and organizes the action on stage. The sentimentality of *Our Town*'s story of happy families, adolescent love, marriage and premature death – humble American existence as it is experienced in Grover's Corners New Hampshire – is undermined by the interventions of the Stage Manager figure, but is never subjected to critique or cynicism. The result is a drama that, in spite of its formal playfulness, elevates parochial experience and folk wisdom to the status of eternal truths.

Thinking about Wilder's celebration of American community alongside the realities of contemporary globalization led Greig to ask what would 'Our Town' be today? Replacing the insularity and stability of Grover's Corners, is San Diego, a place just as unreal and just as metonymical. Wilder's utopian stable small town community ironically also morphs into a transient postmodern pseudo-community of travellers on the new Boeing 777. Whereas *Our Town* compresses the passage of time to heighten its message, *San Diego* oscillates in both time and space. And finally, echoing Wilder's Stage Manager figure, Greig writes a version of himself into the play that initially performs a very similar function. As the plane descends David Greig introduces his characters: the Pilot in the cockpit; the Pilot's son and his wife, Andrew and Marie in a motel in the desert near San Diego; and the Pilot's daughter, Laura in a clinic in London. Following each introduction, a short scene is played out. Soon though the author's status as confident and omniscient guide is radically undermined when he loses his way on the motorway near San Diego. David Greig just manages to introduce his fourth main character, Daniel an African immigrant to the United States, before Daniel stabs him in the stomach and leaves him bleeding on the roadside. Despite the efforts of his characters to save him, by the end of Act One the playwright is dead, leaving their stories to unfold without mediation. Bizarrely the author has become a victim of his own narrative.

If by his own admission in *San Diego* is in some sense autobiographical, motivated partially by Greig's first visit to America, then the fact that the play is quite obviously not about its namesake city is another aspect of its deliberately disorienting dramaturgy. Different facets of the city as a tourist attraction gleaned from the *Blue Guide to San Diego* are delivered by the playwright in Act one. But the facts that 'San Diego has the highest quality of life of any city in the United States,' or that it has served 'as the unnamed backdrop for several episodes of *America's Missing Children*' (7) are utterly disconnected from the characters' experiences of the place. The attractive local details in the guidebook contrast starkly with the travellers' attempts to navigate an alienating urban space that is without defining features that could be anywhere.

Such disorientation is enhanced, as Charlotte Thompson observes, when '[m]ultiple scenes are interspersed in the stage space, requiring an audience to switch attention between the simultaneous narratives' of the characters (2011: 113). Stressing the spatial compressions and distortions of the global village, more than twenty different places are mentioned in the play, but none is presented as a setting. Instead, what the opening production underscored was the non-specificity of the space. Monitors, a palm tree, a drinks machine and piles of suitcases suggested, according to Holdsworth, 'the anodyne sterility of an airport' (2013), the epitome of a non-place. The appearance of the author's name and the play title intermittently on the monitors meanwhile accentuate that '*San Diego* is the play. The characters are trapped in the play *San Diego*' (Fisher 2011: 21).

In a prologue the audience is addressed by the playwright. He is approaching, after a journey of over eighteen hours, his destination, the city of San Diego. As he tells us, in between drinking whisky and poring over his guidebook, he has watched 'a Filipino woman refuelling a 747' (7) in Toronto Airport, and read 'in a two-day-old British newspaper about a Quebecois biologist who had heroically saved a flock of baby geese from extinction' (8). This collage of apparently random observations presages lines in an intricately networked structure. In the course of the play's four acts, Greig plaits five main storylines around clusters of characters. The concurrent narratives of the Pilot and Amy the prostitute, Laura and David, Andrew and Marie, Innocent, Pious, Daniel and Patience and a 'Conceptual Consultancy' converge in a number of thematic hubs.

A problematizing of authorial authenticity is prominent in the play's first act. Wearing a T-shirt with his name printed on it, the actor performing David Greig is soon joined by other characters also wearing shirts bearing his name. As Holdsworth details, this 'self-referential device . . . immediately raises questions around the status of the playwright, authorship and the blurring of fiction and reality' (2013). Greig wittily subsumes the 'death of the author' into the play's opening scenes, relegating himself to the sideline by murder. However in Act Three, like a *deus ex machina*, the playwright intervenes to sort out an impasse in the Daniel and Pious narrative. His interference enables the quest to find Daniel's mother to reach a conclusion, but it also allows for a second meeting between Daniel and David Greig. Daniel comes from Jos in Nigeria, the place where the Greig spent part of his childhood, and bears a scar caused by a white boy who threw acid in his face. The game of recognition played out between the fictional David Greig and Daniel is marked by an undertow of suppressed guilt and insidious accusation and Daniel's role here is as volatile and ambivalent alter ego. This meeting between First World and Third World figures, engineered by the playwright perhaps in an effort to establish harmony or assuage guilt, is usurped by Daniel when he tells him

> I came to San Diego to kill you. . . .
> You are no longer in control
> San Diego, from now on
> It belongs to me. (107)

The political symbolism of this exchange in a post-9/11 world is hard to avoid. Describing his motivations in incorporating so much of himself in this play, Greig states: 'I think what I am trying to do in this play is to negotiate between . . . two approaches, the presence and the absence [of commentary], the channel and the critical intelligence' (McMillan 2003). Although open to the charge of self-indulgence, it is a significant gesture that destabilizes a safe external position of judgement and acknowledges a complicity in the conditions that the play critiques.

In *The Speculator* I suggested that America could be read as a metonym for globalization, in *San Diego*, I would contend, this notion is carried forward. A fundamental aspect of the play is its treatment America as a land of opportunity, a hub of flows of desire that are disseminated across the globe linking diverse places and people. It is a world where globalization is catalysed and sustained by patterns of consumption, and underpinned by the dictates of free market economy. Diverse forms of consumption, in the shape of air travel, tourism, entertainment and marketing, form another crucial set of motifs here. Commenting on one of the issues that engaged him as he was working on this play Greig admits:

> One of the key things I was thinking is that the cheap labour on which economies depend used to live in the working class areas of 'our towns'. But now it lives in another country; either in an underworld of migrant labour that most of us never see, or literally in another country where the work is done. (McMillan 2003)

The comforts and securities apparently guaranteed in modern consumer society are shadowed by a world that is disturbing and insecure. In the play this world constantly intrudes, distorting and disrupting the smooth surfaces of First World privilege. The first suggestion of this dynamic is the passing reference to the Filipino woman refuelling the plane in the David Greig's prologue speech. Later, this underworld of exploited labour and economically motivated migration is elaborated through the narratives of Pious and Innocent, and Daniel, three illegal immigrants from Africa. Pious and Innocent are first introduced in debate over Innocent's will and to whom he will bequeath his possessions: a melon, a knife, a guide to San Diego, twine and a zippo lighter. The comedy around a homeless migrant's material anxieties is punctured by the visual reminders of Daniel's attack on David Greig – a bloody knife and the much-cited guidebook. In various humorous scenarios Pious and Innocent vainly attempt to integrate Daniel into the labour market, sweeping sand from the roads, processing meat, and working at telesales. Each time Daniel proudly refuses to become a menial worker, much to their frustration. Pious and Innocent respond with a vision of the dire consequences of refusing to service a structure of relations where meat, sand and telephones are all bizarrely connected. 'You have no idea' says Pious angrily,

> If we don't answer these phone calls then the Americans will just store up their thoughts until their heads are full and then one day it'll all come pouring out in a great torrent of gibberish and they'll talk and talk and talk until they deflate like balloons

And then they'll lie exhausted on the streets with the meat piling
up in warehouses and the desert lapping at their ankles (58)

It is a bleakly humorous, somewhat hysterical, image of the American
way of life in which entropy, chaos and violence hover held at bay
only by the endless toil of invisible and exploited outsiders. Their
dispensability is brutally illustrated when police arrive and shoot
Innocent for possession of the murder weapon.

Meanwhile patients in the clinic in London, Laura and David
embody different pathologies of consumption. Laura's cannibalization
of herself visibly constitutes a grim twist in strategies of abjection
by transforming consumption into a means of self-destruction and
disappearance. Laura is self-conscious in the way she objectifies her
body, which she examines like a butcher. She is also bleakly self-
mocking during therapy: 'I want to be cured' she tells her counsellor, 'In
salt. Or maybe smoked' (48). Laura meets her match in fellow patient
David. David's chronic attention deficiency likewise is a metaphor for
extreme fragmentation of consciousness that seems to characterize the
postmodern world. David's ailment, like Laura's, is both a rejoinder
to and an abdication from reality; while his wise-cracking, subject-
hopping responses illustrate a similar state of aimlessness and a refusal
to choose. As individuals Laura and David are locked into respective
cycles of self-harm, together they tentatively find a path towards
healthier states of being.

This quest for direction is expressed throughout *San Diego* in the
recurrent motif of flight. In a pointedly ironic story that may well be
just another urban myth, we learn that Daniel's mother abandoned
him in Lagos to become a backing singer for Paul McCartney's band
Wings. Clearly associated with references to and images of flight is
a constellation of ideas around mobility, fantasy, faith, nature and
civilization. Air travel is crucial to the dynamics of the global village,
and is the paradoxical locus of both romance and terror. The thrill of
the technology and sheer mechanical power of the plane is humorously
laced through the play's opening scenes. The aeroplane transports both
welcome and unwelcome visitors – again tourists and vagabonds – to
the land of opportunity, some in comfortable seats and some clinging

to the undercarriage. It is also at the crux of the post 9/11 hijack film in which Andrew is starring which points to and resolves Western anxieties about terrorist attacks in a sequence of narrative clichés. Concomitant with the aircraft as a complex symbol of human achievements is the natural wonder of the migratory flight of geese.

If flying for most human beings is an act of faith, then the geese's migration is a genetically programmed mystery. And in obvious contrast to the birds, the characters in the play struggle to discover a 'natural' sense of purpose and with feelings of helplessness. This sensation fosters Marie's paranoia about her baby son's health and drives her into an obsessive spiritual quest that paradoxically leads her away from her child and husband. Marie's longing for God in a post-sacral age itself is a form of performance where simulacra replace reality; she dresses as a nun and finally finds spiritual release in a film set Bedouin encampment in desert beyond the city.

Simultaneous with Marie's crisis of faith, the scenes dealing with Andrew's film and the 'Conceptual Consultancy' suggest other levels of wilful fantasy and suspension of disbelief that are deflated by the sharp humour of Greig's writing. The brainstorming session of the consultancy at work on a 'redesign concept' (95) for the airline ruthlessly satirizes postmodern marketing and its pretensions to creating belief structures in order to bolster consumption. Here a parodic global village – the aeroplane – is projected as the only space where people have a sense of identity, direction and togetherness. In a world where time and space are no longer stable, the aeroplane becomes the zone of 'co-ordinated universal time':

The cabin of the aircraft is the only space where we can be certain that we belong – we have a ticket with our name on it
   On the seat in front of us there is a map which shows us clearly where we are going
   And we are going forwards (82)

But the world in which '[t]he aircraft is your village' (83) is blatantly one of broken family ties and individual co-travellers who have nothing in common apart from their purchase of a ticket to the same destination.

The abundance of non-places and communication breakdowns in *San Diego* is dramatically balanced against characters' yearning to belong somewhere or to someone. Laura repeatedly attempts to contact her father who never answers the phone. Their failure to connect with each other physically and emotionally is poignantly rendered when he visits her in the mental hospital and she asks him to take her home. But none of the places he can offer – his flat in Surrey, a cottage in Fife, her mother's home in Hong Kong, the gîte in Provence – is home. Laura flees the mental institution with David to try to find a place she remembers from her childhood where she watched geese flying. At 'the goose place' Laura overdoses, but is saved by David; the inference is that home is perhaps not so much a physical place, but a relationship.

By contrast Daniel, one of the several abandoned children in the play, is like the Greylag goose Pious and Innocence name him after on a mission to find his mother. Echoing the Quebecois scientist's adoption of motherless goslings mentioned by the playwright in the prologue, Daniel is adopted by nurturing foster parents who become more meaningful than his biological mother. The play closes with juxtaposed images of nurturing and connection in a final weaving together of more hopeful possibilities where as David Pattie puts it, a new geography 'is mapped out by the experience of the individual interacting with other individuals' (2008: 150). In contrast to the closed locale of *Our Town* then, *San Diego* proposes transitory spaces of transnational encounter in which alternative relationships may serve to sustain fellow-travellers in a world of corrosive consumerism.

Lost and Found: *Pyrenees*

Pyrenees also delves into questions of the geographies of identity and communication across borders of various kinds, but counter to the perambulatory modes of the plays just discussed, the focus is very much upon a linguistic terrain. Produced by Paines Plough with the Tron Theatre Company, Glasgow and directed by Vicky Featherstone in 2005, the play was part of a season of work titled 'This Other England' to mark Paines Plough's thirtieth anniversary. At one level it certainly probes, with Greig's characteristic irony, the notion of nationally circumscribed identity. At another it works as a companion piece or sequel to *The Cosmonaut's Last Message* although this is not evident until midway through the play.

In *Pyrenees* Greig returns to the compact and lyrical dramatic structure, he employed in *Outlying Islands*. Condensation occurs across the fields of setting, characters and plot. Action takes place on the terrace of a hotel in the Pyrenees. The hotel is quiet as it is off season and serves as a refuge and temporary residence for the characters. Marilena Zaroulia likens this setting to the non-places so common in many of Greig's works, because it is a space where identity is unfixed (2011: 45). That said, a mountain hotel in the South of France is not wholly characteristic of the transitory spatial anonymity of the non-place. In this space the amnesiac protagonist is offered hospitality and seeks to discover who he is. Beyond the terrace are the mountains; their presence is suggested (and later described by the characters) rather than represented, their symbolic significance subtly building as the play develops. Commenting on the dramatic appeal of mountains, Greig has linked them with attempts to escape, and also nervous breakdown (Lawson 2005). Here, the Pyrenees are place where the Man is discovered unconscious and where springtime climbers risk their lives as they attempt to reach the summit. The action that unfolds centres on this unknown man, Anna, a representative from the British Consulate in Marseille, the Proprietor of the hotel, and a woman named Vivienne. Anna interviews the Man in an effort to ascertain whether he is British. In the process, they share their stories and an undefined sexual attraction develops between them. They are attended by the play's comic provocateur, the Proprietor, and are later interrupted by Vivienne, who claims that the Man is her husband. Tension builds between the two women culminating in Anna suffering an attack of epilepsy. Finally, the Man allows Vivienne to claim him as her husband, Keith Sutherland.

The thematic currents of *Pyrenees* flow around how identity is established and performed in or beyond language, in relation to a past or to a culture or nation. It is a concern revisited in *Damascus* which will be discussed in the following chapter. Anna records the Man's voice believing accent may provide the necessary clue to who he is. She has been told 'that people carry a landscape in their voice' (244) but the man's voice is too soft to provide anything distinct. Threaded through their exchanges is an acute attention to vocabulary illustrated in the repetition of the word 'dither' from the Man's self-description, in his groping for the word 'burn' meaning stream or his use of the oddly expressive 'clanjamfrie' (274) to signify mess. Anna listens for accent cues but she cannot read the landscape. Her failure to recognize Scottish usage is a confusion that is reflective of her own confused sense of origins.

Immediately adjacent to this impression of linguistic identity is an event that does not submit to description, but is equally pivotal. The Man's experience in the snow is likened to rebirth. Vainly trying to communicate it, he can only compare it to 'having been scourged' and awaking with 'an intense understanding of exactly who I was' (272). But verbal analogies are as slippery as the mountain's rock faces so when Anna compares the sensation to the moments before an epileptic fit, he is deeply insulted. He defends his experience as spiritual; alone on the mountain his individual identity became meaningless, for him it is not some mere breakdown, but a breakthrough to a new consciousness. This 'a place that language cannot grasp, a place beyond representation, a non-place, a utopia,' Zaroulia interprets as sublime, linking it to Greig's avocation of theatre as a space of possible transcendence (2011: 33).

Another map of identity is indicated obliquely by the Proprietor and presented directly by Vivienne – that a person is the sum of his or her past. Describing the Man as a pilgrim, the Proprietor ominously warns Anna that anyone who has reached the age of fifty always has '[s]ome act which he would yearn to erase' (261). Through the character of Vivienne, Greig allows the connection with *The Cosmonaut's Last Message* to emerge explicitly, although phrases from Keith's speech in the former play are discreetly planted in the Man's dialogues creating a

layered effect for those familiar with both works. Vivienne is the bearer
of a possible past for the Man, and not one he particularly welcomes.
It is a past of mediocrity, betrayal and failure, diverted into a desperate
attempt to escape by staging his own suicide and roaming through
Europe. Finally, after hearing about the pilgrims' way to Santiago
de Compostela, his flight becomes a pilgrimage. Vivienne gives the
Man a name and a story, but most importantly she embodies a form
of unconditional loyalty. As with Anna, he confesses to feeling 'an
undertow' in her presence, although in this case non-sexual, something
indescribable that reminds him of the snow and it is this that convinces
him to accept her account.

The final grid upon which identity is traced in *Pyrenees* is national
and cultural allegiances and characteristics. Recalling the theme of
the Paines Plough anniversary season, it is a topic subjected to comic
deconstruction throughout the play. The Man's sense of placelessness
coexists with a conviction that he is British, proved rather humorously
by his 'feeling of pride in the British Diplomatic Service' (248).
Further discussion of what it means to be British develops as Anna
asserts that she is Welsh followed by a delightfully contradictory
summary of her life:

> To be honest, I say I'm Welsh, my father came from Wales. I was
> actually brought up in Essex. . . .
> And then I went to school in Yorkshire . . .
> And then I went university in Brighton.
> And then I joined the Diplomatic Service, so I've lived in Tel
> Aviv and in Gaberone and now here I am in France.
> But if pressed
> I think of myself as Welsh.
> Whatever that means (269).

The constructedness of such a claim to a specific, regional identity is
obvious. And the elision of the numerous locations that might make up
a contemporary sense of self is so deliberately artificial that it becomes
farcical. It also, of course, belies any pursuit of a singular, authentic
identity defined in terms of place of birth not only for the Man, but

more generally. Just as in *The Cosmonaut's Last Message*, Greig uses the figure of the Proprietor for thematic amplification. Pedro identifies himself as French, English, Spanish, German, Portuguese, Italian, African, Galician, New Yorker and Basque as well as both male and female. Via the Proprietor a multitude national, cultural and racial stereotypes are playfully referenced, undermining the limitations of their clichés and, as so often is the case in Greig's work, underscoring the inevitable and necessary plurality of identity per se.

The conclusion of *Pyrenees* has been read in some very different ways. For some 'the play dwindles into mysticism' (Billington 2005). For Aleks Sierz in *Rewriting the Nation* (2011) its 'meditation on human communication, national identity and feelings of connection . . . ended on a note of muted reconciliation' (2011: 175). Zaroulia, by contrast, focuses upon how 'the utopian emerges through a negotiation of place and belonging in a globalised world,' and sees the Man's acceptance of the identity Vivienne offers as a retreat from transcendence to the everyday (2011: 34–5, 47). Yet, the Man's postmodern pilgrimage concludes with a poignant and deeply emotional conciliation, that is not wholly a capitulation to the mundane. Vivienne's absolute devotion and truthfulness is an extraordinary testament to the possibilities of redemption and forgiveness. At closer range, there is something quite wonderful about it that is easy to overlook because it is so unobtrusive. While she prints the memory of their past onto the Man's temporarily liberating tabula rasa, she also allows something new to emerge. The final scene mingles tenderness, regret and embarrassment with a dash of quirky humour. The Man's rueful acceptance of Vivienne's description of his life and their self-conscious physical contact is offset by the Proprietor switching on his strings of coloured lights and the 1983 pop hit 'Africa' by Toto. It is a moment redolent with a whimsical postmodern humour and the ironies of this choice are outlined by Greig in our interview. In place of an epiphany, Greig suspends his characters between pop and possibility – reaching for each other across the disorientations, coincidences and erased certainties of the present. Steve Blandford sees in this a 'metaphor of the reconstruction of a personal past, the rebuilding of memories, unavoidably connected . . . to questions of national identity in a bewildering, shrinking globalized context' (2007: 154). Perhaps it is that inconclusiveness that has prompted Greig to begin on a third play to complete the journeys begun in *The Cosmonaut's Last Message* and *Pyrenees*. Provisionally titled *Volvo*, and to be directed by Vicky Featherstone, it promises to reconfigure these plays yet again as elements in a trilogy that has now been developing across three decades.

Homecoming: *Brewers Fayre*

Bringing lost characters home is a motif already at work in *Brewers Fayre*, a short piece first performed at the Traverse Theatre in 2009 directed by Greig himself. In *Pyrenees* that sense of alienation and disorientation is metaphorically distilled in the image of two sixty-somethings holding hands listening with embarrassment to a pop song. An equally embarrassing pop song, Rihanna's 'Umbrella' – which incidentally topped the charts in 2007 during one of Britain's wettest summers – makes its way into the fabric of *Brewers Fayre*, but by contrast it is a work that anatomizes contemporary consumer society with a wry directness. A 40-minute show involving four performers and the use of PowerPoint slides, it overflows with a plethora of issues from depression, unemployment, marital crisis, cyber dating, environmental catastrophe, teenage angst, bad grammar and consumer culture. Twenty-five brief scenes produce a collage narrative composed of speeches and interactions between five characters: an unnamed counsellor, the Elaine, her husband Ian, their teenage daughter Christine, and Anthony whom Elaine has met online. Using a technique that, as we have already seen in Chapter 2 he carries forward in *Fragile*, Greig experiments here with PowerPoint to dismantle the spectator-performer divide. Elaine's speeches up until scene twenty-two are to be delivered by the audience, foregrounding a choral effect that gathers them into the production of the story. This was vividly counterpointed by Greig's involvement in the Traverse performance where he took Ian's part in the play.

Brewers Fayre is a quirky piece about feeling lost, vulnerable and dissatisfied in a very familiar contemporary world. It is Christmas time and Elaine, overwhelmed by the feeling of hopelessness at home finds herself searching online for someone to have an affair with. The website she subscribes to promises instant wish fulfilment – 'Soon you will be meeting real partners and entering a whole new world you never imagined was possible' (495) and paradoxically, a cautioning disclaimer on the potentially destructive effects of martial infidelity. Meanwhile, her depressed and agoraphobic husband has lost his job and is drowning in an apocalyptic sense of doom exacerbated by listening to the news on the radio. Their daughter Christine is angry that their lives have changed and wants 'things to go back to how they were before' (502); before her father's redundancy and the bank took their things, before, as it were, the flood of 2007. Young and sporty, Anthony is little more than a beautiful running machine, a self-deprecating reference to one aspect of Greig's own passions.

By making Brewers Fayre the hub linking each of the play's fragments Greig works a seam of rich ironic potential. He appropriates the name of this chain of British pubs, a place emblematic of generic consumerism and makes it the space of crisis and resolution for the play's characters. It is at the centre of the narrative climax where an unexpected sequence of events brings the family back together. Her car broken down on the other side of the Forth road bridge, Elaine makes her way through the snow towards its neon sign and her illicit meeting with Anthony. Torn between guilt and desire, she finds herself reflecting on the lack of apostrophe in the venue's name and the abject nature of her quest for some sense of connection with another human being. Inside, competing with the rising din of Christmas karaoke Christine, who has spied on her mother's correspondence, is busy scaring off Anthony. Meanwhile back at home, Ian decides on the basis of a Wikipedia search that the world is probably not about to end and manages to leave the house to help his family get back home.

A restaurant chain, the internet and a pop song are the resonant co-ordinates in *Brewers Fayre*'s intensely commodified world, and maybe this is precisely the battlefield of the imagination that Greig talks about in 'Rough Theatre'. This chapter began with a play inspired by the share markets and the opportunities presented by the New World in the eighteenth century. In *The Speculator* the potential power of global systems of connection, exchange and commodities are powerfully rendered through temporal disjunction and a metatheatrical knowingness. That sense of disjunction is mapped more concertedly in *The Cosmonaut's Last Message* onto place and identity. Meanwhile *San Diego*'s collage of images and experiences in a postmodern globalized no-man's land offers a bleak analysis of powerlessness in and the trivial absurdities of contemporary consumer society. These are balanced against a cautiously positive affirmation of alternative, if contingent, communities and relations of care or compassion. That compassion also guides *Pyrenees* and the play's ironic unravelling of identities, national, linguistic, personal and performative. Finally, in *Brewers Fayre* there is no pretence that the everyday effects of the contemporary context can, or even should, be ignored. Crucially what happens to these co-ordinates in *Brewers Fayre* and the other plays discussed here is a resistant distortion of the routes they offer for navigating our world. And it is in this that the critical and transcendent possibilities of the imagination lie.

CHAPTER 5
EAST/WEST

Contact Zones and Cosmopolitanism

The challenges of globalization entangled with those of politics, ethics and aesthetics are further distilled in Greig's Middle East work, and that work's reception. They are no small challenges; the orientation of these plays and collaborations along an East–West axis, especially in the post 9/11 environment, means that they provoke, directly and indirectly, a host of questions about the exercise of power (military and cultural), about transnational encounters, about the very possibility of mutual understanding and the practical feasibility of cosmopolitanism. My heading here refers to Mary Louise Pratt's notion of contact zones as 'social spaces where cultures meet, clash and grapple with each other, often in contexts of highly asymmetrical relations of power' (1991: 33), an idea that I think is particularly useful in attempting to interpret both the plays discussed below, but also the more general cultural and political contexts in which they participate. Clearly there are multiple terms that speak to these contexts. Contact zones are a feature of multicultural environments and may give rise to forms of intercultural exchange among people within a country or between people in different countries. Increasingly, as seen in the previous chapter, with the advance of globalization, these zones are less plainly determined by national contexts and more by the complex politics of mobility. The prominence of types of transnational experience and states of cultural hybridity in so much of Greig's work was the guiding impetus of the collection Anja Müller and I edited – *Cosmotopia: Transnational Identities in David Greig's Theatre* (2011) – and some of the points made by contributors to that book are threaded through what follows. However, this chapter will concentrate on following

Greig's engagement with the Middle East specifically and the issues that this engagement has given rise to.

Both transnationalism and cosmopolitanism are terms surrounded by extensive debate and disagreement. If transnationalism for some is a way of labelling a form of 'pluralistic utopia' freed from the constraints of nationalism, then for others it may appear to be 'a patronising and homogenising force' (Müller and Wallace 2011: 3). As we have already seen, Dan Rebellato holds up cosmopolitanism as a means of counteracting the negative progression of neoliberal globalization. Yet the commitment to tolerance and justice in a culturally diverse and deeply unequal world meets many obstacles in practice, and frequently implies 'a sustained tension without a harmonious resolution' (Müller and Wallace 2011: 6). Greig's attempts to creatively test out a space in which mutual exchange might happen, sometimes within the dramatic situation, sometimes beyond it, indicate both the benefits and the pitfalls of entering contact zones between cultures. Although the most obvious major plays to elaborate East/West relations are *The American Pilot* and *Damascus*, it is important to note that his work around the topic has developed in different contexts since 2001, so it is above all not static in its attitudes. These big plays are surrounded by a constellation of smaller projects that highlight the playwright's shifting approach to those relations over the last decade.

First Attempts: *Not About Pomegranates* and *Ramallah*

Greig's first journey to the Middle East in 2001 was the result of an invitation to work with George Ibrahim at the Al Kasaba Theatre in Ramallah along with British director Rufus Norris. The project took place as part of the Royal Court Theatre in London's programme to forge links with Palestinian theatres and to support writers. Their purpose, together with Ibrahim and the company, was to create a 'comedy about the intifada' (2008: 208) as a means of alleviating some the sense of depression that was prevalent. The extraordinary nature, some might even say naivety, of such a project perhaps only properly comes into focus when current events in the region are highlighted. Beginning in late September 2000, the second or Al Aqsa intifada continued until 2006 with the loss of nearly 6000 lives, the vast majority of whom were Palestinian. By the time Greig and Norris arrived in Ramallah in the summer of 2001, Israel had just begun to use warplanes to attack Palestinian targets, and the death toll of Palestinians and Israelis was rising rapidly with atrocities such as the lynching of two Israeli army reservists in Ramallah in October 2000 still very fresh. A series of appalling suicide bombings continued throughout 2001. It is therefore not surprising that experience of living in Ramallah even for a short time was intense; at once frightening and exciting, 'No other experience of my life has shaped my writing so much as that month' Greig states on his website.

The play they created was *Mish Alla Ruman (Not About Pomegranates)* which was performed in Arabic and is not in print. Set at a checkpoint in the West Bank in early 2001 and featuring thirteen characters, the play is a sprawling intergenerational comedy about two families, a few bystanders, an Israeli soldier and a lot of pomegranates. Amid the absurd everyday restrictions that govern their lives, they carry on trying to realize their ambitions, do business, fall in love and so on, all with mixed results. The play is undoubtedly a farcical comic excursion, but is very much a product of its context and moment. Inevitably comedy seems an insufficient match for the grim realities of the intifada and, in retrospect, is even less so given the state of world politics after the September terrorist attacks. Yet more important than the play itself, was the experience of working with young theatre-makers in a war zone, in particular Raeda Gezaleh and Marina Barham of the INAD theatre company (now Al Hara Theatre) in Beit Jala. As Greig describes in 'Rough Theatre' it was the other theatre being made in the region, at great risk, and his encounters with young writers and performers in workshops that touched him deeply and made him rethink his ideas around theatre and politics. A crucial dimension to this was not so much the content of the performances he attended, but the realization that the communal act of making and watching theatre in the midst of violent conflict was itself an act of resistance that could temporarily transcend the brutality and cynicism outside (Greig 2008: 208–10). As

I have shown at different points throughout this book, the outcomes of this experience and realization are processed variously in Greig's subsequent plays; one of the most direct attempts comes in the shape of a short piece called *Ramallah*.

Ramallah was first presented, directed by Ramin Gray, at the Royal Court Theatre as part of an evening entitled 'City States,' one of the theatre's International Playwrights events in March 2004. Five short plays by writers who had participated in the international programme were given rehearsed readings in celebration of its work. *Ramallah* is only ten minutes long and is an ambivalent celebration of the outcomes of the programme and its intercultural objectives. It is a blatantly autobiographical scenario framed as a straightforward two-hander. The man has just arrived home from a journey to the Middle East. The couple taste the local wine and food he has brought back. The woman has been occupied in his absence with their home situation and recalls him to the business of work, overdrafts, busy routines with children, and the plums from the garden. The man is full of the sensations of the place he has visited, the things he has tasted and seen, and the people he has met. He describes the experience of watching a performance in a shelled theatre and his sense of vulnerability and fear. When questioned by the woman why he has taken such risks he frustratedly counters: 'The least I can do was piss myself for half an hour on their behalf. Get a flavour of things' (108). Momentarily the worlds of home and Ramallah are held alongside each other, and in some respects they echo each other in their references to family and fruit. The difficulty lies, inevitably, in the discomfort of the realization that, as a person from elsewhere a privileged Westerner one can experience or indeed taste Ramallah and still go back to the safety of home. The play concludes with the man's recognition of how lucky he and his partner are. *Ramallah* is of course not a full play and was never intended to be more than a brief contribution to the Royal Court's programme. It is nevertheless a sardonically self-critical snapshot of the conflicts intrinsic to how to represent and respond to the West Bank from an outsider's position and an acknowledgement that perhaps it is not even really possible. Despite its initial limited purpose, *Ramallah* has had some afterlife; revived in 2010 by Glasgow's Tron Theatre as part of a programme titled 'From the West Bank,' it was grouped with two other short pieces, Raja Shehadeh's *An Imagined Sarha* (adapted for stage by Greig) and Franca Rame's *An Arab Woman Speaks*. In this context, its portrayal of Western ambivalence, even indifference, gains a sharper outline.

Meanwhile, Greig's approach to the political complexities of representation and cultural interchange are evidenced, less by a burst of further writing about the Middle East, than by an attempt to be a conduit for voices from the region. In fact, in 2004, more significant than *Ramallah* is his adaptation of Palestinian writer, Raja Shehadeh's diary of Ramallah under siege, *When the Bulbul Stopped Singing*. Directed by Philip Howard and produced at the Traverse as part of the Edinburgh International Festival, the play won a number of awards for its highly personal and reflective insider perspective. It was also the first of an ongoing set of collaborations which see Greig engaging with the Middle East through the adaptation or facilitation of other writers' work, a practice he continues, as we will see, up to the present.

Power Play: *The American Pilot*

Although *The American Pilot* is a piece that points in a somewhat different direction to the work just discussed, it is similarly aligned on an East/West axis. After September 2001, world politics swerved towards a heightened awareness of terrorism and the threats posed to the West by the East specifically in the shape of Islamic fundamentalism. Operation Enduring Freedom, begun in October 2001, saw the invasion of Afghanistan by an alliance of Western states with the aim of crushing the terrorist group al-Qaeda, and overthrowing the Taliban regime that protected them. It was the beginning of a complex and ongoing set of conflicts now habitually labelled the War on Terror. Considering the transformation of conflict in the closing decades of the twentieth century, Mary Kaldor has argued that, 'a new type of violence has developed, especially in Africa and Eastern Europe, which is one aspect of the current globalized era'. These conflicts, she describes as 'New Wars,' are characterized by the erosion of the boundaries between war, organized crime, human rights abuses; they are the postmodern versions of warfare where distinctions between aggression and defence are no longer clear, where private and corporate interests cut across ideologies in convoluted and obscure ways, where globalization provides the context for new forms of identity politics (Kaldor 2006: 1–2). The War on Terror heralded an era of 'New Wars' in earnest. It is in this context and as an early response to these impulses that *The American Pilot* must be read.

Greig has described the genesis of this play on a number of occasions. In early 2003 in the midst of struggling to complete *Pyrenees*, he was reading Heiner Müller's play, *The German*, and was struck by a powerfully resonant image. In Müller's piece, a soldier in the Russian Army in 1914 is awestruck by the figure of an advancing German. Greig felt instantly that the corresponding figure today would be American and went off to compose *The American Pilot*. As he says in an interview with Peter Billingham, the play is in a sense a response to the Iraq war which had not yet begun, but was patently on the horizon (2007: 90). Crucial to the reception of the play, however, is the lag between the time of its composition and that of its production. Turned down by the Royal Court, it was not until 2005 that the RSC mounted the play, directed by Ramin Gray, as part of their end of season celebration of 'New Works'. Revived by the Soho Theatre in London in 2006, *The American Pilot* then went on to be produced in the United States in New York in 2006 and in Seattle and Minneapolis in 2008. The differing receptions and interpretations the play received will be discussed later, for now it is perhaps enough to observe that they must be understood against both the rapid escalation of violence and the political patterns at national level. At the time of composition, the play was prophetic in the sense that, at that point, the videoed execution of hostages had not occurred, and the depiction of the War on Terror as a crusade against evil had to some extent masked the complexities of interests involved.

The American Pilot is, perhaps, more clearly than any of Greig's works to date, a play about power in a 'New Wars' era. Arguably *Dunsinane* revisits this territory with its interrogation of the politics of invasion, peacekeeping and regime change, but the approach is fundamentally different. Whereas in *Dunsinane* the method is allegorical, and as a result a Scottish frame of reference is always present; here the method is metonymical. Specifically, the figure of the pilot works as a synecdoche of American cultural and military force that each of the local characters and the audience is obliged to face and respond to. The double nature of the pilot – as a person, a body on stage – and as figuratively representative of a set of relations beyond it is the motor of the play. In a dramatic manoeuvre that we have seen in much of his work, Greig overturns the dominant perspective, and instead offers a plurality of possibilities united only by the fact that they emanate from those who conventionally are silenced, sidelined or demonized. In giving the disenfranchised control over the narrative, *The American Pilot* permits a reversed encounter with the Other that raises a host of questions about how to act, and the brutalities of dreams and reality in an era of globalized conflict.

The setting of the play is unspecified: a farm in a 'rural valley in a country that has been mired in civil war and conflict for many years'. In the RSC production costumes loosely referenced Afghanistan and Greig has stated that the place he had in mind was the Panjshir Valley (Fisher 2011: 21). This makes sense given the current affairs context, but as we shall see most reviewers read the play in the light of the Iraq war. The scenario in some basic respects reprises that of *Europe*. The appearance of an ousider transforms the fates of all the local characters; they have no choice but to react. The American's presence provokes in the Farmer human sympathy, in his wife Sarah a sense of vague foreboding, in their daughter Evie's excitement and attraction. For the Trader, who recalls the character Morocco of the earlier play, the situation is a business opportunity. For the Translator, the American churns up feelings of anger, remorse and self-disgust. For the Captain, he is a problem that must be solved.

As was noted by a number of critics and is flagged by Greig himself, the play is a Brechtian parable or fable. Pertinently, Michael Billington's review of the first production describes the format as a *Lehrstück* thus aligning it with the dramaturgical model that also informs *Europe* and, as seen in Chapter 2, a number of other early plays. Similar motifs can be excavated – the response to the Other along a spectrum from naivety to violent rejection, the dynamics of hospitality, the matter of ethics in a politically unstable environment. Yet there are some important structural differences, primary among them is the way the Other here, in the shape of the pilot, is viewed only from the outside and, as it were, in translation. The choric speeches of *Europe* are exchanged for a construction that alternates between the mimetic and the diegetic, showing and telling. In each Act dialogue and monologue scenes are layered in a regular oscillation between action and direct address. Each of the local characters, consequently, is seen externally and internally while the pilot is never afforded the luxury of interiority, of directly speaking to the audience or of a developed individuality. The parable quality of the piece is underscored by the conundrum the dramatic situation presents. As is clear from the monologues, the events that have happened are in the past and gradually we learn that there are few survivors, so the characters speak from an indeterminate and, in most cases, posthumous position that ruptures any naturalistic recourse. In the opening production, directed by Gray, this was further emphasized by the lack of set and by the fact that the full cast of performers remained on stage throughout. This destabilization of naturalism is fundamental to the space of debate opened by the play, in particular the questions it poses about the relativity of experience, justice and truth.

As already noted, the American means something different to each of the local characters. The Farmer's opening monologue highlights his physical beauty, he is like a golden angel fallen from the sky and his physical presence is 'unsettling' (3) causing a confusing swarm of unwelcome emotions. Several scenes later Evie concurs that he 'seems to glow' (13), as does the Captain towards the end of the play. To Sarah he is but a natural phenomenon, 'a light breeze that shakes the grass a little in one part of the meadow' (10) nothing more, another body to be tended. Common to these responses is that they address the pilot as a person, however romanticized. The Farmer, Sarah and Evie each offer, in varying degrees, kindness and hospitality. In their exchanges with him, Janelle Reinelt sees an 'affirmation of civil possibilities among strangers' (2011: 212), fragile but vital. By contrast the others are alert to the American's metonymical significance. At worst he is the face of the American imperialism that supports the dictatorship with which they are at war; at best he is perhaps a solution to their problems.

Jason Reinhardt drops into their world, as Billingham aptly describes, as a *deus ex machina* and the image of intervention from above is brutally reprised when the US forces arrive at the play's conclusion to rescue him and in the process killing all but Evie and Sarah (2007: 120). So while his presence is initially 'unsettling' ultimately it is decimating. Because of his presence an uncomfortable contact zone between East and West is briefly opened and it is, to return to Mary Louise Pratt, a space of contention characterized by 'highly asymmetrical relations of power'. Pratt's concern is for what she calls the 'literate arts of the contact zone' that risk '[m]iscomprehension, incomprehension, . . . absolute heterogeneity of meaning,' (1991: 36) and although the context is not identical, these are clearly not only features of the communication situation within the play but also pertain to its reception as I will discuss further on.

The mountain community is simultaneously remote from and connected to modern life, even while the wider world may be indifferent to their plight. The play cleverly suggests the reach and unevenness of globalization though references to the media – its prime cultural vehicle. Evie's knowledge of America has been gleaned from watching television, while the cartoon character, Daffy Duck, is instantly recognizable to Sarah and her husband as they look at Jason's family photograph. The MP3 player is less familiar. To the Captain the hip-hop and rap music emanating from it is as incomprehensible as code, but the suggestion is that the problem is generational rather than cultural. As soon as the Trader manages to connect the device to the system in the Captain's jeep, the younger people are happy to listen to some of the 4000 songs stored in its memory. Ironically, where physical invasion is feared and resisted, this cultural invasion is accepted and consumed.

Global media culture thus generates ambivalence throughout the play. The Farmer is wary of television and the messages it bears; by contrast, the Trader hopes that media exposure will bring pilgrims or tourists to their village thereby boosting their stagnant economy. What is really at stake is power, inevitably. Access to the media is potentially empowering and changes the terms of old wars – notably the Captain still holds on to the old-fashioned belief that negotiating is rational and prisoners should be ransomed. The Translator argues for the much more up to date use of the media as a weapon – they will video the beheading of the American and will have it broadcast internationally. As the Captain remarks, it is a perilous strategy: 'At the moment our cause is misunderstood by a handful of diplomats. Now we have the chance to be misunderstood by the entire population of the world' (34). It is only Evie's hysterical intervention that spares Jason's life, and prompts the Captain to switch his attention to her use as a figurehead for their campaign. Bizarrely Evie interruption is a passionate pro-American plea: 'America is on our side . . . America is watching us . . . We can be American' (60). Billingham highlights Evie's speech as act that 'embodies the efficacy of a global, colonial propaganda which offers a world of popular culturally-mediated commodities while reducing the individual to a homogenized commodity: 'American'' (2011: 75). In Chapter 4, I cited anthropologist Arjun Appardurai's assertion that one aspect of globalization is the way people are induced to imagine their lives in particular ways by the mass media and that often these imagined possible lives have little to do with their real opportunities. Clearly Evie's vision of an idealized consumer society that America will deliver to the valley falls within the ambit of such media-generated fantasy. Notably, it is not the feasibility of these claims that draws the disillusioned rebel, the Captain, but the magnetic quality of their fervent tone.

The dissemination of cultural forms, military power, political messages, and naively visionary beliefs is dogged by what is lost in translation, cynicism and what the addressee might merely fail to comprehend. Interestingly, the shared quality of both proposed broadcasts – the beheading and the visionary speech – is emotionally charged, visceral spectacle. Their potential value thus lies beyond reason, and both entail violence; the former would sacrifice the pilot, and the latter Evie, albeit in a more indirect fashion. Yet finally we are reminded of the extent of the locals' disadvantage in the information market and how access to the channels of global communication is lop-sided. The absolutely superior force of the American military explosively cuts short these flawed attempts at self-representation and their implicit bids for agency before they can even begin recording their message.

Responses to *The American Pilot* span a range of positions and highlight the equivocality of its shape as a *Lehrstück*. While Billingham remains ambivalent about the treatment of otherness, and the possibility that the play's conclusion is possibly a 'reactionary, sentimentalised fatalistic resolution' (2011: 179), conversely Verónica Rodríguez argues that the play aesthetically intervenes in the ethical dilemmas inherent the 'global media saturated era' (2012: 14). Meanwhile Reinelt highlights the tension between dreams and reality and how tentative reciprocity is overwhelmed by 'the violence of these darker forces of globalisation and local terror' (2011: 212). Zaroulia continues along these lines with a more developed exploration of 'the process of labelling the Other as a threat hampering any possibility of hospitality' (2011: 41).

Reviews of the productions also tell a heterogeneous story. In Britain, reviews of the RSC shows were generally complementary, so for instance Michael Billington's is fairly representative in its assertion that here is a 'provocative' play that 'goes beyond simplistic propaganda to explore both America's cultural colonialism and its residual mystique' (2005). Reactions to the three productions of the play between 2006 and 2008 in the United States were predictably a good deal more mixed. Elyse Sommer's review of the New York one in *CurtainUp* is positive, stressing its balance and use of figures to develop its fable. Marilyn Stasio in *Variety* combines a fairly favourable account of the play with rather patronising references to Greig as 'scribe'. In contrast Charles Isherwood's *New York Times* review found the play too schematic to be effective, 'more pedantic than discomfiting, despite the ugly immediacy of the events it portrays'. As Greig himself discusses in the interview later in this book, inevitably plays signify differently depending on the audience. By the time *The American Pilot* was performed in the United States sadly the atrocities it anticipated had become realities. Nadine Holdsworth sums reception context by remarking that '[t]here is no doubt that real life events that had originally given Greig's play gravitas and political significance, within a couple of years had the capacity to make the play seem naive and potentially opportunistic depending on the cultural context and presiding political zeitgeist' (2013). Perhaps it is more apt to stress the power dynamic that shapes reception at the crux of which is the authority to name or describe others. As the Translator tells the Captain, 'We're all terrorists now'. When the Captain insists he is a soldier, he is told 'You no longer have the power to decide what you are' (33). Few enjoy being essentialized as a type, fewer still appreciate the suggestion of complicity with unilateral, violent militaristic power. Isherwood's review, in particular, strives to reintroduce American experience as the primary one, in exact opposition to what the play offers. Particularly striking is his desire for a specific as opposed to generic reality that he argues is lacking in the play especially when daily 'real soldiers (and real civilians) are mired in predicaments of a similar kind'. Note how civilians, the vast majority of casualties in both the Afghan and Iraqi conflicts, merit only parenthetical inclusion. To my mind the fact that *The American Pilot* provokes such diverse responses testifies to the potency of its attempt to say something about the contact zone between East and West. Admittedly it is difficult territory, and no audience or commentator could be expected to hold absolutely neutral views, yet to criticise a parable for not being naturalistic seems beside the point. Combining Greig's preference for non-naturalistic method and discursive theatricality, *The American Pilot* is political theatre for a globalized environment where it is imperative to challenge default modes of thinking and treating the Other.

Intercultural Miscommunication and *Damascus*

The critical dissonance around *The American Pilot* pales by comparison with that stirred by Greig's next play, *Damascus*. Already in a presentation at the 2005 Strange Behaviour symposium on the topic of the connections between theatre and geography, we find him working through a recent experience of teaching playwriting in Syria for the British Council. 'Doing a Geographical' is a revealing essay partly because in the story of his visit to Aleppo there is a detailed account of a chance encounter with a young Syrian man whom Greig meets on a walk through the city. This Zacharia is obviously the model for a central character in *Damascus*, Zakaria, and good portion of the conversation Greig remembers with this man makes its way into the play. Also striking is the essay's ambivalent reflection upon the dynamics of the process of cultural outreach, how the intention of the programmes he was involved with was not to 'engage with and learn from local theatre culture,' but rather to propagate a set of representational techniques that would enable the transfer of the resulting work to a Western (specifically Royal Court or Traverse) stage. Greig traces this directly to the forces of globalization: the simultaneous desire to see stories from around the world in British theatres, and an anxiety around the hazards of appropriation. Consequently the strategy is to 'train the subjects of globalization in the methods of telling their own particular local stories' as a means of accessing some authentic representation. Greig concludes with the suggestion that such intercultural programmes that send writers as emissaries and teachers perhaps mistake 'physical space for metaphysical reality' (2005). That ambivalence notwithstanding Greig continued to participate in these programmes and to support writers from the region in this way through to 2007 when he led British Council/Royal Court-sponsored workshops in Syria and Tunisia.

Damascus emerged as an 'unexpected by-product' of this cluster of impulses, exchanges, experiences and Greig's continuing engagement with the Middle East. One of its aims, as Greig states in a *Guardian* interview with Charlotte Higgins, was 'to challenge received western notions about people in the Arabic world' (2009). The play was commissioned by the Traverse Theatre and premiered in 2007 for the Edinburgh Festival directed by Philip Howard. The production travelled to New York and then transferred to the Tricycle Theatre in London in 2009. In his contribution later in this book Howard gives a lively account of the play's journey from Edinburgh through to the controversial 2009 British Council tour to Syria, Egypt, Lebanon, Jordan, Tunisia and Palestine.

The dramatic scenario revolves around a brief visit to Damascus by the British, or rather Scottish, Paul Hartstone who is meeting with representatives from a local college in order to try to sell them his English language textbook series. From this basic premise, Greig imagines a funny but ultimately tragic intercultural encounter between Anglo and Arabic worlds, expressed in the exchanges between Paul and the Syrian characters, Muna, Wasim and Zakaria. As Dawn Fowler wryly observes, despite the rich cultural heritage of Damascus and its biblical associations, all Greig permits us to see is a rather generic hotel lobby (2011: 139). The world beyond this space is signalled by calls to prayer and a muted television broadcasting updates on an unspecified, but violent, 'current situation'. As we have seen on numerous other occasions, Greig resorts to a narrator figure to break with a naturalistic frame and to complicate the dramatic situation through direct address. Elena is the play's omniscient narrator, functioning literally and figuratively as an accompanist, reviewing the events enacted by the other characters, providing a series of fragmented contexts and framing the play with statements that are directed to both the characters and the audience. Above all she inhabits the implausibly exaggerated role of outsider. *Damascus* is patently a play about difference – linguistic, cultural and political – and the difficulty of arriving at a place of mutual understanding between West and East. Beyond that opinions on its achievements diverge widely. Is it just a satiric tragi-comedy on British political correctness or is it another example of appropriation, of Orientalism? To my mind the key to the conundrum *Damascus* allegedly presents is a recognition of the pivotal role of different forms of irony – structural, dramatic and verbal – within the play and as elements to its decoding.

Questions of presentation, representation and interpretation are self-consciously centre stage in the interactions between the play's characters and to Elena's interleaved monologues. Greig highlights this in the published text with a prefacing quotation from the poet W. S. Graham: 'Language, you terrible surrounder of everything'. The quotation is attributed to a collection called *Implements in their Right Places* – in itself an ironic slip since the title is *Implements in their Places*. W. S. Graham's poem discloses his ambivalence about language and his inability to control its effects:

> what is the good
> Of me isolating my few words
> In a certain order to send them
> Out in a suicide torpedo to hit?
> I ride it. I will never know. (2004: 244)

Such ambivalence about the impact of a 'few words' finds potent expression in *Damascus* and is also a feature of the play's troubled reception.

Paul is the engine of structural irony and his role as misguided, naive protagonist is quickly established – the phone conversations with his wife and his boss Sean outline his neurotic and insensitive tendencies even before he speaks with any of the Syrian characters. As a representative of The Language Factory company and author of an ESL textbook, most prominent among Paul's ironic endowments is his monolingualism. He enters a context where he is utterly at the mercy of translation and therefore faces serious challenges in decoding or understanding what is going on around him. Throughout much the play, comedy is generated by the obvious disjunction between what is said and what is translated, what is said and what is meant, what is claimed and evidence to the contrary. Paul's first meeting with the Dean of the college, Wasim, showcases the language barrier as a source of discomfort and as a tool of thinly veiled aggression. Knowing Paul cannot understand Arabic, Wasim continues in his attempts to seduce Muna, offering her his newly composed 'erotic poem' in Paul's presence and generally disrupting her attempts to take the textbook seriously or to conduct a professional meeting. Muna's superior language skills nevertheless permit her to silence him before Paul. Her translations of Wasim's statements are for the most part blatantly not translations at all, and as the performance is in English the audience are privy to the joke. The only point at which she does translate is when Wasim and Paul attempt to speak to each other in French and Paul fails to understand Wasim's comment that during the British Mandate his grandfather shot an English soldier in Jerusalem. So the entire scene is built around the dramatic irony of a stilted and distorted communication situation where the audience has complete access to both sides while two of the main characters understand only part of what is going on.

The scenario is reprised later, with variations on the theme of language and interpretation but the direction of translation is largely reversed and the tone is less imply comic. The three have returned from a poetry event in the city and, inspired by Damascus, Paul demands that Muna translate his ideas for Wasim. Here again Muna takes liberties, abbreviating and simplifying Paul's eloquent and enthusiastic comparison of the city's 'interconnections and accretions' to language and 'a desire to tell the truth' (64). Muna's version reduces his ideas to the mundane, the buildings are 'higgledy-piggledy' and the elaborate metaphor is boiled down to a simplistic simile, 'Writing is like Damascus' (65). Unsurprisingly Wasim, already full of frustrated sexual desire and disappointment at failing to win the poetry prize, groans 'How much more of this do I have to endure?' (65). Paul, unaware of his addressee's response, presses on arguing that their students should 'have the right to live in Damascus. A Damascus of the mind'. Finally, in an unexpected turn Muna communicates the spirit of Paul's speech to Wasim in a beautiful, literary register with explosive results. Wasim violently rejects what he sees as Paul's arrogance, telling him in no uncertain terms 'there is no such thing as freedom of speech' that he is merely a tool of 'Anglo-Saxon idealism' (66). Once more Muna mitigates the force and intent of the message so Paul does not experience its full impact.

Verbal misunderstandings are matched by the multiple examples of textual instability. Writing in the play appears in three guises: the 'Middleton Road' textbook, Wasim's poetry and Zakaria's film script. Each connects to a complex network of cultural and political conditions. Most obvious is 'Middleton Road'. Paul's enthusiastic, but very rehearsed, marketing monologue about his 'completely integrated English language learning system' (14) quickly reveals how language is never culturally neutral. The acquisition of speaking and writing skills is wedded to a knowledge of 'contemporary multicultural Britain. Not,' he hastily qualifies, 'the old – you know, homogenous – very much the UK now' (15). Implicit to this package is the acceptance of certain assumed norms and these are rendered obvious when the book is presented in a non-British context. Paul's text celebrates a version of liberal, tolerant Britishness through a cast of cheerily unproblematic and politically correct characters. It also lays claim to a certain universality that is immediately undermined by Muna's request for changes to facilitate better 'cultural and political understanding' (25). Yet, Muna is also in the business of representing a market for such a product through an appeal to assumed universal norms. She emphasizes the quality and freedom of their education system and how 'important for the Arab world that we have young people who are able to make their way in a globalised marketplace' (25). In particular she is attentive to the depiction of a woman in the textbook wearing a niqab. What is intended by Paul as an image of tolerance between members of a community is perceived by Muna as a debilitating validation of the 'codes of patriarchy' (43). Her requests for changes to the book reveal perhaps more about her own values and concerns, than a generally accepted set of codes in her society. The way she is treated by Wasim clearly indicates the sexism that she struggles against and is implicitly connected with her sensitivity the potential difficulties experienced by professional women in the Arabic world. She challenges the disrespect for parents taken as routine, if undesirable, by the fictional inhabitants of Middleton Road, and she rejects the way a teenage character expresses his desires and ambitions through the codes of rap music. Whereas Paul sees the rap merely as a joke, Muna sees it as a mode of encouraging individualism and materialism. The viral spread of the rap form through the channels of globalized popular culture was already referenced by Greig in *The American Pilot*. Here Muna highlights the way form and content are conjoined (summed up as being famous, living in luxury and sleeping with lots of women – sentiments thumped out in the selected rap tracks used in *The American Pilot* as well). Indisputably, despite the grating of an old-fashioned Marxist critique, she has a point. Unfortunately, her rejection of individualism and materialism as being 'not in line with our values' (45) seems impossibly out of synch with her earlier claim that their students should participate in the 'globalised marketplace'. Similarly her assertion that young people in Syria do not engage in sex before marriage is comically belied by both her own and Zakaria's stories.

What is noteworthy in this whole exchange around the 'Middleton Road' text is the way Greig allows the radically different perceptions and contradictory agendas Paul and Muna espouse to surface. Paul tends towards the inclusive, tolerant and ostensibly politically neutral; Muna repeatedly sees a network of issues connected to power. Ironically,

Paul's version of British culture, while apparently not homogenous, assumes an agreed set of values; Muna brings a cultural perspective that is so acutely aware of lack of consensus that at times it seems detrimentally over-sensitive. Both are a mixture of fact and fiction. Strikingly, Paul finds it difficult to know how to decode Muna's comments. Her code switching deliberately places him in an uncertain interpretative space. One moment she lacerates him for British hypocrisy, the next she teases him about his self-excoriating Western guilt, then just as quickly swerves back to severe critique. This reaches its apex in their discussion of the Rabbi Samuels character in the textbook. For Paul the character's emigrating to 'a sunnier place' is merely a way of teaching the future tense. For Muna it cannot be separated from what she vigorously renounces as 'the illegal Zionist colonisation and campaign of occupation against the people of Palestine', to which Paul doubtfully replies 'Are you serious?' (51). As we can see Muna is not necessarily always right or completely honest throughout their discussion, but Paul's politically correct representation of multicultural Britain suddenly seems blundering when compared to the complex cultural and political balancing act Muna is engaged in.

Wasim's poem, by contrast, points towards a network of questions around the artist's role, creative freedom and compromise. What initially seems to be a cynical ploy to seduce his colleague turns out to also be an attempt to connect with 'the language of the street' (26) and with a happier, more certain, past. The post-mortem of the evening at the Writers' Union annual dinner permits a deeper appreciation of Wasim's conflicted approach to writing and his disillusionment. He finds his former friends old and 'complacent' and ruefully remembers a time when they used to argue over the qualities of revolutionary art (58). If Wasim's views earned him six months in prison fifteen years earlier, now he is unsure where he stands at a time when even poetry competitions are implicated in the production of propaganda. When Muna accuses him of cowardice, his answer is poetically redolent with a sense of painful compromise: 'Doubt, hesitancy, timidity, uncertainty – these are the ways we go towards the truth' (94).

Finally Zakaria's Arabic 'script of [his] life also containing mythology' (34) serves to show the underside of the glossy promotion of language skills in the global marketplace. Indeed Dawn Fowler sees the character as a victim of globalization whose 'experience of the west is mediated by absurdly exaggerated, elitist and aspirational cultural references while he feels trapped in an endless cycle of low-paid labour' (2011: 145). Throughout the play Zakaria's expression of existential discontent and thwarted desire is hobbled by his command of English and also by his inability to dissimulate. His intense longing to escape to some idealized Western place in one way or another is unrolled in a series of comic scenes with Paul that again rely upon verbal and situational irony, and intercultural embarrassment. Zakaria's fantasy of success in Hollywood, improbably to be facilitated by Paul, is so at odds with the realities of their situations that it is laughable. Yet the comic disjunction between naive desires and reality evaporates when he discovers that Paul has left his life story by the bin in his hotel room. Zakaria's suicide brings the play to an abrupt and shocking close – the intensity of his need to escape is instantly translated from comic to tragic in a manner that brutally challenges audiences to re-evaluate their earlier responses to the character.

From the outset Paul is presented in various ways as a haplessly insensitive character. His repeated phone calls to his wife late at night and early in the morning, his complaint to his boss about being sent to 'a war zone' (10), his intermittent sense of smell, his mistaking Indian whisky for Scotch provide ready evidence. Above all, the discrepancy between the tolerant liberal political correctness of his textbook and many of his actions serves to satirize Western blindness and hypocrisy. But with Zakaria, that tactlessness has appalling consequences. Tragic irony resonates in Paul's drunken claim that they 'understand each other [. . .] they] have a connection' (101) just moments before Zakaria discovers his discarded script.

The motif of interpretation is enhanced by the narrating figure, Elena, who provides both an ever more hyperbolically contradictory identity and musical accompaniment. If questions of accurate representation and access to truth are constantly circulated in the characters' discussions of language and writing, then the music in the play adds another layer of incertitude. Elena plays a myriad of interpretations of widely varying musical compositions, in numerous styles around the clock. From sentimental versions of European pop music to Euro-pop arrangements of nineteenth-century romantic composers, Elena's piano creates multiple atmospheres in the generic space of a hotel lobby, aurally undermining a sense of stable, singular or authentic identity there. At the same time she verbally mediates between past and present, allowing the complex and multi-ethnic past of the region to seep into the picture. Elena provides a blow-by-blow account of Zakaria's last night, as well as the history of the gun he uses to kill himself. Ironically, the gun has more mobility than Zakaria ever will and its trajectory serves to mark how he 'has no noble cause to fight for, no strong belief system except greater individual freedom and it is this which causes his destruction' (Fowler 2011: 146). Along with the memory of the smell of 'Blood and whisky' Elena closes the play with a rhetorical question that draws attention to her own artificiality while withholding any easy comfort: 'What else could a transsexual Ukrainian Christian Marxist cocktail pianist possibly say that would make things any better for you?' (116)

Damascus premiered at the Edinburgh Festival in 2007 where it won a Fringe First award. Already mixed with positive responses were some critical notes that mainly address the structural coherence of the piece. Lyn Gardner praised the play's humorous challenge to 'liberal notions of a multicultural Britain' and the way it 'revel[ed] the gap between what we think we know about the Middle East and the reality' but felt the play lost momentum in the second half (2007). Similarly, Mark Fisher's positive review was leavened by a questioning of the narrative validity of the suicidal conclusion (2007). However, real reception turbulence occurred when the British Council mounted a tour billed as 'the first UK play to tour to the Near East and North Africa as part of the British Council's theme aimed at presenting UK plays that have been influenced by Arab culture' (*British Council Magazine* 2009: 6). As both Philip Howard and David Greig in their contributions to this book describe, it was a rawer experience of an intercultural contact zone than they had perhaps anticipated. Like Paul in the play, Howard and Greig found themselves obliged to edit the production in the interests of 'cultural and political understanding,' so the ironies at work within the drama seemed to fold back upon its makers, while issue of misunderstanding escalated swiftly.

It is to be expected that sensitivities run high in zones of intercultural contact and especially when that space is highly politicized. The suspicion that a privileged outsider might be speaking for your culture and even critiquing it is always potentially incendiary and *Damascus* seemed to fall into that category for some of its audiences and critics. This led some to condemn the whole project as a play of caricatures, 'uninterested in anything specifically Arab or anything specifically human' (Fordham 2009). More moderately, Joyce McMillan, who attended both the Scottish and the Syrian productions, commented on how if in Britain the play looked like a 'searing piece of self-criticism directed against the well-meaning ineffectual westerner abroad. To audiences in the Arab world, though it inevitably looks like a thumbnail sketch of their entire culture, summed up in three troubled characters' (2009). This would seem to be the eye of the storm even though *Damascus* is clearly not a documentary depiction. As close attention to the play reveals that the Syrian characters are complex and diverse rather than simply troubled, while it is the British character who is lampooned. Consequently is vital not to conflate Paul's character with Greig's intentions. Yes, when Paul tells his wife of his newly discovered appreciation of Damascus, he falls back on an orientalist romanticization of the place, but the scene is yet another instance of situational irony. Undoubtedly, as is raised by Joseph Fahim, 'the play is laced with post-colonial guilt,' but this is something Greig himself openly acknowledges and argues that the play is 'an attempt . . . to take one step beyond where we are with post-colonial guilt' (Fahim 2009) Conversely, another important dimension to the play's reception specifically in Syria, made obvious by the outbreak of civil war in Syria in 2011, is the fact that the characters' political ambivalence touched a nerve with regard to the governing regime – an unwelcome image for some members of the play's audience. Certainly *Damascus* invites reading in a metaphorical sense as a play on the tensions between East and West and contending perceptions and agendas, but the position taken is an open one. Despite its difficulties it is, as Joyce McMillan asserted at the time, a cultural dialogue worth having.

'Foreign Imaginings' and *The Miniskirts of Kabul*

Questions of cultural dialogue also surround *The Miniskirts of Kabul*, a short play commissioned by Nicolas Kent at the Tricycle Theatre. The play premiered in 2009 as part of a series of plays devoted to exploring the history of Afghanistan, titled *The Great Game* – a term used to describe 'the strategic rivalry and conflict between the British Empire and the Russian Empire for supremacy in Central Asia' in the nineteenth and early twentieth century (*Great Game* 2010: 9). As Kent declares in the introduction to the ensuing volume of plays, the impetus behind the project was the continuing conflict in Afghanistan and a general ignorance of the region's history. Very much a Tricycle political theatre project, the aim was to catalyse debate as well as to raise awareness, an objective that also underwrote the 2010 tour to the United States. The result, described by Philip Fisher as 'a long day but ultimately very rewarding for anyone with an interest in political or global issues', was questioned by others for the lack of Afghani writers (Clapp 2009) and potential colonialism of the programme (Fricker 2009). *The Miniskirts of Kabul*, directed Indhu Rubasingham, was but one element in the twelve-hour programme of plays presented, but what makes it stand out is its acute awareness of the problem of perspective.

The play depicts a meeting between an unnamed Western writer and Mohammad Najibullah former president of Afghanistan on the day of his death, the 26 September 1996. The woman and Najibullah discuss his role in Afghan politics. As Greig describes in the interview later in this book, in order to write the play he felt he had to 'embrace the falsity' of the situation – his situation as a Westerner communicating something meaningful about Afghan history – and to make that gesture the foundation of the drama. As a consequence *The Miniskirts of Kabul* is structured around an imagined meeting between writer and historical figure, knowingly acknowledged by the fictional writer – 'It wasn't possible to arrange a meeting any other way' (130). Severing the bonds of plausibility enables an unorthodox and speculative encounter 'which explores the sacrifices that can be made for moral and political purposes' (Fowler 2011: 146). Najibullah is invited to describe himself, his past and his politics for although the writer has read about him she cannot imagine what it was like to be him. And he surveys his choices with a pragmatic eye. This contrived act of empathy facilitates the sharing of a part of the story of modern Afghanistan, a country that is, according to Najibullah, 'the creation of foreign imaginings' (134). A Western gaze is illustrated in the writer's questions about dress habits under Communism but also in the play's title and the citational game played with the reference to American archaeologist and anthropologist Louis Dupree's 1973 history of Afghanistan. The writer in the play cites this source and asks Najibullah to verify its truth to which he incredulously responds 'Have you come all this way . . . to ask me about women's fashion?' (141). The seriousness of gender politics is undercut momentarily when Najibullah asks the writer to imagine the Spice Girls as the sound of shelling draws ever closer. Transitory humour notwithstanding, the politics of dress in Afghanistan is interlaced with a broader and deadly lack of consensus about self-determination and social change. And since 'Afghanistan has a complicated relationship with time' (138) the suggestion is clear – progress can just as easily be reversed here. The clothing motif remains at the play's conclusion when Najibullah dons traditional Afghan costume in preparation for the confrontation with his enemies. The extreme violence of his final moments at the hands of the Taliban is narrated by the writer who, in the absence of facts, finds she must once again imagine his response. *The Miniskirts of Kabul*'s merit lies in the self-consciousness acknowledgement of the impossibility of empathy without the intervention of the imagination while at the same time offering a glimpse of the ethical labyrinths of recent Afghan politics.

New Directions: 'One Day in Spring'

Greig's work as a theatre-maker in a broad sense continues to bear the imprints of the lessons learned in the course of his various attempts to engage with the East and, specifically, the Arab world. This chapter has surveyed its progression from provisional forays in the shape of *Not About Pomegranates* and *Ramallah* to provocative explorations of power in *The American Pilot*. The latter play clearly can be seen to redeploy Brechtian strategies of narrative performance. With *Damascus* Greig certainly faced a crisis in his attitudes to the feasibility of making theatre across cultures. As he describes in interview here, the accusations of orientalism levelled at him because of that play painfully revealed the hazards of writing in a contact zone. *The Miniskirts of Kabul* consequently foregrounds the artificiality of its situation to problematize historical perspective and understanding.

Despite the risks attendant upon Greig's efforts to theatrically explore the contact zones between East and West, these works more generally attest to the necessity of cultural exchange as an important tool in creating a space for debate between identities and for imagining the possibility of cosmopolitan contact. With the 'One Day in Spring' season of plays at Òran Mór in 2012 we see Greig using his contacts and experiences with young writers from Arabic world to support and develop exchange flowing from East to West. A co-operation between the National Theatre of Scotland and A Play, A Pie and A Pint, 'One Day in Spring' brought together work by writers and performers from Syria, Lebanon, Morocco and Egypt that reflected upon the Arab Spring. Its purpose as Greig remarks, was to attempt to provide a three-dimensional perspective on current events in the Middle East and North Africa that was not available in the media. The project, curated by Greig, included work by Mohammed Al Attar, Jaouad Essounani, Abdullah Alkafri, Abdelrahim Alawji among others that tackled questions ranging from violence and repression to homosexuality. The season concluded with a piece created by Greig and a pair of Egyptian performers. The performers offered audiences twenty-four lessons on how to be a revolutionary assembled from fragments of stories and scenes contributed by writers from the region. In this instance, Greig's chosen role is less as author and more as facilitator. As he notes, one of the themes that emerged was the tension between the urge to speak and violent silencing of that possibility. Making a space for the voices and stories of these writers and performers and propagating those stories has clearly become his preferred approach to East/West intercultural dialogue.

CHAPTER 6
PERSPECTIVES

Writing and the Rule of Opposites: David Greig in Conversation

CW: You've often mentioned how spending part of your childhood abroad really shaped your sense of identity, yet you are without doubt deeply rooted in Scotland. So how would you say your sense of belonging has changed over the years, and how do you see yourself now in relation to the Scottish theatre community and your participation in that community?

DG: It's very interesting to think of it that way, as a changing thing. It has changed and the manner of its changing reveals some of my own predilections. So I notice for example that my writing, as I've settled longer in Scotland, I now really have been writing in Scotland for about twenty years, and to some extent one obviously becomes at home in that literary environment. When I began I felt awkward about writing in using dialect words, or writing anything in accents. Now much more I am alright about doing that. I think that's a sense of sure footedness, that I feel OK on this landscape. I'm never going to be somebody who naturally will write in Scots or in dialect. In fact one of the great other liberations is that the more that I've felt at home the more I've also felt oddly liberated to write in English, if you like, without any self consciousness about that either. So there's a linguistic freedom that has emerged over the last four or five years of writing, in the sense of a realization that there isn't anyone looking over my shoulder saying you should write this way, you can't write this way, this is Scottish or isn't Scottish. Once you shake that off, it's a good thing.

One of my current ways of thinking about the world, is the rule of opposites; whatever one says, one's very aware that one is also saying it because of its opposite, the sense that everything must make up a whole. So if I spend a lot of time talking about being Scottish the less I perhaps really feel it, the less I talk about it the more sure I am of it. The pie chart of identity does shift for me as I move through time. At the moment I do feel quite at home in this culture, established within it in literary and theatrical terms . . . and that's now something that's started to worry me.

CW: Really, why?

DG: I notice glimmers of the feeling of wanting to run away from that, wanting to rebel against it. I mean it's an interesting, hopefully a relatively creative tension. Even this situation we are in at the moment is emblematic of a certain point in a writer's career when particularly a male writer can say, well here I am, look at how important I am. I find that very uncomfortable. I think it's good to fuck that up. There's something important in not feeling you've arrived.

A writer's own awareness of where they sit within a culture is a factor in the way that they write. Some people perceive themselves as outsiders, some people yearn to be accepted and it gives them fuel. So it's not wholly self-indulgent to have a sense of awareness of how one feels about that. In my case, I think that I became aware over the last four or five years that within Scotland, and to some degree more broadly, I had become, in a sense, the establishment. The Scottish National Theatre was established, and I was part of that. When the Scottish National Theatre is doing three or four of your plays and your plays are being done by major companies in London, you can't be an outsider. You might wish that you were, but you're not. What you do about that is then an interesting thing. And I'm not even sure that I know . . . But I'm also very aware that if I look at the writers in Scotland who were generationally ahead of me, writers such as Chris Hannon or Jo Clifford or Ian Heggie, Liz Lochead and so on, in five years time, who knows, we could be in a very different environment. For different reasons factions come and go, at the moment I can get plays on, but I've seen playwrights go out of fashion, and then come back in. So I don't think if you are a Scottish writer you ever truly feel . . . like an insider or safe, if that word is an appropriate word. I think there's always a feeling that it's all a bit contingent and circumstances can move on.

But there's another thing, I do feel very profoundly that within Scotland communicating with the audience, that there is an audience who is interested in my work, who've seen a lot of it, who are interested to see things that I might do and have enough familiarity with the work that they can come on a bit of a dance with me, they might come in a bit of a direction . . . and that's a different form of safety. So to put it in a crude way: I might write something and wonder how the *Guardian* might review it, but I'm actually much more interested in how the Traverse audience or the Traverse audience at the festival or the Scottish audience, how they might take it.

We are a small country; there are five million people in Scotland. The regular theatre-going audience in Edinburgh and Glasgow and the Central belt is probably in the range of hundreds and thousands, but not that much. So it's not to say you could literally know every one of them but to some extent there is a group. Certainly something I've become very aware of now, because I am more involved with the Traverse, and the NTS and to some degree with the Citz, I have a real feeling that we have to give some credit to an audience as being part of what shapes the dramaturgy of a theatre and that's a good and interesting dialogue to have. It's not about pleasing an audience, it's about if an audience is hungry and accepting of variety, of newness, of risk, then give them variety, newness and risk.

Take David MacLennan's A Play, Pie and a Pint series, which has done many new Scottish plays over the last five years. He's developed an audience who come every week, there's a new play every week and they come every Wednesday. That is brilliant for a writer because you have a feeling you can go mad, you can do what you want, if it's terrible they'll still come back next week for someone else. So you've not spoiled anything. If it goes brilliantly, they'll enjoy it. And that's a case where an audience has created partly a genre of the 45 to 50 minute play where there are avant-garde works, there are very, very mainstream works, even pantomimish stuff. So I think the audience need to be given a bit of credit for the creation of those works.

CW: It seems very community focused doesn't it?

DG: Well, I suppose because when I'm writing a play I have a sense of who they're for, and I have a sense of those people and they are as present in the telling of the work as when a storyteller is talking to an audience and he is making it up.

CW: It's directed?

DG: Yes, and I'm anticipating their reaction and I try to push them, pull them, move them. Another example is the almost literal authorial audience with *Dunsinane*. *Dunsinane* moved from Hampstead, and then was performed at the Lyceum and the Citz. It was a different play. It was a different play because from playing to 200 people in London, who saw it as an interesting allegory about Iraq, to 800 people in Scotland who saw the play, possibly even mistakenly, as a major statement of Scottish identity at a time of flux. That electrified the room, and the room felt fundamentally different. It was about different things, different notes sang out. It was very exciting in a way, but it did make me realize that one is not in control of that . . .

CW: you can't stabilize it . . .

DG: Absolutely. Nor could I therefore complain about it. I wouldn't have, it was exciting but rather unnerving.

CW: So do you feel you have learnt much from your involvement with the NTS?

DG: Huge amounts. I'm constantly thinking about theatre, theatre writing broadly and the more I'm involved – I do more direction and things that get described as curatorial, dramaturgical or however you think of it. It's still not something I'm quite able to put into words, but I think that there is a sort of particle physics of theatre that differentiates it from other art forms, literary forms. Each form has its own physics if you like; it has a particular movement. What I mean is it's not just about a play or the dramaturgy of a play, it's about the relation of bodies on the stage, about the relationship of the audience to actors, about the relationship of an audience to actors they know compared to actors they don't know.

It's interesting that we are talking a lot about the audience, but it is something that obviously plays a lot on my mind at the moment. When I think about theatres and audiences and my writing, or my directing or whatever, there is an element of trying to understand the storytelling relationship and that involves knowing, empathizing, putting yourself in their shoes for a moment and seeing where they might be at, so then you might ask why am I telling this story? What effect do I want to achieve? What's actually going on here that is making me speak? And then once you've got that you set off in a different way, perhaps you cast a different actor or perhaps you spin something towards comedy where you might have done the reverse.

CW: So you think basically it's a progression of experience and being sensitive to those conditions.

DG: Yes . . . What I'd hate it to sound like is second-guessing or giving the audience what they want, and perhaps if it is badly handled that is what it is. More and more in my writing, I have two strands to the way that it develops – one of the strands is that I very self-consciously narrate my projects. The story that gets told in the play is never that story, but there is a thing about that performance that I need to keep doing because it keeps a sense of mutual shaping is going on. And maybe this is the point, between me and whoever, every time I do that to my producer, my friend, to my family, to whoever, the story becomes something beyond me. Then I make a play out of it and I use all my skills in dramaturgy to tell that story as well as I can. But the story has kind of, I'm not sure I even know what it is . . .

CW: it's evolving

DG: Yes and it's a shared project. So the performance element is about losing authorial control. Because if you are in performance you can't plan, you're improvising, you're responding to the moment. Obviously a playwright can't literally perform, but that's a way by which performance enters the writing process for me. What appears to be an obsession with the audience at the moment is an obsession with surrendering to performance so you lose the self-conscious control that can make things rather dull or unsurprising.

CW: Laterally connected with that, a feature of so much of your work is the ways in which a journey or mobility opens new experiences but also involves risk. It's obviously a motif you've gone on with. What drew you to that motif and do you think your idea of it has changed over time?

DG: I think it's innate in me. But also writing is itself literally every step, every foot, like in poetry, putting a foot down and making the poem or prose becomes the route. Another metaphor I've used a lot for playwriting was mountain climbing. So I would talk about a play and I would say look it feels like you glimpse in the distance a mountain, you want to climb that mountain. Then you spend a lot of time just getting to the mountain to the bottom of it. Then of course the closer you get the less you can see it. And then you start to put up a route and then you might come back down and put up another one. Eventually by a very windy route you get to the top, but partly by getting to the top you see that there's probably a quicker route, so you come back down. You hopefully write the play that gets you to the top. Then you have to get back down, which is production, making it. And then eventually, there comes a point where maybe five years later you are back where you were before and you can look at it and say, I did climb that, or not. But that's a metaphor that again shows for me there is the play and there is the route, and the route is your writing. What I'm trying to get at is that somewhere under there is a landscape and in my metaphor I'm not sure what that is. So the metaphor of the journey is partly repeated because I remain interested in journeys and I find that it's only in disconnection that you find out who you are. How can you find out who you are, how can you find the border of yourself unless you are in a place where you're not the same or not at home?

CW: But it is also a very central motif in your work, in terms of what characters do in fact not all but most of your plays involve travelling and moving . . .

DG: Certainly, yes. I'm writing number three of the *Cosmonaut* series and that is a journey home, that's also journey play. There is another thing, another rule of opposites, whenever faced with a question of how to write a play think what's the obvious thing to do and then do the opposite. And to some extent, it's another part of the particle physics of drama. Surely the most exciting thing is to try to do the thing that appears impossible to do? So to me, why would you do a play in which a person is essentially in a room, because you are a person in a room already, there's nothing new there. If that room is now the summit of a mountain, or a train or if they're moving that's interesting, just to animate the space.

CW: One of the first phases of your work is a delving into the legacies of modern European history and the transformation of Europe in the 1990s. *Stalinland, Europe, The Architect*, but also *Petra* and *Dr Korczak's Example* all tease out major questions of European identity in one way or another. Does the idea of European identity still interest you?

DG: I would have thought it didn't and then the moment you said that I realised that I've got this big piece which has been preoccupying me for the last year and a half that I'll write shortly which was inspired by being unable to let go of Anders Breivik. I thought I was obsessed with him because I was interested in the nature of evil and why people do things, and men in particular. Perhaps a reason is that he cites Europeanness, he's part of this notion of Europeanness as being something threatened by Islam. What he does by attacking Norway is he also attacks, my slightly jokey but relatively serious utopia, he attacks perfection in a way. It's the worst sort of family tragedy in a way – the middle son of the family who decides to attack it. That's what he did, when he was attacking Norwegianess, Norwegian social democratic ideology, he was attacking his family essentially. And his family, Norwegian social democracy, is Europe as welcoming, multicultural, open, tolerant and secular. He was attacking it, at least nominally, on behalf of some other Europe. It's the same story in *Europe*; it's the same one again and again. So, I don't know why but I suppose I am drawn to that story because part of me who likes to feel rooted worries the other part of me . . . That tension is always there between rootedness and defensiveness. So yes, European identity maybe still is there.

CW: You've obviously talked a lot about politics and written on how you navigate this creatively without being pigeonholed. It does seem to be still something that has to be wrestled with . . .

DG: What I would hope very much is that I don't have the illusion that I am not interested in politics. At the same time I am very firm in knowing that that which I say I believe in a newspaper article or when I speak or try to promote a particular political ideal that my writer self has no responsibility towards it. My writer self may reveal other things that I may have no control over and that in the end my prime responsibility is to that, that's what I always have to remember.

CW: A term that keeps coming up in discussions of your work is globalization. Has your thinking about theatre and globalization changed since you wrote 'Rough Theatre'?

DG: That being the notion that theatre is a good tool . . . the Rough Theatre idea for me keeps evolving in the sense that the notion of theatre not as a separate building or room or the paraphernalia about it, but simply an unbelievably primal way in which we explore the nature of what it is to be human and – God, that's fucking pretentious – what I mean is, how else is that enacted except by the idea of character that can be adopted for a moment and played with? So it seems to me that is unbeatable by screen, it is unmediatable, it is not unmarketable but the market can't destroy that. It's cheap, it's a technology we are all familiar with.

There's another question though and that is – is theatre a good place to discuss the notion that we are all truly global and so on? That's more complicated because I don't know. On a purely practical level I've tried very hard and the work which has not always been my most successful has been the work I have tried to deal with what I perceived to be the realities of globalized life. So *Damascus* is a play about cultures interacting. It did well in some ways but it's not a play that's done a lot because it's very difficult since you need half a cast of Arab actors and half a cast of British ones. That relatively daily occurrence of crossing a cultural barrier is actually very difficult to put on stage.

CW: Obviously some of your plays have presented stories that are political in a big, broad sense but, strikingly, of late you have written lots of short plays that focus on specific political issues. These pieces are polemical and recall Brecht's Lehrstücke. How did these plays come about and do you would see them in the mode of the lesson play?

DG: Yes, a bit. Why I really liked them was that they were a challenge. So let's take *Miniskirts of Kabul* as a prime illustration. I realised with *Miniskirts of Kabul* that I'd been given a task that was explicitly to educate about a politics which was absolutely anathema to everything that I had said I'd do and so I thought that's interesting – how am I going to do this and still be what I say I am? And I realised that the problem with *Miniskirts of Kabul* is that a. its remit was to be educative and most people try and hide that and b. how do I know anything about Afghanistan and what it is like? There was a moment when I realised that the answer to writing it was to absolutely embrace the falsity, to allow that to be what it's about and to enjoy that. So when Nick asked me to do something about nuclear weapons I did it again that way. And then *Fragile* was the formal experimentation that came out of *Brewers Fayre*, but involving the audience literally in saying the lines and so on.

CW: Did you find those experiments with technology to be a success?

DG: It really was much better than I ever expected in both cases and with *Fragile* especially. I honestly expected some hostility, but it really felt as though the audience genuinely loved two aspects of it. There's a slightly liturgical aspect to it. They loved the joke of it as well, there was a knowingness and the PowerPoint becomes a kind of character, a kind of wink. So in *Brewers Fayre*, when you've been saying these lines and then suddenly you get a massive speech and then someone stands up from among you and speaks there's a sigh of relief. In *Fragile* there's a bit where the character goes 'all my life I've fought against this and all my life I've been defeated'. I absolutely knew the kind of audience who were going to turn up to *Fragile* would be lefty people of my generation and I knew getting them to say those lines would be an act of . . . they wanted to say that, I could feel it and it felt as though they were getting something off their chest.

CW: And it's an inspired way of navigating that question of audience participation which frankly may be terrifying.

DG: Yes, although in both instances I said to them you've got to say to people at the beginning that it's absolutely fine not to do it, that we only need a small proportion of the audience to do it and it will work. But I kid you not, every time I've seen it if anything it's hold them back. And I love sitting next to people and hearing them and it's a choir so the voices fall together, but within it you hear different voices and expressions and they really are acting and it makes me really delighted.

CW: To go back to those political plays, they really are responding to specific big issues and the contrast between the dimensions of the issue and the play form is striking. Were they all commissioned?

DG: Apart form *Kyoto*, yes. *Kyoto* came about because of the failure of *Futurology* which was a real attempt to . . . I still do think that climate change and issues around that are so enormous and enigmatic and all encompassing that to not approach it at all just seemed almost criminal, so we tried with *Futurology*. Graham and I, we tried to create something that was an old-fashioned popular agitprop show which failed. Actually, I think that was not intrinsic but partly in the way it was presented. So *Kyoto* is literally an offshoot of *Futurology* which was set at a fictional climate conference and one of the sketches concerned a couple – essentially I just wrote the scene that was alluded to.

CW: And it brings the enormous question down to individuals

DG: Yes. I don't think *Kyoto* is 100 per cent successful, but I think it's funny that the radiator suddenly stops working and then the lights and then they're just suddenly not sure where they are and actually what's happening. That seemed about as good a metaphor as I could get. But trying to make it small again was a reaction to it not having worked when I tried to make it big. And the rule of opposites worked to reconsider the biggest problem facing mankind, and the way not to do it was to do a big show.

CW: So *The Letter of Last Resort* followed a similar trajectory bringing up some incredibly difficult ethical questions in miniature?

DG: That was the one that I just thought, I can't do it. Nick kept asking and I said no until he encouraged me to meet a submarine captain. As a lefty of course I don't think we should have nuclear weapons, but if we have to have them I'm very glad it's him who drives the submarine. He was a very thoughtful, quite practical proper British officer type. Absolutely lovely chap, very funny, and I really liked him . . . So that was one of the things, just him, and then I thought I can't write this until there's a moment when I believe nuclear weapons are a good thing, until I have that moment then there's nothing for me to say. So I had to reach a point when there was genuinely a part of me that said this is interesting and the point was when I realised soldiers don't like nuclear weapons, soldiers like to fight. A nuclear weapon's job is to not fight that's the whole point of a nuclear weapon; it exists only to not be used. Its use is its own failure. Once you get that it becomes more interesting to write about, and the letter is a true thing.

CW: Another major strand in your work has been the Middle East. Do you feel you are reformulating engagement with that?

DG: There are different things for sure. One is the young writers with whom I work were almost all on the front lines of their struggles, and what I felt instinctively that there was this generation that we should be listening to. Because at that time I felt we only saw the Middle East in terms of potential al-Qaeda fanatics or brutal dead hand regimes. Yet, there is a set of kids who if you only speak to them, they are not going to kowtow to you in America but they are open, they're on Facebook you can talk with them. I certainly didn't predict anything, but I had sensed the energy. So that was one way of re-reading the past. Then literally working with young writers and what they'd written about claustrophobia about needing to break out and I followed that up with the season in Òran Mór, 'One Day in Spring', where we had commissioned new plays and used plays that already existed.

The other side was the tour of the play *Damascus* to the Middle East and that journey which was very bruising for me. I had the experience particularly in Syria when the play would go on and in the post show discussion I would get shouted at and then afterwards young people would come up to me would go, 'it's our teacher, so we can't speak in public but you're totally right in what you're saying'.

CW: So you found yourself in the midst of an internal politics as well?

DG: Totally. I think the version we toured to Damascus had Zakaria shoot himself at the end. In one version we had him set fire to himself at the end. But in both versions the big thing we were told in every Arab country we went to was our young people are proud to be Syrian or whatever, they would never commit suicide, in our culture young people don't do that. And what was the spark that did it? It was a young working-class boy setting fire to himself! If I have an edge of anger it's that I took a lot of shit for making that up and my only defence against it when I was accused of orientalism, I was accused of all kinds of things, my only defence was – I met Zakaria in the citadel in Aleppo and he said, 'I am dead Mr David I am dead inside' and I thought, he is a suicide boy. So the only defence that I could offer was I was an outside eye. But with twenty young writers writing plays many of which discuss suicide my use of that image and storyline was not false. All I could say was that is what I saw. Afterwards I thought maybe I am an orientalist and certainly I did become very anxious about cross-cultural dialogue. I started to wonder about what cross-cultural dialogue actually was and was there ever a context in which it could really exist or was it always a kind of . . .

CW: appropriation or misrepresentation?

DG: yes, but there was also the accusation 'you put this representation of this culture' and I said 'have you seen any of the other representations of your culture?' I've probably got this wrong but it's a more honest attempt than having a Hollywood terrorist. So there's a bit of me that said, isn't the irony of cross cultural communication that the conflict emerges in the people trying to talk and the people who aren't even bothered to talk to each other don't get it. Finally it was just too much, so I totally withdrew. And then almost a couple of years later all this blows up again and suddenly it felt, not a vindication – it would be insanely hubristic to describe it like that – but it does make me re-read that story in a much less self-critical way. I was right about that energy being there.

I used to say to people with *Damascus*, imagine if there was a show called 'Edinburgh' by an American funded by the CIA – because that's the foreign office if you're Arabic and the British Council is the foreign office – so imagine that show arrives in the biggest theatre in Edinburgh, it's got a budget ten times the sizes of any we have here, it doesn't have any Scottish actors in it but it has a lot of Americans doing Scottish accents. What are you going to think? Of course you're going to think it's rubbish . . . And that's maybe unavoidable.

So I suppose in terms of learning, with 'One Day in Spring' I came at it in another way. Doing Raja Shehadeh's pieces, that's the way I would now engage with the region. Increasingly I'm not interested in asking novelists to write plays; I know how to make plays. Give me a short story, give me a memoir, and I'll make a play of it. But I need the writing to be you. That's where I'd now look and *One Day in Spring* was that. It was a multitude of writing voices that were not me, but I was making a show of it. When I worked with Raja I did that too.

CW: That seems to connect well with your ideas around the transcendent possibilities of theatre, but also the oscillation between tangible and intangible.

DG: That's the particle physics of theatre. What I feel now and enjoy is the concrete: the actor moves from there to there, something happens in your emotion and that my job is to manipulate the concrete. So you can say she enters wearing a red dress, you can't say she symbolises death. You can't do anything with that, but you can make her wear a red dress. And I like the red dress because I might think it symbolises death, you might think it symbolises blood. But as long as it's about the red dress, it's got all the energy of theatre. When it's about 'this is a symbol of death' you've crushed it to one thing, and maybe that's why when I describe the story as a separate thing I try to tell, there's a level at which story is concrete too. Story is concrete, the realm of the story is the realm of the concrete and you can manipulate that in the same way you can manipulate the position of an actor. But if all you are doing is concrete that's hopeless, you are doing that to produce the intangible.

CW: Looking at your work in sequence I would say that you've moved away from things that are more abstract up front towards stories that are suggestive but much simpler on the surface. Would you agree?

DG: I still think it was literally a switch point. I've always wanted ambiguity, openness, I used to think you got that by not doing story. Now I think the opposite, you get it by doing story, in a sense that is what *Mainstream* proved for me. It's like playing an instrument – in *Mainstream*, I was sawing away but not quite knowing, thinking wouldn't it be brilliant if you didn't play a tune, but you played fifty different tunes fragmented. And then the astonishing thing with *Mainstream* was that somehow there was still a story – that was amazing. How could it be? It's not there, the fragments can't be arranged together to make a story and yet there is a story. So what I understand now that is that story is so unbelievably powerful and concrete, that the way to really make it strong is to pull and test it; then the audience are part of the team of making this story and it's exciting. So a piece like *Yellow Moon* is on the surface is just a story, but actually every chapter of it is told in a different tense or perspective so some is from Leila, some is a ballad, some is from newspapers. That was a very self-conscious thing; I would not allow myself to use the same voice twice.

At some point I will probably stop doing this, but right now I feel that once I've got the story, I can play such formal games because of the confidence I have that the audience will come with me. That's really exciting. So *Glasgow Girls*, the musical book I'm doing, that's a story about these asylum seekers and girls in Glasgow defending their friend from deportation . . . it took me ages to think I'd got the story, but once I'd got the story, the musical was allowed to tell itself. The feeling that once you've got confidence of story you can then really fragment which is what I was doing with *Mainstream*, but just not knowing I was doing it.

CW: Let's turn to *Midsummer* and *The Strange Undoing of Prudencia Hart* since they are both very much part of this. You've been talking about how a story can unfold and told in different ways by people participating in it. These plays fuse a sense of crisis with celebration and self-exposure in a playful way that doesn't submit to being read in terms of big issues. And they've been very successful too.

DG: Yes, it's also kind of letting myself off the leash. Once I trusted that I wasn't David Mamet – he was like the parent I had to overthrow, I don't know why . . . But there was this moment where I remember thinking, I can't do it any more. I can't pretend I don't like words; I'm going to write an opening speech that tells and does not show. I'm going to throw a hundred adjectives and adverbs where one would do; I'm going to break every rule I've been told. And actually it was like coming into myself – I felt *now* I'm speaking. There was a moment when I started to realise, whose approval do I need? It's not to show off, but rather to say that if one trusts one's writing voice, then one can go and do it, whereas in the past I felt I had to plan thoughtful things and ideas. Now, I just try to approach the energy of what you need to approach and it will come out.

CW: Do you find music to be linked with this? Because it seems the musical references in your work also break with what might be expected, the everyday hops in through music.

DG: There's a lovely bit for me in *Pyrenees* and it's a story I am telling against myself. In *Pyrenees* a song comes on and it's Toto's song 'Africa'. Well it comes about because that's what came, so I went with it. And then I got very embarrassed about it and after we did the first read through for rehearsals I wrote a second draft in which I changed the song to a better song. I thought these are people in their sixties, it's a sixties song they would have listened to and this is better because it's about snow . . . it'll make me blush if I say it. You should probably promise to use asterisks! So I changed it. And then when we read it, I could feel the company and the director going 'What the?' And so I immediately said, 'I'm terribly sorry, I don't know what came over me' and I changed it back. But the point being 'Africa' works, if it works, because as I wrote it, it was the right note, I didn't know why it was, it just was. Now I can look at it and say, the character lived in Africa and he doesn't know that, that's why it connects. Also the banality – it's the funniness of them going 'this must be a clue' and really listening to the song. And there's just no clue. Nothing! And that's something funny. The moment you go away from that the note is just horrible and tries to be meaningful. But it's also this slightly shamanic thing that you need when you're writing. You need to be unselfconscious in the moment of writing and it's an example of that.

Yet to be unselfconscious you have to trick yourself, it's a constant effort, it's an unbelievable effort to get into those states, so that's the dance. Not to say, that's the sort of thing I did last time and it worked so I'll do it again.

The story with Kylie was that as I was constructing it I had to keep riding the rhyme horse. So although I'd told the story lots of times before, I pretty much knew the story before I was writing, I was literally writing in rehearsal, trying to keep a scene ahead of them. And because I had to write in rhyme I couldn't control where it went, which is why it becomes about that. But the moment when I thought, yes, the muses exist was at the very end. I knew she was going to sing 'Can't get you out of my head' and there was this moment I realised the pun, not so much the devil's ceildhe as the devil's kylie. Obviously you could read it and think that's what I had first but absolutely not at all. The pun arrived as if it had just been a piece of treasure that one only needed to find. And I love that, I don't know what you do with it, you just have to throw yourself in and trust that you keep going. But more seriously, I like the conundrum that Prudencia is a woman who loves folk but doesn't like people. I like that contradiction. And Kylie perhaps points up how we love the folk song but the idea that it's karaoke basically is another matter.

CW: Some responses to *Prudencia* highlighted the satire on academics – was that your intention?

DG: Actually that annoyed me because many of my friends are academics. I knew some of them didn't even bother to read the play because they thought he's suddenly gone academic slagging, and I really don't think that's true. I think we end up on Prudencia's side in that we like the idea that there is beauty, whatever it is. I do think she gets put through quite a wringer about that. The fact that she's forced to sing Kylie does prove that Colin's argument about folk and folk studies is pretty strong. But they all get a bit of a teasing. Also, what I tend to find is the people who most love *Prudencia* are themselves Prudencias. She's me and I'm her. That's the condition of being literary; it doesn't matter if you are a poet or an academic.

CW: I was wondering about *Midsummer* – for me there is an echo of *Ulysses* here especially in the repetition of 'Yes, I say yes' which is reminiscent of Molly Bloom's monologue. And they seemed alike in a celebration of wandering a city.

DG: I like that analogy. And you talked about crisis before. *Midsummer* is absolutely an exploration of crisis in the old Greek meaning – the point at which you have to go forward or die. There's also a parallel with *Prudencia*, there's that moment of change from one to another when the gap of possibility opens up. They're also both about stripping identity, so in *Midsummer* they both believe you can't change and they have to go through this to realise yes, it's fine you can do it. And I think that Prudencia is similar, she has to realise that she doesn't have to be what she thinks she has to be. In terms of self-exposure and one's inability to avoid telling one's own story in whatever one's writing where you are naked effectively, I'd say that's a theme that's running through quite a lot of the work in the last five or so years. The sense of having spent the whole of your twenties and thirties establishing an identity and realizing that just the moment when you think you know what you are is probably the moment you have to change. I literally had a year, a few years ago, when I said to myself, every single thing I catch myself saying or thinking, I'm not the sort of person who does that, I will do it. And that was a kind of response to that.

It goes back to the yes thing. It is a celebration that this is not it and you can change. But there are two layers in *Midsummer*: there's the story and the telling of the story. The telling of the story is funny and it's told, particularly when Matthew and Cora do it, in a delightful, flirty way and you just know everything's fine and they can wheel about and do jokes and play. If you just did a film of the story, and not the telling of it, it's about as bleak as *Leaving Las Vegas*. It's about two alcoholics, essentially, on a binge, desperate and lonely. But the play never feels like that because you can trust that these characters wouldn't tell you this story if it went wrong. The other fun thing with *Midsummer* is that it's consciously in dialogue with the romantic comedy; it has its cake and eats it. It allows you to enjoy the romantic comedy while being self-aware. *Prudencia* is self-consciously in dialogue with the ballad form, *Glasgow Girls* is self-consciously in dialogue with being a musical, even *Yellow Moon* is a bit aware of being a road movie. There's an element of using the genre to give me something to play with – which again might have to stop.

CW: Let's close with an image that you've used several times is that of a forest; the forest as an ecosystem with accretions of growth, as a metaphor for culture and theatre. Would you apply this to your own work?

DG: Well, I also like the metaphor of the city and accretion that is used in *Damascus*, because both understand that there is not a guided planned self that creates everything. So if it's me that we are talking about as a writer there is no . . . the ecosystem model allows for the fact that it is a multitude of influences, there are a hundred voices going on, there's a constant shifting of things and seasons and so on. But at the same time there is an underlying landscape that perhaps you could argue is being explored. Anything that takes it away from the idea that an individual mind can control and plan and lay out a play. No, you can't and if you try you'll fail. Even if the attempt and failure might be interesting, it is still a mixture of organic and chaotic and collaborative, and that collaboration partly can come about because the voices in our heads are shaped by other people. So if you write a play you are still collaborating even when you don't think you are.

Edinburgh, 14 September 2012

'Geographies of the Imagination' in David Greig's Theatre: Mobility, Globalization and European Identities

Marilena Zaroulia

> Theatre cannot change the world but it can allow us a moment
> of liberated space in which to change ourselves.
> (David Greig, 'Rough Theatre')

Writing in 1994, David Greig described playwriting as an experience of 'internal exile', where a writer crosses borders between the real and the fictional, producing what Greig calls 'geography of the imagination'. According to him:

> This geography maps a place in history, memory, fantasy . . . It is
> in the interweaving of the two worlds, the real and the imagined,
> that the writer experiences home. In a sense, writers walk the
> boundaries mapping and exploring the space they share with
> others. (1994: 8)

For over two decades, the Scottish dramatist has consistently attempted various ways of expressing this 'geography of the imagination' in his numerous plays for the theatre. He often sets his plays in small, ostensibly insignificant locations, such as the hotel in *Pyrenees* (2005) or the disused train station on the border in *Europe* (1994) that is emblematic of the playwright's approach to place in a globalized world. However, by using these small, unknown locations as the stage of the characters' stories, he indicates how the flow of global capital and its consequences can penetrate people's everyday lives in locations across the world. Furthermore, many of his plays distort linear understandings of time and space and present a number of challenges as texts for performance. In other words, Greig is a playwright who attempts to represent the whole world onstage, in ways that, in the context of British theatre, are reminiscent of Complicité theatre's work, particularly *Mnemonic* (1999) and *A Disappearing Number* (2007).

In contrast to other contemporary British playwrights who have captured the state of the British nation through various dramatic forms including and beyond social realism, Greig's prolific career offers an anatomy of the world, negotiating relations between place and individual or collective identities in a context of globalization. Greig's understanding of what defines Britain and particularly Scotland in the present historical moment is firmly bound up with an appreciation of how global experiences of late capitalism and the subsequent diffusion of ideologies have changed the limits of the nation and contributed to discourses of transnationalism. In other words, Greig's emphasis on 'geography of the imagination' not only implies an aesthetic or dramaturgical choice, but also encapsulates the complex politics of his drama, as this often bridges the local and the global, the particular and the universal, the current and the transcendental, the banal and the sublime, the Marxist acute critique of social reality and the adamant belief in a utopian elsewhere that is yet to arrive.

This chapter suggests ways of reading this 'geography of imagination' while assessing how specific plays respond to experiences of globalization and transnationalism. It is impossible to cover all the aspects of these complex phenomena; therefore in this chapter, I will focus only on how experiences of place and mobility shape and are shaped by processes of globalization and produce notions of transnationalism. In other words, I shall attempt to unpack the politics of Greig's 'geographies of the imagination' by analysing in more detail the tangible geographies and relations produced across the globe. In the first part, I discuss two epic plays written at the turn of the third millennium – *The Cosmonaut's Last Message to the Woman He Once Loved in the Former Soviet Union* (1999) and *San Diego* (2003) – with reference to two key questions: What does it mean to live in a world 'on the move' and how does the condition of a world in flux impact on experiences of belonging to specific communities, cultures and nation-states? In order to offer some thoughts on these complex questions, I will be referring to two key terms – non-place and strangerhood – proposing that many characters in Greig's work can be seen as strangers, who challenge the established notions of belonging to a place by often occupying what

French anthropologist Marc Augé has defined as 'non-places'. I do not intend to celebrate strangerhood, conceptualized by sociologist Zygmunt Bauman, as a transnational way of being that transgresses isolated and problematic attachments to the nation. Instead, I ask what is the significance of the travellers, strangers and other subjects 'on the move' in these texts while suggesting that the Scottish dramatist seems to have an ambivalent position on strangerhood as a consequence of mobility, which is accelerated by processes of globalization.

Questions of travel and border crossing in the 'world village' are also central in the second part of this chapter, which examines how Greig's representation of cultural and national identities is particularly related to politics in post-1989 'New Europe'. In this second part, I discuss two of his earlier texts, written during the shifting international *milieu* of the 1990s: *One Way Street* (1995) and *Europe* (1994). I question how characters experience their belonging to a changing world, following the end of the Cold War. In this context, it is not the people but the borders that move, thus constructing new nation-states and making people feel like strangers in their own hometowns, causing new flows of migration or requiring new ways of mapping these landscapes. How do characters in these plays adapt to this changing reality? What makes home and what is the particular significance of emotion for understanding national belonging – and potentially, a belonging that stretches beyond the nation's borders?

Both parts of this chapter examine the complex interrelation between cultural politics, identities and feeling. I explore how this dynamic is manifest in plays that happen in a specific place or in plays that take place in a number of locations. In my reading, Greig's 'geography of the imagination' is tied to a strong negotiation of feeling – both for the characters and the audiences – that often shapes experiences of national and transnational belonging. The politics of emotion is crucial for a comprehensive understanding of Greig's dramaturgy, as the work's affective dimension and power trigger and enhance the reader's or audience's appreciation of the world of the play and how this might correspond to the world they inhabit. But before I focus on the chosen texts in relation to identity and cultural politics, I will offer a brief introduction to two key critical terms: mobility and place as a way of exemplifying notions of globalization and transnationalism. It is precisely in this dialectic between routes and roots that Greig's 'geography of imagination' and his critique of the contemporary world emerge.

Place, Mobility, and Globalization

The experience of human identity has always been bound up with a sense of place and the practice of dwelling. Place is a location where relations are built and history occurs; it is the space that becomes meaningful through human activities happening in it. As cultural geographer Tim Cresswell suggests in his short introduction on place (2004), place often signifies privacy, ownership, hierarchy, authenticity, memory and a sense of belonging. Place determines the way that we perceive the world and the way that we understand ourselves in the world, constructing our point of view. Place, Cresswell reminds us, signifies a material location but also a way of looking at that specific location, in both ontological and epistemological terms. Thus, place determines identity and human interaction.

Marxist cultural geographer David Harvey (1990) has proposed a different conceptualization of place as a form of capital, a *fixed* form of capital in a world dominated by capitalist systems of production and consumption and forms of capital that flow. Following Harvey's approach, definitions of place as a form of capital require a negotiation of relations of power. Reading place not as a neutral location where human identities grow but as a locus of conflict and antagonism is crucial, bearing in mind contemporary crises of displacement and the number of refugees. However, in both ways of reading, a sense of place emerges as an embodied relationship with the world, for it signifies relations, connections and individuals' involvement with a certain location. Greig's dramaturgy negotiates place in both ways: as a space that constructs humanity and history as well as a battlefield where relations of power and uneven development are staged.

However, there are numerous arguments that in the present moment, individuals' sense of place is replaced by an overwhelming placelessness, as people move all the time and their relations with places have become temporary and functional. Mobility is considered the reason for this drastic shift in definitions of and relations to place. This 'blank space' (Cresswell 2006) acquires a number of meanings but in short, it signifies movement and is considered the opposite to place. As a multitude of flows of people cross paths throughout the world on a daily basis, new hybrid experiences of place emerge, whereby people of different cultural backgrounds and practices inhabit a place already populated by individuals who have come from elsewhere or have never moved away from this place. Hence a place that is no longer bounded due to practices of mobility stages new forms of identification and potentially struggles over community and difference.

Tensions around place are certainly not new; human civilization has historically been shaped through dialectics of place and mobility, the need for dwelling and desire for movement. The history of Europe in particular has been shaped through experiences of mobility, triggered by sociopolitical changes, such as industrialization, poverty, war and class struggles or revolutions. In the present moment, it is this movement's speed and degree that are more intense and this is why mobility is perceived as process and product of the vicious cycle of globalization.

Globalization is another term that operates as a 'blank space' acquiring divergent significations: economic, cultural, military and political. Harvey's view (1990) that globalization is a key factor in the making of postmodern societies through 'time and space compression' remains an influential approach to the phenomenon. Similarly, Fredric Jameson's assertion in his seminal study on postmodernism that 'it is arguable that our daily life, our psychic experience, our cultural languages are today dominated by categories of space rather than categories of time' (1990: 16) summarizes the radical shift that occurred in capitalist, Western world, particularly in the past three decades. Technological progress and the rapid growth of the free market contributed to certain celebratory views – particularly during the 1990s – about the making of the 'world village' or what German sociologist Ulrich Beck has termed 'world society' (2000).

It was argued that individuals not only had the opportunity to access and consume goods from across the world, but also that globalization presented a significant opportunity for the expansion of human consciousness beyond national borders. Various political institutions and neoliberal policies paved the way not only for the dominance of global capitalism but also for arguments that the persistence of nation-states threatened the possibility of crystallization of a global consciousness. The cosmopolitan citizen, 'who freely interacts and negotiates between cultures [and can be] regarded as the embodiment of the transnational condition' (Müller and Wallace 2011: 3) was advocated as a desirable mode of agency. Nonetheless, this perspective often served the global, capitalist *status quo* and did not signify anything more than a privileged, world elite that travelled and consumed worldwide. In contrast to this attitude, which promoted universalising, homogenizing and often neocolonialist politics, others emphasized the imperative of protection of national and cultural identities and authenticity, thus promoting an isolated sensibility, parochial localism, or even xenophobic nationalism, which was equally dangerous as any banal cosmopolitan attitude.

In a context of what appeared as a borderless world, it was easy to assume that everyone is 'on the move' because of choice: travel for leisure, work, studies, in short travel for pleasure or achievement. In the post-1989 European context, that of European Union expansion and integration ostensibly replacing the Cold War divisions, the word travel replaced other words such as migration, exile and homelessness. However, after the Civil War in the Balkans and the violent displacement of people in the former Yugoslavia, this celebratory attitude towards the forces of globalization shaping 'New Europe' was contested. The 9/11 terrorist attacks and the subsequent War on Terror as well as the rising number of conflicts across the world further exposed the risks and ruptures that underpinned globality. Such factors reignited the debates about migration in a post-colonial world of uneven development. Instead of assuming that all people can travel and cross borders, it is now clear that mobility is differentiated:

Some people are more in charge of it than others; some initiate flows of movement, others don't; some are more on the receiving end of it than others; some are effectively imprisoned by it. (Massey 1994: 149)

At the time of writing, the global financial crisis further precipitates this frantic movement across borders, challenging notions of place and identity and further exposing the inequalities that the global, capitalist edifice maintains.

Against this backdrop, Greig wrote the plays that this chapter studies. These plays balance between two aspects: on the one hand, the realization or representation of what the contemporary world *actually* is, a world of uneven social development. On the other hand, human relations evoke hope and aspirations for a different kind of world: a world of equal development, free movement across borders and a world where the principle of hospitality can be fulfilled. This tension between the *as is* of the contemporary world and the *what if* of the dramatic world underpins the politics of Greig's dramaturgy, its affective power as well as its transnational or cosmopolitan sensibility, not as a vague principle but as a lived experience.[1] Indeed, when discussing cosmopolitanism or transnational sensibilities in Greig's work, it is not an abstract ideal that serves the global, capitalist hegemony but instead it is 'habits of thought and feeling that have already shaped and been shaped by particular collectivities, that are socially and geographically situated'. (Cheah and Robbins 1998: 2)

Travellers and Strangers: *San Diego* and *The Cosmonaut's Message*

A man is on a plane travelling for the first time to San Diego, California. He is reading from a travel guide, because, as he says, 'I always like to know the facts about a place'. His name is David, a character based on the playwright. Before he arrives, the fictional David Greig provides very important information about San Diego:

> Despite being such a great place to live, San Diego has featured in almost no fictions, films, novels or plays, but it has served as the un-named background for several episodes of *America's Missing Children*. (7)

These first lines indicate how Greig captures the 'geography of the imagination'; although he seems to present the reader with specific information about the location where the play is set, he actually presents San Diego as a place with an ambiguous identity. Later on, when the playwright's fictional persona disappears – perhaps as he is punished for attempting to consume the place as a tourist rather than really engage with the people in it – San Diego becomes a place that could be anywhere, an open space where a number of different characters pass by and meet.

Inspired by the playwright's visit to the United States, *San Diego* is the epitome of a travelling play, a play-critique of mobility and its impact on identities, exemplifying the tension between the need to move elsewhere and the quest for home. The play explores identities in a changing, transformative place where every character is 'on the move' and relations of care between each other produce new forms of identification and belonging. It develops motives that have dominated the playwright's work since the 90s. As he has admitted: 'I do seem to come back and back to a neutral space into which people bring with them their pasts and their cultures and countries' (2011: 14).

In *San Diego* most of these neutral spaces are anonymous but recognizable because they could be anywhere in the Western world. According to Augé, hotels, airports and motorways are non-places, 'spaces that cannot be defined as relational, historical, or concerned with identity' and are 'the real measure of our time' (1995: 77–8). They are functional spaces that efface any possibility of expression of individual identities. Instead, they merely 'create a shared identity of passengers, customers or Sunday drivers' (101), but that does not mean that they promote collective identities or the construction of communities. Augé associates the proliferation of non-places with travelling in the postmodern world, what he terms supermodernity. In his anthropological theory, travelling signifies a lack of relations, since the focus is not on the place but on the ways in which individuals relate to themselves in rapidly changing landscapes.

For Augé, 'the traveller's space may be the archetype of the non-place' (86); it is a solitary, non-relational space where the only spectacle is not the place but the individual in the place. Greig develops a similar argument in his manifesto for a 'rough theatre', suggesting that this kind of travelling becomes a tool for the growth of global capital.

> We are encouraged to dream of destinations. Our imagination begins to place us in cities to which easyJet has opened up a new route. We take photographs of ourselves at the destination. The destination becomes a part of our self-description so that we can say 'Prague is my favourite city' just as easily as we might say 'Nirvana is my favourite band'. (2007: 214)

In *San Diego*, when Amy cannot locate the Pacific View Apartments, where the Pilot is planning to spend the night, he has to go out on the motorway and look for her. It is there that he meets David, who has been attacked by Daniel, the illegal immigrant who arrived at San Diego to find his missing mother, and tries to save him. The hotel's anonymity and the Pilot's subsequent adventure opens up the opportunity for a different kind of travelling, what Greig terms a 'journey narrative' (2008: 208), which presents an experience of travelling that does not reinforce global capitalism, as newspapers' travel supplements do, but presents a more complex picture of mobility.

The characters' movement – from San Diego to London to Lagos to the desert to a beach in Scotland – is a consequence of globalization or colonialism but they cannot be approached as tourists, leisure travellers who are subject to the predicaments of global capitalism. Instead, they experience travelling in a more complex way that moves beyond Augé's critique of the non-place. When they pass from the non-places, they are not deprived of their identities; instead, they encounter themselves in a new light and open up to a process of transformation, due to their encounters with Others.

Nonetheless, in a context of proliferating non-places and lack of roots, certain characters in *San Diego* seem to feel like strangers. For example, Laura, the Pilot's daughter, confesses her envy for the geese that fly north and know where they are going, whereas she feels that she does not belong anywhere. Bauman has read the stranger as an ambivalent term, which is neither a friend nor an enemy but exists outside normative ways of order through binary oppositions. Greig seems to suggest that the only way to escape strangerhood is by developing intimate relations and replacing functional interactions with caring actions that will transgress the non-places in a world that is constantly on the move.

Laura's opportunity to stop feeling like a stranger is presented at the end of the play, when she travels to Scotland with her lover and fellow patient, David. Her exclamation that 'it's definitely the place' (109) recognizes this beach as home, but trying to protect this image of perfect home, she attempts to commit suicide. The encounter with the stranger, though, is a catalyst of change. David saves Laura's life, transgressing his own clinical condition and committing an act of care. Greig's engagement with routes and roots, travellers and strangers is also evident in the story of Daniel, Pious and Innocent. This story gives a different image of strangerhood, moving beyond the recognizable or privileged subjects of the contemporary world – Laura, Pilot, David. Having stabbed the fictional persona of the playwright, Daniel, or Grey Lag, cannot be classified as a friend or an enemy. He is an illegal immigrant, an angry stranger, particularly after the murder of his friend Innocent by policemen; Daniel's ambivalent identity subverts established systems of thought and existence and expresses the unequal relations that define the contemporary world: 'in San Diego, do they suppose that we are ants? . . . . Do they suppose that we are dogs? That we love them? Do they suppose that we are cattle? That they can eat our bodies?' (87)

At the end of the play, having realized that neither San Diego nor his mother was what he had imagined, he decides to leave, but in the meantime, Pious – an outsider himself – has become his mother, assuming responsibility and caring for Daniel. In the play's last scene, Pious helps Daniel to get ready for his illegal flight back to Nigeria, on the wings of the airplane. Pious's sentence 'my little goose is leaving the nest' (117) reveals the intimate bond that has developed between the two men, alludes to the universal condition of motherhood but also is a sharp comment on travel, as socially produced yet unequally distributed movement.

As I have suggested elsewhere (2011), these eternal strangers make us encounter our responsibility, raising questions about transnationalism as a political attitude. If transnationalism signifies a process of crossing national borders, Greig's work seems to be asking us a more pressing question: to consider the ideological and cultural borders that we might need to transgress so as to achieve a cosmopolitan, transnational attitude. Assuming responsibility through acts of care is a way of crossing borders; however, this does not signify attempts at integration or assimilation, neutral indifference or acceptance but raises the question of hospitality; how hospitable can we be to Others who have now appeared on the border and managed to cross it?

The intimate relations between Laura and David, Daniel, Pious and Innocent become a temporary metaphorical home for these strangers who are not only people 'temporarily out of place'. They are '*eternal wanderers*, homeless always and everywhere, without hope of ever "arriving"' (Bauman 1992: 79). Moments before the airplane's landing at the end of *San Diego*, the end of the journey and the return to the 'real world', Laura's and Daniel's stories are unfolded simultaneously with another moment of intimate connection between the Pilot and Amy walking on a beach in San Diego. Greig invites the audience to see in the relations between these characters and their travels an image of a different, better world. A world where 'the stranger' is located in and shaped by multiple contexts, while triggering acts of hospitality, care and responsibility which derive from the realization that the identity of 'the stranger' can never be totally defined or closed in its representation. The encounter with strangers makes people aware of the fluidity that defines identity and allows them to cross-fixed national and cultural borders.

San Diego's final scene makes audiences metaphorically travel elsewhere; its affective power through the evocation of care and intimacy as forces that flow in the world, beyond global capital, produces – even for a brief second – a different sense of belonging that exists beyond the nation and derives from 'a global perspective as well as local engagement, sees what divides us as well as what connects us' (Rebellato 2002: xxi). Doreen Massey (1994) has suggested that place should not be perceived as static but as part of a wider network of interactions between places and people. In Massey's theory, this way of appreciating place in a context of postmodern, global mobility allows for what she calls a 'progressive sense of place', where the place where we stand is understood as part of the wider world, connected to it and making an impact on it.

> Instead of thinking of places as areas with boundaries around, they can be imagined as articulated moments in networks of social relations and understandings, but where a larger proportion of those relations, experiences and understandings are constructed on a far larger scale . . . . And this in turn allows a sense of place, which is extroverted, includes a consciousness of its links with the wider world, which integrates in a positive way the global and the local. (1994: 7)

Following her argument, mobility and globalization help us redefine identity and relations through 'articulated moments'; series of moments where what happens here might have an impact elsewhere and is part of a wider network that extends the boundaries of a specific, tangible location. Thus, these 'articulated moments' are a metaphorical way of crossing borders without moving away from a location and designate a transnational way of being.

The last moments of *San Diego,* where Daniel's airplane flies over the Pilot's and Amy's heads, wakes up Marie from her prayer and coincides with David's 'thank you God!' exclamation as Laura returns to life, capture these 'articulated moments' of connection between people, places and actions. In a similar way, *The Cosmonaut's Last Message* expresses this world of 'articulated moments' but this time with action that 'bounces between Earth and space like a satellite signal' (Greig 2011: 25). The play captures the constant and often-desperate attempts at communicating between people, who are in non-places, feel estranged or out of place due to the frantic experiences of what Augé describes as 'time and space in excess'. Nastasja's shouting at the airplane in the middle of London when she is deserted by one of her lovers and Oleg's desperate detonation of the space capsule as a signal to the woman he once loved show that both characters' lives are shaped by the place where they are but are still subject to past influences or events in other places across the world; at the same time, their actions have an impact on other people across the world.

Like *San Diego, The Cosmonaut's Last Message* articulates a world in flux which challenges fixed notions of identity. In the same way that Laura dreams of the perfect place where geese fly north, Keith in the *Cosmonaut* promises Nastasja to take her 'somewhere beautiful'. The desire for a transcendental moment of beauty and real connection between people seems to be the only possibility for home, in a world of frantic movement. The 'articulated moments' and connections between people across borders are even more obvious in this play through Greig's device of doubling: Keith and Bernard, Vivienne and Sylvia are characters in different places in the world, but performed by the same actors. By situating the daughter of the Russian cosmonaut as the stranger at the heart of capitalist London, the play recognizes the rapid changes that occurred in Europe since 1989. However, by employing what Rebellato calls 'ghostly doublings' as well as some linguistic echoes, Greig emphasizes that the whole world is interconnected but also hints at the possibilities that theatre offers to present different realities, depending on the choices that a director might make. These dramaturgical and performative possibilities also indicate the theatre's political power to escape the totalizing forces of global capital and banal transnationalism.

Feeling European: *Europe* and *One-Way Street*

The Cosmonaut's Last Message opened at the end of a decade that saw seismic shifts in Europe and concludes Greig's overt engagement with the future of Europe; *Europe* and *One Way Street* demonstrate how Greig's theatre not only maps people's movement across places but also contests the established notion of place as a fixed, stable entity. *Europe* represents 'history, nations, places and identities in a dynamic state of process' (Holdsworth 2003: 25), which implies people's appreciation of the place – their 'sense of place', to return to Cresswell – radically shifts. The play articulates homelessness, a transition to new ways of being and a tension between nostalgia and hope, past and future. In other words, it stages the opposition between the global and the local and the ways it emerged in Europe after the fall of the Berlin Wall, through the metaphorical story of the station on the border, where no trains stop anymore – a place that runs the risk to be eradicated by the forces of history.

Returning to Massey's theory, what was necessary in Europe in the early 1990s was to replace 'a very problematical sense of place, from reactionary nationalisms . . . introverted obsessions with "heritage"' with a 'progressive sense of place' (1994:6). Massey's call for a 'global sense of place' is pertinent for understanding *Europe* as a parable for new ways of conceptualizing the Old Continent, a process that was bound up with literal or metaphorical notions of travel.[2] Place and mobility are no longer binary opposites; on the contrary, the desire for movement and stillness shape new forms of identification and community. For Fiona Wilkie, the play 'pursues the implications of disconnection – in transport links, in personal relationships, in versions of nationhood, and between competing social ideologies – for understanding a contemporary European sense of identity' (2011: 157). Indeed, *Europe* tackles both mobility and immobility and their impact on identities, those who leave (Katia and Adele) and those who stay behind (Fret and Sava). Through images of travel by choice, forced displacement or unavoidable stasis, *Europe* presents different forms of European identification, recognizing the fluid and unstable nature of identity as tied to place and time. The characters' relations to the derelict train station and the disconnection between them correspond to the material and emotional factors that contributed to the making of new European consciousness, where Europe emerged both as a 'space of imagination and emotion' (Passerini 2007: 110) and the stage of unequal relations among people.

A year later (1995), Greig in collaboration with Suspect Culture wrote a text that responds to the same issues but in a minimalist way: *One-Way Street* is defined by a nostalgia for lost modernity and openly dialogues and pays tribute to two important European philosophical and literary figures, Walter Benjamin and Charles Baudelaire. The play follows the journey of an English man, John Flannery in East Berlin, in his attempt at writing a tourist guide of the city, after the fall of the Wall. However, as we move on alongside Flannery in his '10 short walks in the former East' journey, we gradually get lost and a new sense of geography emerges through the interweaving of places, actual moments in East Berlin and Flannery's memories and imaginations from the United Kingdom. By means of this 'geography of the imagination', the borders between Berlin, a place located at the heart of European past and present history and imaginary of European identifications, and the United Kingdom seem to disappear and are replaced by multiple encounters between Flannery and other characters. These encounters, though, are manifest in the body of one actor only (Graham Eatough), thus producing a new way of mapping identity; in this way, the human body articulates a different kind of topography, produced by people and places and potentially suggests a way of reading identity and difference through the commonality of the human body.

Flannery creates a 'map of his life' – just like Benjamin did in the original text – through a subjective mapping of the landscape while his 'ordinary man' view of Berlin constitutes a comment about the history of Europe, or rather a transgression of Europe's histories. Most importantly, though, *One Way Street* presents a different form of identification for the central character – leisure traveller: his feelings for people in the city and particularly his ex-lover Greta shows how belonging is not about a specific place or its borders but belonging *with* other people. For Luisa Passerini, the feeling European sensibility is bound up with experiences of community that are not produced by national affiliation but other kinds of sharing that move away from national borders. Indeed, Flannery is both connected and not connected to Berlin but his belonging is certainly produced through the small 'articulated moment' where he transgresses his British identity and develops true connections with other people.

Greig sets the end of the play in the revolving restaurant at the top of the TV tower in Alexanderplatz to illustrate Flannery's uneasy relation of belonging. As David Pattie has argued (2008: 150), this is 'a location both firmly poised in Berlin and separate from it, and Flannery is similarly poised between versions of himself'. *One-Way Street* captures Greig's interest in experiencing identity through feeling. As Passerini has noted with reference to feeling European sensibilities, in strong affect-imbued moments a subject does not 'possess something defined as an identity, but rather it is the subject who is possessed' (2007: 98). The performative choice of using one actor to perform a multiplicity of characters hints at these intense moments of 'possession' where travel does not signify only passing through places but also engaging with people. This is another way of representing human interaction beyond culture and nations, thus indicating how small, lived experiences might offer a way of transgressing – even momentarily – the most enduring ideological, sociopolitical and cultural borders.

The Battlefield of Imagination and the 'Anywhere' of Theatre

Writing about space in performance, Gay McAuley has observed that 'while theatre can take place anywhere, the point is that it must take place somewhere' (McAuley 1999: 2). She recognizes theatre's imaginative and material qualities: although theatre as an art form can happen in any kind of location, what is important is that it needs to happen in *a* tangible, specific location. Theatre cannot remain in the realm of the imagination; every play – in the case of text-based theatre – must be transposed on a spatial, aural and inhabited space, which may be the theatre stage or any place that can host a performance. Thus, how can theatre, which is based on representation and occurs in a specific, fixed space, articulate experiences of mobility, migration and displacement and the changing notions of human identity that these experiences bring about? Rebellato has identified the 'massive disparity of scale between the stubborn localness of the theatre and the awesome scale of the whole world' (2009: 3) as the factor that might limit any discussion of the link between theatre and globalization. Nonetheless, when we are in the theatre, we are physically in one location but often – by suspending our disbelief – we imaginatively travel elsewhere, to the place where the play happens. In other words, the act of watching theatre is already a form of travel, a way of transgressing the specific and the global.

Greig, in his manifesto for a 'rough theatre', suggests a way to bridge this disparity between local and global, fixity and flow, mobility and place, routes and roots. He approaches imagination as a 'battlefield' and calls for a theatre that will introduce new ways of imagining and resisting powerful discourses and ideologies that determine what is imaginable and what is not. According to him, 'theatre is a very appropriate weapon in the armoury of resistance' (2008: 219). By scrutinizing travel and the processes of crossing borders, which are often manipulated by the forces of global capital, his plays produce geographies of imagination in order to present a strong political alternative.

While staging the action in San Diego, Berlin, London, Oslo and other tangible places, Greig gestures to a different place, a place that we can arrive to only by travelling in our imagination, while watching a performance or reading a play. In particular, *San Diego* – exemplary of what Rebellato has defined as the 'site-unspecific text' – stages *nowhere* in order to indicate what could potentially *be* there. Greig is writing about place and passing by places in order to produce a new sense of place that seems placeless, yet exists in the theatre that presents 'a space of endless possibilities' (2008: 211). In this way, Greig's 'geographies of the imagination' celebrate theatre as an art form while evoking a different but actually existing world.

'Who's Scotland?': David Greig, Identity and Scottish Nationhood

David Pattie

The Matter of Scotland

On 28 August 2011, *The Guardian* asked a number of prominent Scottish writers (Iain Banks, Janice Galloway, and A. L. Kennedy among them) about the future of the union between Scotland and England. Their responses were interestingly uniform; all came out, in some cases rather tentatively, in favour of independence, if only because the relationship between the two countries had exhausted its usefulness. All, to a greater or lesser extent, endorsed a view of nationalism that was in line with the broadly left-of-centre consensus in Scottish politics, culture and society. As arguably Scotland's most prominent playwright, David Greig was asked to participate. He was as wary of the idea of a national identity founded on ethnicity as the other contributors; his idea of Scottishness was of something rather more communitarian

> The Scotland whose independence I seek is more a state of mind: cautious, communitarian, disliking of bullying or boasting, broadly egalitarian, valuing of education, internationalist in outlook, working class in character, conservative with a small c. It's a polity formed by the virtues of the manse. And, given that the virtues of the manse are not dissimilar to the virtues of the mosque, the gurdwara or the Women's Institute, it's a multicultural, shared, open polity.

There is something usefully unfixed about Greig's idea of Scottishness. It is not an entirely evanescent concept; it is located in an attitude to the traditions of the country, and to the people who inhabit that country – but it also, implicitly, includes other voices, other traditions, woven around the central idea of a Scottish identity. There is something in this description, also, which chimes with longstanding ideas of Scottishness as an identity which tries to escape fixed definition: of a national identity which places itself, self-consciously, on shifting sands.

Greig's relation to Scotland is a complicated one. Born in Edinburgh but raised in Nigeria, when he returned to Scotland he found, in his own words, that he 'stuck out like a sore thumb' (Fisher 2011: 15). In an interview in *New Theatre Quarterly* in 2011, Greig has said that

> [being]/not being Scottish is a matter of profound uncertainty for me. It's perhaps the defining plank on which my identity is built and yet it's uncertain. It's wobbly. So – this issue inevitably crops up in my plays. (Rodosthenous: 5)

The question – of being or not being Scottish, of laying claim to an identity which is simultaneously a fixed point of reference, and something profoundly unstable – isn't something that Greig has wrestled with on his own. It is a question with which Scotland has asked itself, over and over, for quite some time. As David McCrone has pointed out, internal debates over the status of Scotland might not have been conducted in the language of fervent nationalism, but neither have they been dry exercises in constitutional negotiation

> What is striking about constitutional debates in Scotland – and they have been going on for almost 300 years, not simply the last 30 – is how debates connect self and nation. There is a strong current of argument that Scotland's constitutional status is both a cause and effect of imputed senses of self . . . (2005: 70)

Scottishness, at various times, has been the sign of an unacceptable past that modern Scots eschewed; an exotic panoply of mistily romantic images (the tartan, the heather-strewn mountains); a covering descriptive term, signifying dour practicality; or a short-hand description of a feeling of indefinable difference – we do not know who we are, but we know what we are not. It has never been widely used as a term which describes a stable identity; Scottishness always seems in transition – located somewhere in the past, or in an as-yet-unrealized future, or in an attitude to our neighbours and the wider world, or, sometimes, in a damning indictment of Scotland itself (Renton's assault on Scotland as a 'nation of wankers', in Irvine Welsh's *Trainspotting*, for example).

This is not a new phenomenon. For the past three hundred years, it could be argued, Scottish identity was dizzyingly unstable; during the nineteenth century, for example, one could be at the same time distinctively, proudly Scottish, and a loyal part of the British imperial state. The same uncertainty manifested itself during the Scottish literary renaissance of the 1920s. The poets Hugh MacDairmid and Edwin Muir might have seemed to hold diametrically opposed views on the matter of Scotland (MacDairmid enthused by the potential of the nation, and Muir dismissive of a land that had lost all sense of itself), but as Paul Robichaud has pointed out:

> In their search for an authentic identity for modern Scotland, both MacDiarmid and Muir quite literally draw a blank. The quest for a stable essence of Scottishness lying within the nation's symbols and history discovers a terrifying and dispiriting emptiness. (2005: 141)

A 'dispiriting emptiness' which is also anatomized and excoriated in Tom Nairn's 1977 polemic, *The Break-Up of Britain*. More recent interventions in the debate – David McCrone's widely influential *Understanding Scotland: The Sociology of a Stateless Nation* (1991), Cairns Craig's discussions of Scottish literature and culture – define Scotland as an anomaly; a nation with some of the structures of a state, but no fixed national identity. One might even say that there is an emptiness (which, however, does not need to be thought of as a dispiriting absence) at the heart of Scottish political life. For example, rather than a commonly agreed cluster of national myths and signifiers that Scots clutch to our collective hearts, Scottish nationalism is more likely to manifest itself in rather looser ways; in particular, the newly successful SNP has pledged itself to an idea of civic nationalism – a version of Scottish identity which embraces many individual and group identities, all bound together by a Scottish institutional polity. Scottishness, for Scotland's main nationalist party, is not a matter of the correct accent, or the correct ancestry; it is multifaceted and impossible to categorize. It is not a fixed identity to which we adhere, but something far more indefinable and evanescent. Wherever and whatever it is, Scotland is never here and never now.

In November 2011, the National Theatre of Scotland hosted a panel discussion on Scottish playwriting, at the Royal Lyceum theatre in Edinburgh. Paul Henderson Scott, a veteran advocate of Scottish theatre (and a man who campaigned long and hard for the formation of a Scottish National Theatre in the 1980s and 90s), made a case which was, at base, simple and clear. One of the defining features of a Scottish play was that it should sound as though it came from the country; the voices that spoke on stage should do so in Scots – a rich literary language, refined by the Makars (a generation of Scots poets who produced their work before Chaucer inaugurated the English poetic tradition) and revived by MacDairmid in the 1920s; a common, demotic and democratic language, despised by those both outside and inside Scotland who regarded the country as always, by definition, subordinate to England.

Greig's contribution was more hesitant ('any project of definition is going to be fraught, and open, essentially to ridicule . . .' as he put it). Rather, one could more usefully understand the nature of Scottish drama by looking at the territory, (or the environment, as Greig put it) in which the work developed. This didn't mean that a Scottish play simply meant a play written and produced in the country; there were features which had come to define drama in Scots – a mixture of high and low speech, a poetic, allusive turn of speech, and the idea of direct address to the audience. These features, though, were not inherent in all Scots writing. Greig traced them back to the Scottish literary renaissance of the 1920s and 1930s, and the revival of Sir David Lyndsay's sixteenth-century satirical morality play *Ane Pleasant Satyre of the Thrie Estatis* at the Edinburgh festival in 1949. However, this moment (and the others cited by Greig – *The Cheviot, The Stag and the Black, Black Oil*, John Byrne's *The Slab Boys*, the plays of Chris Hannan and John Clifford in the 1980s, Liz Lochhead's *Mary Queen of Scots Got Her Head Chopped Off*, and more recent work, such as Gregory Burke's *Black Watch*) did not lay down a marker, pointing to the true nature of Scottish drama; rather, they were attempts at a definition of Scottishness, but each one was of necessity partial. For Greig, there was no one experience, no one location, and no one language which could be used by writers or artists who wished to lay claim to an essentially Scottish identity. This was inevitable, given

the marginality of this culture, the differences in language, the archepelagic nature of its different communities, the fact there is no one city that was truly able to dominate any other. I think out of those tensions artists were required or forced to . . . grow in a peculiar way . . . Each author had to find their own way through all of those different restrictions or opportunities . . . ('Staging the Nation roundtable')

Hunting down the true nature of Scottish identity was an impossible task; creating a play which could capture the complexity of this small nation was similarly beyond the power of any one writer. For Greig, any play – indeed, any work of art – which took Scotland as its setting or its theme would have to negotiate its way carefully around the absences, the elisions, the marginalities, the complexities, and the sheer uncertainties that have always accompanied any attempt to define a Scottish identity.

Caledonia Dreaming (1997): Sean Connery's my Sensei

. . . When I look back, we must have known; devolution was just going to happen. You just knew it. You didn't know when or how, but you just knew . . . (Fisher 2011: 18)

Scotland – at least as a named, identifiable location – did not really feature in Greig's earliest work. There are traces of Scottishness in the plays – the characters in *Europe*, damned to economic irrelevance by forces beyond their control, the jerry-built tower blocks in *The Architect* – but they remain in the background:

All the pieces were set in these anonymous places and were not written in Scots or any sort of Scots idiolect and entirely disconnected from Scotland, apparently. So it may be that had I not come back, I would somehow have been forced to write about Scotland. It freed me from that. I don't know if that's true. All I can say is that there was unquestionably a need to come back to Scotland and, being back in Scotland, all I did was question notions of rootedness and notions of Scottish identity as represented on the stage. (Fisher 2011: 16)

In this, Greig was not alone: rather, as noted above, he was reconnecting with a very intense and complex debate which had, by this time, spread out to all aspects of Scottish culture. It was not that a nationalist tide had begun to sweep its way across the country; rather, national consciousness, of a kind, emerged in Scotland in the 1980s and 90s almost by default. Most Scots rejected Thatcherism; and Thatcherism – a peculiarly harsh mixture of Victorian values and economic determinism – was associated, by both the Scots and the Prime Minister, with the Union as it then existed:

> In Scotland, the Union was sacrosanct and not up for discussion. With as much dogmatic certainty, Thatcher refused to concede that there was a 'national' dimension to Scottish politics and believed that the issue was simply between unionism and nationalism . . . For her, there was no half-way house: 'As long as I am leader of the party, we shall defend the union and reject devolution unequivocally'. (Finlay 2008: 170)

After a prolonged tussle with such an intractable political philosophy, the prospect of a new government, promising a change in the political and social constitution of the country, was welcomed by the majority of Scots. Thatcherism and its after effects, however, posed a question for Scotland. As a set of inflexible ideas, it was useful, albeit unintentionally; it provided a fixed point, against which debates around national identity could develop. It gave us something to define ourselves against; its passing posed an implicit question – Thatcherism was what we were against, but what were we for?

Greig's as yet unpublished play *Caledonia Dreaming*, written for and performed by 7:84 Scotland in 1997, did not provide a neat answer; rather more usefully, it explored the bundle of fears, wishes and hopes that lay behind the question. It was the first of his plays to be set unambiguously in Scotland; not only that, but it is based around a figure who has come to stand for Scotland. Sean Connery is the closest that Scotland has to a national archetype: born in a working-class area of Edinburgh, with a Protestant mother and a Catholic father (and able to trace his ancestry, on his mother's side, back to the Highlands); an internationally successful actor, and a generational icon; a vocal supporter of Scottish independence, and a tax exile; and a man who manages to make every single part he plays (Irish American cop, Russian submarine commander, et al.) sound indefatigably Scottish. When Stuart, a Labour MEP, is looking for a figurehead for his bid to bring the Olympics to Edinburgh, he and his staff run through a series of available options. Billy Connolly is not serious enough; Donnie Munro, the lead singer of the band Runrig, is 'good, but not the dream'; and Irvine Welsh is instantly dismissed, in a damning set of heavily end-stopped lines ('Never. Mention. That man's name. In this office. Again . . .'). Stuart is looking for a man who incarnates Scotland: not an easy task, given the bifurcated nature of the nation:

> **Stuart** Scotland is modern – yet old.
> Urban – yet rural.
> Friendly – yet canny.
> Strong – yet compassionate.
> Who is it.
> Who's Scotland. That's the question we need to answer. (41)

The answer, though, is already there; only Sean Connery, of all potential figureheads, can reconcile such diametrically opposed attributes. He is the only true avatar of Scottishness: no wonder the other characters are drawn to him; no wonder that, when they finally meet him (in one of the funniest, and most unexpectedly touching, scenes in the play), they are struck by an almost overpowering sense of awe:

> **Eppie** He looked familiar.
> **Lauren** He looked welcoming.
> **Darren** He looked like my dad.
> **Stuart** He looked like he was in charge.
> **Jerry** He didn't need to speak. (83)

The symbol of Scotland, appearing like a returning god, at the symbolic centre of the capital city (the limousine carrying Connery pulls up next to the characters by the Heart of Midlothian, in Edinburgh's old High Street); perhaps the only man who can show the country the image of its own, best, most familiar and most comforting self.

Except that Connery is not there: he never appears on stage. At the heart of the performance, where the archetype of Scotland should be, there is an absence, an empty space into which the characters project their hopes and their longings. Darren, a young man from the council schemes in Oxgangs, wants to be Connery's PA; Jerry, the doorman at the Caledonian Hotel, wants Connery to hear him sing; Eppie, a discontented member of Edinburgh's cosy middle-classes, wants to rekindle an erotically charged moment from her past (which, inevitably, included Connery). Lauren, originally from England, does not have the same emotional investment in the actor that the others have: an Edinburgh call-girl, she is enlisted by Stuart in his quest to discredit a political opponent (Stuart, equally inevitably, comes to realize that Connery would provide him with the face and voice that could best reflect Scotland back to the world). Obviously one actor, no matter how famous, cannot incarnate these conflicting desires; by implication, no one image of Scottish identity can carry the weight of national aspiration. Ultimately, what is important is not what Connery can give the country; what is important is the aspiration he represents. Connery, the *ur*-Scot, is a symbol for all the undefinable aspirations of a country coming to accept a new idea of itself; a country, as one of the choral speeches that thread through the play, makes clear, that is learning to say yes, rather than no

> We're the yes, yes campaign.
> We demand new questions.
> Questions whose answer is . . .
> Yes Yes.
> Just to hold that word in my mouth for once.
> Yes. (17)

Victoria/Outlying Islands: The Highland Archetype

> **Victoria** If I could step out of my body. Leave my skin on
> the hillside. Walk into some new life. But I'm half in and half
> out of the ground. Place holds me. The shape of me. In the
> mountainside (172)

In an insightful 2008 chapter on Scottish theatre, Nadine Holdsworth
identifies the importance of the Highlands in contemporary
representations of Scottishness. As she points out, this vast hinterland,
home to a tiny percentage of the country's population, has variously been
a symbol of a romantic, lost past (the place where that unlikely thing,
the essential Scottish soul, might be found), or an endemically
backward prison, removed from the struggles and achievements of the
more modern Lowlands:

> Crucially, the Highlands have been politically contested sites,
> as evidenced by key historical events such as Culloden, the
> Clearances, and the impact and consequences of the discovery
> of North Sea oil in the early 1970s. It is a place associated with
> many of the battles and narratives of resistance embedded
> in the Scottish psyche in the face of the greater political
> and economic might of England following the 1707 act of
> union . . . (Holdsworth 2008: 127)

The Highlands, then, have always been an important constituent
element in Scottish identity – but because that identity is not static,
the image of the Highlands is also unfixed. They are archetypes;
they have been seamlessly incorporated into various contemporary
branding exercises (the default beginning of a Scottish holiday
advert will be a slow pan across romantically brooding mountains,
accompanied by some quasi-Celtic music), but they are endlessly
flexible and endlessly contested. Rather like the figure of Sean
Connery in *Caledonia Dreaming*, everybody thinks they know

what the Highlands mean; but they don't mean the same thing to everyone.

Victoria (2000) is the first of Greig's plays to be set in this shifting landscape:

> The physical presence of history is unavoidable in towns and in cities. But perhaps in smaller places, places more remote from the capitals of nations, history is refracted and revealed in a different way, its effects inscribed more subtly in the landscape, and in sharper relief in the lives of the people. Of course, in the West Highlands, the twentieth century and its effects are set against a haunting absence brought about through clearance and emigration, and also against the presence, in the mountains and the sea, of a much larger geological time – both of which serve to contextualise the recent past and our dreams for the future. (*Victoria*, Author's Note).

The play follows the inhabitants of an island in the Western Highlands; its three acts are set in historically propitious periods: 1936 (during the Spanish Civil War and the rise of Fascism in Europe), 1974 (a period of political and social crisis; a period in which the natural resources of the Highlands, and especially the oil in the North Sea, was touted as a potential source of economic salvation), and 1996 (the year before the election of a Labour government promising a vote on devolution). However, it is not that the play simply reflects historically significant periods; if *Victoria* had been structured to capture moments that were historically revelatory, the acts would perhaps have been set in 1939 (the outbreak of WW2), 1979 (the election of Margaret Thatcher, and the year of the first, botched devolution referendum), and 1999 (the year when Scotland voted yes to devolution). Each one of these dates – 1936, 1974, and 1996 – is a year in which the world is changing, but the nature of the change is unclear.

Victoria captures a country in flux, and that sense of uncertainty is reflected in the characters' shifting relationships, with each other and with the landscape they inhabit. The grand house and estate of the first act, occupied by the local aristocracy, is the centre around which the other characters revolve; in the second act, it is the locus of a struggle between the fading forces of post-war collectivism and the rising tide of proto-Thatcherite individualism; in the third act, it is owned by the representatives of a new class, the economically dynamic entrepreneur – who can exercise their power by exploiting and destroying the landscape (the very element which, in the iconography of the Highlands, is supposed to be eternal). The conflicts within the play – intergenerational, class-based, and between those with radically divergent views of the past and the future – play out against a landscape which has no fixed identity. The play's title characters – in each act, a woman called 'Victoria' (played by the same actress) – reflect the idea of a landscape and a culture that is constantly in transition. In the first act, Victoria is a minister's daughter, anxious to leave a community she finds enclosed and stifling; in the second act, she is an American geologist, brought into look for mineral wealth in the mountains; in the third act, she is the daughter of the geologist and Euan, a local businessman. Her name, in the Highlands, has its own iconic resonance; the image of the Highlands as an unchanging, wild, romantic backdrop was largely created in the nineteenth century, when the area became the favourite playground of Queen Victoria (and, following her example, the British aristocracy in general). In the play, though, the name carries with it no sense of certainty; the Victorias are radically different characters, and each has a unique relationship with the setting of the play. In the first act, Victoria wants to escape from the place (but, as we find out at the play's end, toward the end of her life she is drawn back to it); in the second act, Victoria bears the information which will transform the landscape, but she feels a spiritual connection with it, which for her is linked to an idea of the continuity of the location; in the third act, Victoria both acknowledges the past (she discovers and reads the diaries of her grandfather, who fought in the Spanish Civil War) and disowns it (the play ends as she sets the diaries, her money, and the body of her grandfather on fire – 'I'm your defeat', she says to his ghost (*Victoria*: 172)). Each of them looks at the seemingly inalterable, eternal Highlands, only to find their own hopes and desires reflected there.

In *Outlying Islands* (2002), Greig explores the same territory on a smaller scale, and from a different direction; two young naturalists are sent to a remote Scottish Island on the eve of the Second World War, to take an inventory of the animals and birds that live there. The date, as in *Victoria*, is profoundly significant; the world is about to change utterly, and the impact of that change will extend even to the remotest of places. The island, which has not been inhabited for over a century, is going to play its part in the war; it is going to be a test ground for the possible use of Anthrax in battle. It is not, though, that the island is a natural *tabula rasa*; it used to support a population (whose buildings are still in use, although sparingly), and it is property, overseen by a dour middle-aged tacksman, with the symbolically charged name Kirk (the Scots word for Church – a very apt choice, for such a forbidding, Protestant traditionalist). Robert, the more experienced of the two English naturalists, finds Kirk's attitude to the island (as a God-given gift, which he can dispose of as he wishes) repellent; but his view of the island is equally skewed – in particular, by his naive embrace of Darwinism. Both Kirk and Robert are prey to versions of the same illusion – they assume that they understand the island; they look at their immediate surroundings and see them operating in accordance with immutable laws – for Kirk the laws of God, and for Robert the laws of nature:

> **Robert** Our purpose here is the close observation of nature, Mr Kirk.
> **Kirk** God put the birds here for man to eat.
> And God, in his graciousness, has afforded me the fowling rights,
> That's all I need to know about nature, boy. (34)

After Kirk's death (a stroke, brought on by a heated argument with Robert that threatens to turn violent), the naturalists are left alone on the island with Ellen, Kirk's niece. They are attracted to her, and she to them; Robert sees this, as one might expect, in purely Darwinian terms (she will mate with the stronger of them first); her choice will be informed by and reflect the natural order – on an island which is as close as one can ever get to an unspoiled state of nature.

Ellen, however, has a far more nuanced perspective on the island than either Kirk or Robert; she is also far less certain of her place in relation to it – or, at least, she is aware of the competing pull of the history of the island, the mythology that surrounds it, and the wider world of which it is a part. For her, the island is not a single thing: it is a hated symbol of her uncle's stifling strictness; it is part of a complex history and mythology; it is the place where her desire for both Robert and John shows itself; and, after her uncle's death, it is the key to an as yet undecided future. Under her influence, John's perception of the island changes; in particular, he comes to lose a clear sense of time

John . . . The summer day stretches on long into the night and just as the darkness finally falls so the first soft light of dawn appears on the far horizon. I am aware of seconds and minutes but hours and days merge into each other and wash away . . . (92)

The tension between Robert's fixed determinism, and the fluid, open attitude to their surroundings that Ellen and John come to share is apparently irreconcilable; however, at the play's end, when Ellen and John act on their growing desire for each other, Robert accepts Ellen's choice – even though the implication of it is that he is the weaker man. Just for a moment, all three come to share a perception of themselves, as people whose lives cannot be fixed in a set history, an all-embracing morality, or a determining scientific theory (they come to experience '[the] falling-away of all things' (107), as Ellen puts it). This realization comes with great pain; Robert walks out into the storm surrounding the bothy, and effectively commits suicide. When John and Ellen have to explain his death to the Captain of the boat that comes to pick them up, they do so in terms that reflect the fact that, for all three of them, the island is not a stable, fixed location

Ellen He ran at the cliff edge
And spread his arms out.
John It was typical of him
Ellen And flew.

John Not thinking.
The complete absence of questions.
Ellen He flew.
John By the time we got down to the rocks on the shoreline, the
storm had taken his body away. (112–3)

Robert's death is ambiguous – simultaneously an acceptance of
Darwinian struggle (Ellen has chosen John, rather than him) and an
acceptance of 'the falling away of all things' (something that happens, at
least for John, without thinking, in 'the complete absence of questions').
At the play's end, the island is about to be removed from Scottish
history altogether (as the Captain says, it will be out of commission
for over fifty years). Its place in that history, however, has never been
determined; neither has its place in religion, or in nature. It is not just
a far-flung, bare Scottish island; it is also a place outside of time. What
Victoria enacts on the widest scale, against a broad historical sweep,
Outlying Islands enacts in microcosm, between a small number of
characters in the most remote of places. In both plays, the Highlands
and Islands – an iconic location in Scottish culture – is a territory with
no fixed meaning in itself; a landscape animated, and made significant,
only by the fears, hopes and desires of its inhabitants.

The Fabric of Scotland. *Dunsinane*

Sometimes I think you can be born in this country. Live in it all
your life. Study it. Travel the length and breadth of it. And still –
if someone asked you – to describe it – all you'd be able to say
without fear of contradiction is – 'It's cold'. (*Dunsinane*: 29)

One of Greig's most recent plays, *Dunsinane,* is set in the immediate
aftermath of Shakespeare's *Macbeth.* When the play begins, the English
forces are just about to storm Macbeth's castle (the matter of their
disguise is dealt with in an amusingly laconic exchange: **Sergeant:**
You –/–Yes, sir?/**Sergeant:** Be a tree [10]); but once the castle is taken,
and the English establish Malcolm as a proxy ruler, the country proves

to be far more complicated, and far more intractable, than it at first seems. The usurped king wasn't a tyrant; the invading forces are not seen as liberators – quite the reverse: and the tangled network of social obligations, kinships and rivalries is impossible for anyone from outside of the country to understand. As an enraged Malcolm tells the English general Siward:

> **Malcolm** . . . There are patterns of loyalty between us – there are alliances – there are friends who say they're friends but work against us and others who say they're enemies but quietly help us – there are networks of obligations between us – there are marriages and births between us – there are narrowly balanced feuds between us – feuds that only need the smallest breath of the wrong word spoken to tip them into war –
> There are patterns between us.
> And into that very delicate filigree you are putting your fist. (108)

As Greig has pointed out, the Scotland of *Dunsinane* is close to the state of post-2001 Afghanistan (about which Greig has written – see the short play, *Miniskirts of Kabul*). An invading army, operating from what are in some ways the best of intentions, finds itself embroiled in a situation that is far more complicated than they had even begun to expect; a situation that their very presence only serves to make worse.

The sharp parallels with post-invasion Afghanistan give the play an uncomfortably topical resonance; but the image of Scotland that manifests itself throughout the play is one with which Greig has engaged before. It is the image around which the characters in *Caledonia Dreaming* circulate: it is the same idea of the country that informs Greig's depiction of the hinterland of the Highlands and Islands in *Victoria* and *Outlying Islands*. It is there in other plays that are set wholly or partly in Scotland (see for example, *The Cosmonaut's Last Message to the Woman He Loved in the Former Soviet Union, Midsummer* and *The Strange Undoing of Prudencia Hart*) or those plays in which Scotland and Scottishness features as a significant element (*The Speculator, Pyrenees, Damascus,* et al). In each one of these plays, Scotland is treated as indefinable (for a further discussion of this, see Pattie 2011). It exists, as I have said elsewhere, in relation; only understandable when seen through the filter of personal and communal identity. Like Sean Connery, or like the mystique of the mountains and the glens in the iconography of the Highlands, it is not there: it does not exist in itself – but that absence is given a shape and a location by the people who engage with it. It is a country that is woven, like the filigree Malcolm describes, from a complex, ever-changing network of interactions, and it is those interactions that give the country a shape – not anything inherent in the nature of Scotland itself.

Directors' Cuts
Philip Howard

Philip Howard was an associate director and then an artistic director at the Traverse Theatre in Edinburgh between 1993 and 2007. Presently he is a joint artistic director at the Dundee Rep Theatre. He has directed many of Greig's plays including *Europe, The Architect, The Speculator, Outlying Islands* and *Damascus.*

I first encountered David's work in early 1993. I was doing some freelance work for the Royal Court Young People's Theatre in North Kensington, London and I had recently been appointed as associate director at the Traverse in Edinburgh, and the then director of the RCYPT Dominic Tickell gave me a play of David which was currently being read and assessed by the Royal Court's Literary Department because he knew I was moving to Scotland and that I would always be interested in the work of an emerging Scottish writer. The play was called something like *The Garden* and, while I can't remember much about its story, I remember the impact it had on me: the work of a (for once) truly distinctive new voice – set in an urban park, I think, sparsely written, cool (in both senses), metrosexual, unhappy, the kind of play you would quote, at the time, if you were trying to define the word 'postmodern'. The play was not, in the end, taken up by the Royal Court – which has consistently failed to support or estimate David – but it did, I think, provide a maquette for a later screenplay he wrote for BBC Scotland, *Nightlife*.

When I arrived at the Traverse in spring 1993 I found they were familiar with David and his work: an early draft of his play *Europe* was sitting on the shelves. Ian Brown, the artistic director, and Ella Wildridge, Dramaturg, had given David some kind of seed commission. While they admired the play, Ian wasn't particularly hungry to direct it himself, and, anyway, I had been appointed to the associateship explicitly to develop new plays and new writers. I asked to meet David and he came over on the train from Glasgow; to this day I remember everything about that meeting, even at which table we sat. I told him I would love to take on *Europe* and direct it, and that I would persuade Ian Brown to this effect.

Of course we can't claim to have *discovered* David Greig at the Traverse: he had already had his play *Stalinland* produced at the Citizens Theatre, Glasgow, after he had brought shows with his Bristol University comrades to the Edinburgh Fringe. But one of the crucial things about *Europe* is that it was produced on the main stage, Traverse 1, which was unusual for a fledgling writer – except that it never felt like a fledgling play, demanding a cast of eight and all the architectural possibilities of the huge, open Traverse 1 space, set loosely in a decaying railway station 'somewhere in Central Europe', covering themes of economic migration, a shifting Continent, the rise of young neofascist movements, worklessness, and David Greig's trope of rail journeys; unfashionably, there was even a chorus. I think it's fair to claim that it was *Europe* which put David Greig on the map.

Subsequently, David has said publicly 'If I had my time again, I would call the play "Scotland". That border town could just as easily be Motherwell'. But, privately, David has testified that one of the reason he set the play 'somewhere in Central Europe' is that it enabled him to sidestep the loaded question of how the young, troubled, working-class but unemployed men in the play should speak. At the time it appears that David was interestingly exercised about his own status as a 'middle-class' writer, tentative about reproducing the voice of his characters: marooning them in the middle of Europe obviated the need to reproduce, say, the Lanarkshire Scots of Motherwell. I don't believe David now would be held hostage by such an apprehension. And the original production featured a mixed company of Black British, Scottish Asian, and white Scottish actors, which drew attention to the universality of the setting.

The success of *Europe* brought David a second Traverse commission. *The Architect*, in total contrast to *Europe*, is a relatively hermetically sealed and conventionally structured family drama, whose eponymous anti-hero is, in effect, killed by his own building once his failure as a husband and father becomes apparent. *The Architect* was produced in Traverse 2, the Traverse's studio theatre, for the simple reason that the space seemed to suit the 'closed' nature of the piece, but the box office pressure of its sell-out performance run necessitated a transfer to Traverse 1 for the Edinburgh Festival later that year. That first production of *The Architect* has a special place in my heart as, without it, I don't think I would have got the artistic directorship of the Traverse later that year, but the play itself is hamstrung by David's reluctance to write the central character's trajectory other than through a series of failed interactions with his own family and a couple of key 'outsider' characters (*Lear* without the King's speeches?), so there is a small black hole at the epicentre of the play. Conversely, this perhaps was the price that had to be paid for David's success in nailing the emotional vacuum at the heart of the family?

I didn't direct another of David's plays for three years, but in 1997 we were approached by a partnership of Brian McMaster of the Edinburgh International Festival and Xavier Albertí of the Festival Grec, Barcelona, with the idea of commissioning David to write a new play with a large scope that would premiere in a Catalan translation in Barcelona in the Festival Grec of June 1999, followed by its premiere in the original Scots/English at the EIF in August, with the same production team for both, but, obviously, separate companies of actors for the two countries. In my view *The Speculator* is one of David's least successful plays, but also, sadly, the only play of David's that I was responsible for messing up. Homegrown Scottish work at the Edinburgh International Festival has a long and perilous history because, almost by definition, it will be a world premiere but without adequate resources or timescale; the first of many mistakes we made was putting the entire project together in eighteen months. David nobly delivered his first draft within the allotted time-frame in 1998, a 'rambunctious' postmodern costume drama about John Law, the eighteenth-century Scottish economist and banker who founded the idea of a central bank in Paris, who for a time was the single richest man in the world, and whose financial collapse triggered a global economic meltdown. A play *spectacularly* ahead of its time, even by David's standards, you might say.

My mistake was to lose my nerve with David's first draft, which was articulated more in the style of a 'masque' of the period: a company of actors; a play within a play, possibly even a play within a play within a play . . .; a very 'knowing' attitude towards the historical setting; not necessarily even trying to be a well-made play. Looking back, I can understand my panic, which had a lot to do with the fact that I would be premiering the play in a language I had not (yet) learnt, and my default position was that the play needed to be A Better Play, by which I meant more conventional, if it were ever to work in its very complex production environment. In this I believe I was wrong. The play duly became more of a well-made play; the production honoured the spirit of the original harlequinade and was certainly never just a costume drama. But something was lost – and the terrifying dramaturgical lesson is that you mess with the very DNA of a play at your peril. Ironically, the show worked better in Catalan than it did in the original English back home in Edinburgh.

Fortunately, the next three plays of David's that we went on to do together turned out to be, in my view, the three best collaborations, starting with *Outlying Islands* for the Traverse Theatre's Festival programme in 2002. This play originated as a radio play for BBC Radio 4, commissioned and produced by Catherine Bailey Ltd. I've always maintained that the best radio plays are those that celebrate the medium so well and so single-mindedly that they won't work in any other medium. Maybe *Outlying Islands* is the exception that proves the rule, because it works beautifully on radio, but equally well on stage; and unlike most radio plays on stage, manages to cloak its radio origins – except possibly for a monologue scene (Scene Five) which, for the first year or so of the production's life, we never used. More importantly than any of this, though, is that it's the play where the writer and director understood one another, and the story and the text, more completely than at any other time. For me, it was one of those rare plays that come along where, as a director, you think 'I would *kill* to direct this play'.

In addition, I rate *Outlying Islands* as the play which made the strongest dramaturgical advances during its making, so that's another reason why I think it was the most interesting collaboration between me and David. It was always one of those plays with a missing scene, but, during rehearsal, David added Scene Six, which I believe single-handedly turned the play from being a remarkable play into a great play. It is rare for a playwright, so late in the process, in the life of the project, to be able to reach right deep inside the play, inside the characters, themselves even, and pull out writing which articulates the core meaning, while resolutely avoiding exposition. The Royal Court's unexplained disinterest in David's work was finally breached: *Outlying Islands* was offered a run in the Theatre Upstairs for the autumn of 2002 even before it had opened at the Traverse in the summer.

In late 2006, aware that I would be leaving the artistic directorship of the Traverse twelve months later, David and I began a conversation about what would be the final Festival programme for 2007. Parallel to this conversation, David's work in and fascination with the Near & Middle East had been steadily growing, since the turn of the millennium. Since 2004, he had been working with the British Council's Near East & North Africa (NENA) Region, headquartered in Damascus, on an extensive programme of developing young playwriting talent across the Arab world. By early 2007 he found himself transferring his energies to a play which soon became the one we did that year, *Damascus*.

I think it's fair to say that the show was perceived to be a success at the 2007 Festival, but it still took me and David by surprise that *Damascus* turned into The Show That Would Not Die. It's not – or so I suspect – a favourite of David's, and I think this might be because *Damascus*, along with *Dunsinane* represent a kind of mid-career swansong for the 'well-made play', the point at which, having proved his ability to meet the challenge of the form, his heart maybe was beginning to tug towards the free-wheeling shapeshifters of *Midsummer* and *The Strange Undoing of Prudencia Hart*. Whether I'm correct about this or not, it's certainly true that *Damascus* took on a life of its own, and over which David felt he was not completely in control. In 2008, a year after its Traverse premiere, the production toured to Toronto, Off-Broadway New York, and Moscow. David and I made a substantial change to the ending of the play for this revival: for the final scene, in which Zakaria shoots himself, the impossibility of working with any kind of stage firearm in the countries to which we were touring encouraged us to try a new idea – that Zakaria would burn the script he had written, and which Paul had not taken seriously, in an on-stage conflagration, rather than take his own life; the image of book-burning in an Islamic context seemed newly right somehow. As it turned out, the ability to do fire on stage *well* against the backdrop of North American health and safety laws was more than the production's resources could effectively muster. So we were left with that most frustrating of combinations, namely that the revival of the show wasn't as good as the original.

All the more satisfying, therefore, when the chance came to undo the change, when *Damascus* was revived again in 2009, at the Tricycle Theatre, London, and then, more importantly, on a six country British Council tour to Syria, Lebanon, Egypt, Tunisia, Jordan and Palestine. The actor Paul Higgins, who had been unavailable for the 2009 version of the show, returned to the lead role, and the original ending of the play – Zakaria's suicide – was restored. The tour opened in Damascus itself, but not before a protracted dialogue had taken place between the British Council's NENA Office, the Syrian Ministry of Culture and David and I, requesting several changes to the text and production (most of which we successfully resisted), including the suicide of Zakaria. We conceded gracefully and easily several cosmetic adjustments to the production, for example any use of the image of the President, Bashar al-Assad.

My fondest memory of the Syrian premiere was sitting in the café of a 3-star Damascene hotel negotiating amendments to the text of the play with Laila Hourani of the British Council, including the scene in the play where Paul sits in the café of a 3-star Damascene hotel negotiating amendments to his education textbook with Muna, his Syrian contact. If Laila didn't know that the character of Muna was, anyway, loosely based on her, then it was certainly what everyone else was thinking. Either way, it was a head-spinning incidence of life colliding with art.

The tour of *Damascus* to the world of its setting was a rollercoaster ride. The opening reception in Damascus itself proved controversial: enthusiasm for the production but sometimes outright hostility at the apparent hubris of a British playwright writing about the Arab world – which, and this is crucial, David had warned about all along. I think, in retrospect, that there was a part of David that didn't necessarily want the tour to happen (the part that had written the play for an audience in Scotland, not Syria) but he wouldn't have felt able, nor indeed actively wanted, to stop it happening. The DNA of a playwright is not wired to *prevent* his work going on. In Tunis the play never happened anyway because the Tunisian Government insisted to the British Council that we play the version with the slight changes we had agreed at the beginning of the tour for Syria. We decided this was a compromise too far and that the idea of Syrian censorship leaking out beyond its borders was intolerable. In Cairo, for whatever reason, the show was a huge hit, with queues of audience and a rapturous reception. David had become a less and less frequent visitor to the tour because he was finding the British Council programme of seminars and talks and never-ending questioning about the play more and more difficult to handle – but at least he witnessed the audience reaction in Egypt.

The final performances of *Damascus* were in Ramallah, in the West Bank, and we had always known that we would not be able to bring the actor Khalid Laith, who played Zakaria, into Palestine, as he is a Bahraini national, and cannot cross an Israeli border, as Bahrain is not a country that recognizes the state of Israel. So we used a local Palestinian actor for the performances in Ramallah who was rehearsed into the show quickly on our arrival. David and I had had a soul-searching conversation in Cairo, in which we agreed that, for the Ramallah performances only, we would again change the ending of the play. We were aware that some things, many things, were more important than our show, and that we were unable to ask a Palestinian actor to use a weapon against themselves, even a stage weapon, even in a fiction. It was the right decision.

It's not unusual for David to be described as the leader of his generation of playwrights in Scotland, but it also happens to be true. But this isn't just about his plays, it's underpinned by his parallel status as a leader in a wider sense: he is a public figure and, for example, he has found himself to be the *de facto* spokesperson for a wider Scottish arts community in the current very public row with Creative Scotland, our national arts funding body. But in terms of his plays, the voice that emerged in the mid-nineties has never really left us: a quite extraordinarily inquiring mind, a chameleon-like agility in marrying form to subject, a harlequin's ability to be Scottish or British or European or a World writer, depending on the force behind the particular piece of work. In an attempt to avoid hagiography, I would say that sometimes David is a victim of his own success: he is a formidable multi-tasker, and famously prolific. And yes, very occasionally he bites off more than he can chew and we sit in the audience and think this would have been even better if he'd been able to spend more time on it.

One of the commonest negative criticisms of the early part of his career is that his fierce intelligence was married to an emotional coldness, that simply his plays lacked heart, that they were 'intellectual'. This is totally wrong, but was repeated often enough to be taken for true. Frequently, in all his plays, and not just the early ones, there is a cool, metallic, spiny incisiveness at work, but I would have thought it blindingly obvious that this is merely the work of a writer – and shared by others of his generation that emerged at the Traverse in the nineties – who mistrusts mawkishness and cheap, cloying, surface warmth. You really don't have to know David well at all to know that he isn't lacking in emotion or empathy.

October 2012

Vicky Featherstone

Vicky Featherstone was the first artistic director of the National Theatre of Scotland. In 2013 she became the artistic director of the Royal Court Theatre. Featherstone directed *The Cosmonaut's Last Message to the Woman He Once Loved in the Former Soviet Union* and *Pyrenees*. She also worked closely with Greig while he was Dramaturg at the NTS.

I first heard of David Greig in a post student haze of people I knew trying to make theatre. He had written a play about Byron and Keats in Italy that a few friends of mine who were training to be actors at Guildhall were putting on at the Bedlam Theatre in Edinburgh for the Edinburgh Fringe Festival. I duly went along and was immediately blown away, not by the production or the performances but by the scope and breadth of writing and the ambition bursting at the heart of it to tackle big ideas, fearlessly with wit and intelligence. I was reminded of him again when I was assistant director at the West Yorkshire Playhouse and a colleague Roanna Benn who had worked for 7:84 in Scotland told me about an amazing young Scottish writer at Bristol University and we did a reading of his play.

The next encounter was my long-term collaborator John Tiffany starting as assistant director at the Traverse and calling me about this brilliant new play he was assisting on. The writer is incredible. You would love him. You've got to come and see it. So I went. It was David Greig and the play was *The Architect*. *The Architect* is not mine to write about in this book. It is Philip Howard's, but in terms of my journey into new writing it was one of the first new plays I had seen by a writer of my generation which seemed mature enough to take on ideas that were part of a truly adult world, yet with a playfulness that prevented them from becoming weighty, preachy or, worst of all, boring. There was a fierce politics at its heart, an anger with the Thatcher years, but the story was treated with such emotional intelligence that it shifted something for me in what theatre could become for my generation. And finally when I met and started working with Sarah Kane it should have been no surprise to me that David and Sarah had studied on the same course at Bristol University and were a huge inspiration and support to each other. On reflection I am unsure of the exact detail of any of these events and the order in which they happened is even less clear. What I am aiming at is the inevitability of my path crossing with David's at some point. He was already in my orbit. I really wanted to be in his.

The Cosmonaut's Last Message to the Woman He Once Loved in the Former Soviet Union – Mark Ravenhill (then literary manager at Paines Plough) and I read this one afternoon in the office and knew immediately this was a play we had to put on. It's form – the multi-stranded narrative, with a rich array of characters, was something which a few writers were experimenting with at the time. It was definitely a backlash to the more common hegemonic lead character in a play, frequently a man and a displayed a desire to create amore democratic ensemble experience and portray a complex and detailed world through which stories weave around imbuing us with a sense of internationalism, a search for belonging, the intimate made epic.

It is the story of Keith and Vivienne. A middle-aged, middle-class couple from Edinburgh. They are stuck. He ends the first half by folding up his clothes and walking into the sea. She goes to find out what happened. Although in David's struggle for theatrical democracy it is obscured by the multi-stranded narrative as the other characters jostle for prime position – the cosmonaut of the title, the business man, the Everyman proprietor, the stripper, the orphan. The author's note to the play is most illuminating and David in his own words is always much better than him in anyone else's . . . among other things, this play is an autobiography. Not that I am a cosmonaut (any more than we all are). In fact I don't feature in the play at all. It is nonetheless writing drawn from life. You – one – tends to arrange the events of life into a story which, if someone asks can be told, a story that makes sense. There are, however, those things that happen to us that seem disconnected from our story. A cluster of events which resonate with us, but which don't fit the story we tell about ourselves and they don't go away. They bother us. So this play is made up of some of those things. None of it happened, it's all true and it doesn't mean anything in particular. He gives 'some examples of the orbiting fragments of life which found their home in this play' – staying in a hotel in Oslo where the other guests were part of an international conference on the banning of landmines, the Russian girl in his primary class he made a name up for and had a crush on, Yuri Gagarin saying he had a good look round for god and didn't see him.

Pyrenees, the next play I worked on with David, was a response to a series of commissions we made at Paines Plough called *This Other England*. Inspired by the Melvyn Bragg BBC Radio 4 series *The Routes of English* we asked several writers whose voice we were thrilled by, to think about English language and how it shapes our identity. Until I received it I had no idea it was the second part of the play about Keith and Vivienne. I don't know if David did until he started writing it. It starts with a man who has woken up in the snow having experienced some kind of blinding fit on the route to Santa de Compostela. He has lost his memory. He feels he is British. In a hotel just about to reopen after the winter, with melting snow around, a young woman, Anna has been sent by the British Consulate to record his voice in order to ascertain through his accent and use of language whether he is in fact British and can therefore be allowed into the United Kingdom. Halfway through the play a woman turns up. She is Vivienne. She has been following the man, who she tells us is Keith through Europe as he lives out his mid life crisis. She is dying of cancer and wants to take him to take her home. He feels Keith is boring and is more interested in the man he now is. *Pyrenees* more than any other play I have worked on gets to the absolute heart of identity and voice. It only has four characters, the ubiquitous proprietor pops up again and is a beautiful and painful cry for who we are and who we would like to be . . .

In terms of civic impact, perhaps more significant has been David's influence on me and choices I have made at the National Theatre of Scotland. David was one of the first people I approached when I was given the job as artistic director of NTS, to write a play of course, but also to become the dramaturg for the company. In his typical self-effacing way, David was reticent at taking on this role. How would it be quantified? What impact would it have?

David is a harvester. He harvests stories, experiences, people, moments and as he himself articulated fourteen years ago in the author's note for *Cosmonaut*, he inhabits those events which won't go away, which bother us. He places himself fearlessly at the heart of his work.

At the National Theatre of Scotland he has encouraged and challenged us on what the National conversation needed to be. He has imagined and realized extraordinary pieces of theatre which have defined us. *The Strange Undoing of Prudencia Hart*, just about to start its fourth version and second world tour, started from a conversation where David said he would like to capture an audience who go to the pub. His version of *Peter Pan* saw Peter become a highland pan and set it in Edinburgh with the Forth Rail bridge being built as a moment of huge change. He brought to life Gobbo, the story of the elf whom he had made up for his own children, which toured village halls in Scotland and he has written *Glasgow Girls* – a new musical about asylum seeker girls in Glasgow who tried to overturn UK immigration policy. He recently curated and made an incredible season of work *One Day in Spring*, influenced by his many travels to the Middle East with the British Council. David's impact on the National Theatre of Scotland deserves a whole chapter in itself. It must be recorded.

I can see David in everything he writes – his travels, his personal interests, his family, his friends. Like the mythical and provocative storytelling that he excels at he exists in a place for me which is real and unreal, somewhere out there in the grand scale of the world and at once precise and acutely focused.

Finally, David and I are working on another project together. It has been a long time in the making. He is always diverted by his own brilliance and rather like a cat that sets up home at many people's houses along the street; I think each person he works with thinks he has eyes only for them. I rather like that. But as he says some things bother us and won't go away. And Vivienne never did get Keith to take her home at the end of *Pyrenees*, so there is a journey we still have to make.

November 2012

Guy Hollands

Guy Hollands was the artistic director at the Citizens Theatre in Glasgow between 2006 and 2011; he now is an associate director (Citizens Learning). He directed a production of *One Way Street* and, at the Citizen Theatre commissioned and developed *Yellow Moon – the Ballad of Leila and Lee* and *Yellow Moon*.

The following text is based upon the transcript of an interview that took place at the Citizens Theatre Glasgow on 15 September 2012.

David and I go back quite a long way as friends and as associates from his days with Suspect Culture here in Glasgow. I redirected *One Way Street* for a short tour of Germany, which was the first time we'd actually worked together I think, and we've just stayed in touch through the years since. Also David had written for TAG before – *Dr Korczak* and *Petra* – and he was one of the few established Scottish writers at that time who was serious about writing for children and young people. I was closely associated with TAG for a long time and then became artistic director so really it made sense that the first new play commission that I set up for TAG was for David to write something for us. The play that eventually emerged was *Yellow Moon – the Ballad of Leila and Lee*.

We knew that it was going to open in the Citizens Theatre's Circle Studio Theatre (so it was a show that would play in the round), that we wanted a show that was for the mid-teens age group and that it would also play in schools and community centres. David and I were both keen to avoid what seems to happen too often when you take a full set into a school – the thing just looks terrible and it takes three crew members to get it in and half a day to put it up and you never get an adequate blackout so the lighting is rendered pretty much useless. We felt it was unsatisfactory to try to replicate in a school the kind of experience you could get in a fully-equipped theatre venue. So essentially this was to be a show that could be performed anywhere and also what goes with that is that there wouldn't be any props and there would be a minimum of costume and furniture – and really that was about it in terms of what we agreed in advance. I've never believed in asking playwrights to write about a given subject or issue or to deliver any kind of predetermined message – as sometimes still happens with work for young people.

David brought many ideas to the table and somehow the story of teenagers on the run rose to the top. I think I said that we could afford three actors and that it would be good to keep the playing time within available time slots in the school day. The first draft was for something like seven actors as I recall, was pretty long and had a number of great songs in it, so it was through a process of cutting that we arrived at what we have which is an hour and ten, four actors and no songs. A performance style evolved for it out of the fact that there was nothing, no props or anything, so we were able to change scenes and location very quickly – the piece required that, it was a road movie for the stage.

Clearly I can't speak for David in this, but it seems to me that stylistically something was confirmed for him in the writing and development of *Yellow Moon*. It felt like he was refining an approach to his storytelling that allowed him to cut to the chase, an approach that believed in and relied on the audience's imaginative engagement and their ability and desire to follow fast-moving narrative told largely through direct address that permitted sudden and surprising shifts of perspective and genre. It's an approach that David has deployed with increasing panache in subsequent plays, not least in *The Monster in the Hall*. One of the many brilliant things about *Yellow Moon* is the way that the Stagger Lee/Stack O'Lee ballad is woven not only into the narrative but also into the structure of the piece and I think it was an aim of David's to try to have each scene told in a slightly different way, so that we frequently get to see characters from a new angle. At the time in 2006 this all felt fresh and new.

Then of course on the back of that success we started talking about doing another one and wanting to do it in the same physical context (in the round, available light, no set or props etc). Clearly, there was an assumption that the stories would have a teenage protagonist or protagonists – that seemed important for the young people to identify with. We have found, of course, that these plays for the fourteen plus age range have been hugely popular with adult audiences as well, there doesn't seem to be any distinction there. It's stimulating to have shows that can bridge that kind of gap and perhaps the most vital of the performances are the ones where there has been a good mix of young people and adults. And that can be especially interesting in the round, in a more open space where people can see each other. Particularly for young people – they're watching other young people watching the show and they're watching other people watching them watching the show, so something special goes on in that conversation. Particularly too because David is very clever at reflecting back something at them that is a true part of their experience, and the writing can be quite unflinching and it's brilliant to watch young people witnessing young characters in those sharp-end situations revolving around sex and identity.

The Monster in the Hall came about because David, who lives in Fife, had become interested in the Fife Young Carers – I believe through a *Guardian* article about an award that they'd won for their work. Anyway, he got in touch with them and had a notion to write a play about a young carer. I got very interested in that idea and we got in touch with Frank Chinn who was the senior arts promoter at Fife Council and then together we organized a three- or four-day residential arts programme for the Fife Young Carers. David met some of the carers and subsequently did some writing workshops with the group. One of the lessons he learnt was that the young carers were keen to have their experience inform a fictional play so long as it didn't portray them as victims and that they wanted the play to be funny. *Monster* is a very funny piece of writing that sets ridiculous challenges for the actors and the director – a motorbike chase was about as difficult as it got. David leaned heavily on farce as the dominant genre in the play so we do all the farce door business only without any actual doors. Which actually works surprisingly well.

The shows were both rehearsed here at the Citizens Theatre. *Monster* also had its final week of rehearsal in a Fife secondary school so that young people could come and watch rehearsals and interact with the professional company while we were there in residence. That was a really positive model that I'd like to repeat given the right circumstances and another appropriate piece of writing. Fife Young Carers saw the first preview and fed their feelings about it back to David and the full company.

Throughout the development of both plays, David showed great trust in the company as we went through quite a number of drafts and I hope he felt that trust was reciprocated. He's a most practical writer to work with – I mean, he's open to contributions from any member of the team and will consider carefully whatever's offered and if he feels a suggestion improves the play then he will incorporate it. The same goes for finding cuts in drafts – whatever makes it swifter, more precise in the telling, he's keen on. Also, David has the amazing ability to be able to write and re-write very swiftly without sacrificing anything in terms of quality. We didn't start rehearsals for *The Monster in the Hall* with anything like a full draft, but I knew it was fine, because we had five weeks rehearsal and I know from experience that David will always deliver something that is extraordinarily good.

Both these shows have generated the most enthusiastic responses from the young people they've played to. David really knows what works for this age group – he knows what's going to grab them – and the pace of the storytelling is really important, that you stay ahead, you demand that they keep up and you don't give them a chance to sit back. The direct address is also very important and useful in that regard. We travelled to Macau and more recently this year toured mainland China with *Monster* and even with an audience reading surtitles they were very engaged by it and laughed a lot. These plays have been brilliantly received in performance and the icing on the cake is that a number of drama teachers now use them in the classroom. It's really gratifying to know that these plays are refreshing the canon of contemporary Scottish drama available to young people and their teachers.

Although they are very different stories in tone, in production style and intention *Yellow Moon* and *The Monster in the Hall* are very similar and that's what holds them together. They were a joy to make and to remake. When you have really good writing everybody knows it and is more confident in the rehearsal room – there's little energy wasted on worrying about the quality of the raw material. It's all there, it's just good and it inspires everyone to raise their game and produce their best work.

September 2012

225

Wils Wilson

Wils Wilson is a site-specific theatre-maker and a director. She developed and directed two shows by Greig for the National Theatre of Scotland: *Gobbo* and *The Strange Undoing of Prudencia Hart*.

I first met David at an initial development meeting for HOME, National Theatre of Scotland's inaugural project which created ten new site-specific pieces in diverse locations around Scotland. A few months later, the artistic director Vicky Featherstone, who had been at that meeting, did the most brilliant bit of matchmaking by saying to us I think you should work together and make a show for NTS. That show became *Gobbo and the Adventure of the Watchmaker*.

Gobbo was developed from the stories David used to tell his children on family holidays. He told these stories in instalment, with a new episode each night. It's significant that Gobbo started life in this way, because although he would plan the stories to some extent, he'd also have to improvise, to react in the moment. He was dealing with a live audience, so if the kids were looking restless he'd have to bring in some sudden jeopardy to get their attention – the hot air balloon would puncture and our heroes would plummet to earth, or the evil villain would reappear – or he'd have to make up a really good joke. Because of this, Gobbo stories had an anarchic feel, and a free-wheeling storytelling style, where anything could happen, the opposite of those improving tales which have at their heart a barely-hidden educational motive. He was also dealing with the whole family, so the stories had to work on lots of different levels, appealing to children of different ages and adults as well.

We set out to take all those qualities into *Gobbo*. We made the decision, which sounds so simple but had a huge effect, of never pretending our audience were not there, in fact we welcomed them and their input. We needed them, or there would be no story. We instinctively avoided the habitual formalities of theatre in order to put the children at the very centre of the event, to make them part of the story. So we sat our audience at low tables, with the performers setting up for a party around them, blowing up balloons, playing instruments, singing and chatting and giving out cartons of juice and jammy dodgers. We wanted to be clear that this story was happening in their space, their actual village hall, there was no sense of an invisible fourth wall, and we would just use whatever came to hand to tell the story. The way the performers spoke to the audience was also very natural, very direct, and the kids and adults instinctively understood that we were making the piece with them, as well as for them.

The characters carried their musical instruments with them all the time and sang and played as often as they spoke; at one point the actors improvised the audience's plot suggestions on the spot; and eventually the kids literally became part of the action. After *Gobbo* we had a sneaking feeling that these techniques and others like them could be happily adapted for an adult audience, in fact *Prudencia* in our minds was always Gobbo For Grown-Ups, with a dram instead of a carton of juice. And through making *Prudencia*, we found that our hunch had been right.

Music is absolutely central to *Gobbo* and *Prudencia*. Scottish folk music was the starting point for *Prudencia* just as much as the ballad stories. David is pretty obsessed with all kinds of music, as I am, and any conversation about a new project between us often begins with a conversation about what the character of the music might be. Aly Macrae, who created the music and performed in both *Gobbo* and *Prudencia*, was part of the development of both pieces from the very beginning, so the music was always there. Aly works in rehearsal, improvising and creating music with the company on the spot, so the music is a completely integral part of the production.

There's a musical shape to David's work in a very fundamental way. There is the musicality of the language and the poetry, the shape and feel of the words in the mouth, which carry real energy and emotion. His work also has a musical or rhythmic awareness in terms of form. It's one of the things which enables him to be very bold in the structure of how he tells stories. He readily experiments with form, and there's a feeling that nothing is out of the question in terms of how a story might be told – if the story demands it, it's on the table.

Making *Gobbo* enabled us to think differently about our performers and how they might tell a story, and in *Prudencia* we started developing the idea of what David now sometimes calls the 'troupe'. A troupe is subtly different from a conventional cast. I think of them as a collection of extraordinary performers, charismatic and highly skilled actors, musicians, movers or dancers, who bring their personalities to bear on what happens on stage. They can tell any story that needs to be told, can transform with a word or a movement, and can say to the audience, hey, I know and you know this isn't real, this isn't even TV, but let's pretend together that I'm someone completely different. That relationship, that shared game, between audience and performer holds huge potential, there can be a lot of humour and joy in it, and it can take you to very serious places. Kids do it all the time, so perhaps it was natural that this whole journey started with a show for families.

Prudencia was developed over a long time, about eighteen months. The Border Ballads were immediately and instinctively enticing because they are a slightly overlooked area of Scottish literature, because they deal with the extremes of human experience including the supernatural and because they come from an oral tradition. They were tales that existed only in the telling, passed on by word of mouth and each teller might embellish the tale depending on their audience, their own taste, the opportunity for a good joke or a dramatic moment, perhaps even in response to current events in the village down the road. The link with the Gobbo stories is clear, and we felt that within that oral tradition we had licence to make our own contemporary ballad, inspired by the originals. And of course the Border Ballads exist as songs as much as they do poems.

NTS organized a research weekend in Kelso when David, Aly and I met a number of local experts on the Border Ballads – academics, writers, singers – and went to the local folk club in The Cobbles pub on the market square. A lot of those conversations and experiences are there in some way in *Prudencia*. David swears we got snowed in, I say we didn't – and I like it that the weekend has become part of the mythology of *Prudencia*, a kind of spin-off ballad in itself. Anyway, we met a wonderful group of highly knowledgeable people that weekend, one of whom was Dr Valentina Bold, who told us tales of collecting ballads in Newfoundland, and about how, as a ballad singer, you need to find your song, the song which speaks of and expresses you. It was meeting her which made our thinking take a new turn and inspired David's idea of putting an academic and a ballad collector at the centre of the piece.

We got to know the ballads, Aly sang them to us, we read about them and tried to learn them. As Prudencia's story emerged, we spent a long time telling and re-telling her story to each other, and, yes, we did get snowed in along the way, and whisky was consumed. Georgia McGuinness, the designer, had joined the team by then, and she filled sketchbooks with images of devils and fair maidens, drunk karaoke singers, snow and generously-bearded balladeers. Eventually, quite near to rehearsals, David suddenly said that – of course! – the whole piece should be a ballad, and it should rhyme.

He showed Georgia and I the first section, which I remember thinking straight away was brilliant, and David was off on the bucking bronco of rhyming verse. That's exactly how he described it (in fact, Prudencia talks about it in the play), saying that the verse starts to take you where it wants to go and the writing takes on a real life of its own. The leap from there to realizing that the devil existed in prose while everything else was in rhyme seemed so right as to feel almost self-evident.

Although we knew the story and a lot of what would happen in *Prudencia Hart* already, David actually wrote most of it very quickly, in the corner of the rehearsal room, while we worked on the scene he'd just written (also very quickly). The great advantage of working in this way was that everything we did in the rehearsal room infected the writing, which in turn influenced the way we were working, in a kind of virtuous circle. Everything, the writing, the personalities of the performers, a tune played or sung in a break, a good joke or visual image, were all there in the same room together. You can feel that adrenalin-fuelled energy in the piece now, even when it has been touring for over a year. It's incredibly powerful, a real ride for the performers and the audience.

Right from the start with *Prudencia*, we knew that dealing with weighty, complex ideas and having a hugely enjoyable night out should be one and the same thing. We were interested in exploring ideas around authenticity of experience within the piece (is a beautifully-sung Border Ballad necessarily more authentic than a deeply-felt piece of karaoke, for example?), but more than that, the whole event, the way that the audience engage with the performers and the piece, is a kind of experiment in authenticity in action. High and low rub shoulders all the time at every level of the piece, which allows the audience to bring all of themselves to the event – the part of them that might drink too much and do embarrassing or silly things, and the part that enjoys a serious discussion about postmodernism or good and evil. It seems a more honest way of talking to your audience, to accept the inconsistencies of human nature – and if you allow your audience to be wholly present, they feel and think more deeply. Perhaps it comes down to this – David and I like audiences. It sounds an odd thing to say, but we really do, we respect and we like them, and we want to engage with them as equals – that's always our starting point.

So to conclude, David's writing seems to me as much a provocation or opening out of ideas as an instruction. He has been involved in every aspect of making theatre – he's run his own company, he's acted, he directs. Consequently, there's a profound understanding in David's work that the script is a part – an extremely important, probably the most important part – of a process, which ends up with actors moving about and talking and singing and dancing – and an audience coming into a space – and props and costumes being designed – and posters being put up in the shop round the corner – and everything that goes into making a performance happen, on a cold rainy night in Blair Atholl or a hot night in Rio de Janeiro. He's got a genuine interest in the creativity of other people and there's always a sense that every moment in rehearsal could have ten or twenty interesting solutions. His creativity isn't something he holds close to his chest. He wants to put it out there in the wind and the rain and the sun, part of the world.

November 2012

CONCLUSION

Progressions and Accretions: Organic, Chaotic and Collaborative

In a recent interview, Greig jokingly admitted the drawbacks of his peripatetic style of theatre:

> The problem . . . with my work is that you look at it and think – where the hell is it? – I can't 'take a line' through it – I don't know what to expect from this guy. For me, it all comes from the same place and, you know, it's a big wide road. I'm going forward; I'm just veering around a lot. (Billingham 2007: 92)

Indeed, as that work continues to accumulate one of the critical challenges it presents is merely trying to keep up. Consequently, this book cannot in any sense be regarded as a summing up; it is rather much more of an attempt to map his journey thus far, to look at the ground covered along that 'big wide road'. The terrain is extraordinarily diverse; the preceding chapters have charted some of its many contours but always with the underlying intention of illustrating that they do link up. That is not to say that there is some preordained route that Greig has planned, but there certainly is progression even when it is non-linear.

With this in mind I have focused on the various accretions in the work – these happen, as Greig himself suggests, organically, chaotically and above all, collaboratively. The experiences and experiments with Suspect Culture – in particular the unravelling of plot, narrative and character – bear outcomes that are processed elsewhere, as well as in a questioning of the strategies of making theatre that is ongoing. I don't believe Greig's interest lies in formal experiment alone, or for its own sake; his theatre is too patently attached to a love of language, a fascination with the power of story, an enthusiasm for human idiosyncrasy and a faith in connection, no matter how flawed, as the interview here so frankly and vibrantly reveals. I do think that his belief in theatre as a space for thought and communication means that he is alert to the pitfalls of torpidity and that this is the source of its formal restlessness.

The journey, begun in the postdramatic explorations of Suspect Culture and of the legacies of Brecht and Barker, has taken lots of different turns, some green roads, some well-paved paths, and has been shaped by Greig's fellow travellers, four of whom have shared their stories here. These points of departure open tantalizing questions about theatre and politics, both the politics of perception and the politics of representation. Those questions pertain to Greig's home territory, Scotland, and his role in the flowering of Scottish theatre since the 1990s. Aleks Sierz is not alone when he claims that Greig's work 'rewrites the idea of a national culture' by 'defin[ing] itself as Scottish by its playful attitude to theatre form and by its theatrical daring' (2011: 9–10). Surely the days when Greig could be seen as an outsider either in a Scottish or in a British theatrical context are numbered, if not already at an end. One of the chief insights that emerges in Greig's contribution to this volume is how committed he is to making theatre for and communicating with Scottish audiences, how central that objective is to the way he perceives his work be it writing, adapting, directing or curating. This may be obvious to those who have collaborated closely with him, but it is a core aspect of Greig's practice that has not been articulated so clearly or fully in print before. And certainly there is a good deal more to be said about the role of the audience, especially in the work since 2005.

Those questions also inevitably resonate in the plays that engage with the globalized world and, by extension, the transnational encounters and dilemmas it produces. As Nadine Holdsworth puts it in an essay in *Modern British Playwriting: 2000–2009*, Greig 'is not just interested in setting his plays in foreign lands and cultures, but of opening up conversations about what it means to engage across cultural boundaries and how questions of ethical accountability, human rights and global citizenship make demands on us all – these conversations may falter and provoke intense debate but the significant thing is that they take place at all' (2013). In this volume both David Pattie's and Marilena Zaroulia's chapters strategically take up aspects of these conversations in ways that harmonize with the interpretations to the work I have advanced. Zaroulia's reflections on how selected 'plays respond to experiences of globalization and transnationalism' are based on the premise that the political potential of theatre is in imaginatively resisting both 'the totalizing forces of global capital and banal transnationalism'. Pattie's positioning of Greig's work in relation to Scotland is significantly not a reductive exchange, but rather an expansive understanding of national identity as relational. In this respect, I would argue, Greig's work is emblematic of the cosmopolitan cultural practice that Dan Rebellato outlines in *Theatre & Globalization*, one that is aware of its roots while continually striving for the possibilities of exchange and engagement with a wider world of human concerns and responsibilities.

Alongside these impulses is a tendency towards the poetic that often uncouples itself from such serious issues. Janelle Reinelt goes so far as to describe Greig as 'a poet in the theatre. He creates a tapestry of allusion and imagery through subtle effects in dialogue, such as repetition, elaboration or reversal' 2011: 216). Surveying the work at length makes this tendency noticeable as a constant and sustained quality, expressed in an interweaving of place names, allusions to songs, images of breathing, mountains, non-places and joking references to Tesco supermarkets, carparks and recyclable bags – ever-present markers of modern consumer society. Greig's fondness for quirky proprietors and strange mediating figures, his ironizing of national stereotypes, his playful incorporation of everyday popular culture and his periodic references to Norway as a kind of utopian otherworld are patterned across twenty years of theatrical projects and lend a characteristic tone to his imagined spaces.

Finally, of late, a pronounced development in his recent plays is a turn towards a music infused, archly self-reflexive storytelling that has proved extremely popular with audiences. This too is hardly accidental and presents a field for further analysis. As Richard Kearney maintains storytelling is an act of sharing, an act of sharing that is fundamentally human and has an ethical dimension (*On Stories* 2001). Throughout this book the matter of ethics has never been too distant; it is this stance that unifies Greig's exceedingly diverse work which continues to pose the question of what it means to be human and how to act. No doubt that impetus will continue to underwrite his creative work. The recent plays' lively and ludic oscillation between showing and telling yet again provide a means of transcending certain dramatic conventions and slicing through the spectacle logic of contemporary consumer society to return to something fundamental – the power of narrative to make connections with audiences. The form of these plays, moreover, recognizes the collaborative energies and imperative of storytelling performance in which the author is but a part. Philip Howard earlier suggested that this fascination with the fluidity and flexibility of narrative performance is perhaps connected with a 'mid-life swansong for the 'well-made play'; time will tell. What is certain is that the technique is yet another significant feature in the protean 'geography of the imagination' that Greig's theatre continues to explore.

CHRONOLOGY

1969 Born in Edinburgh

1970s Resident in Jos, Nigeria

1980 Family move back to Scotland

1987–90 Bristol University

1990 co-founds Suspect Culture Theatre Company

1991 *A Savage Reminiscence* Art is Nice Theatre Company: Hen and Chickens, Bristol

1992 *Stalinland* Suspect Culture: Theatre Zoo, Roman Eagle Lodge, Edinburgh [revived October 1993 Citizens Stalls, Glasgow]
And the Opera House Remained Unbuilt Suspect Culture: Theatre Zoo, Roman Eagle Lodge, Edinburgh
The Garden Suspect Culture: Theatre Zoo, St Columba's by the Castle, Edinburgh

1993 *The Time Before the Time After* Rough Edge Theatre Company: The Bedlam Theatre

1994 *Stations on the Border/Petra's Explanation* Suspect Culture: The Arches, Glasgow.
Europe Traverse Theatre, Edinburgh

1995 *One Way Street* Suspect Culture: Traverse Theatre, Edinburgh

1996 *The Architect* Traverse Theatre, Edinburgh
Petra TAG Theatre Company: Schools Tour
The Stronger (after Strindberg) The Brewster Sisters: The Arches, Glasgow
Nightlife BBC Scotland: BBC2
Copper Sulphate BBC Radio 3

1997 *Airport* Suspect Culture: Traverse 2, Edinburgh
Caledonia Dreaming 7:84: Traverse Theatre, Edinburgh
Timeless Suspect Culture/Tramway: Gateway, Edinburgh
[transferred to Donmar Warehouse, London, 17 March 1998, as part of the 'Four Corners' season]

1998 *Local* Suspect Culture: Tramway, Glasgow

1999 *Mainstream* Suspect Culture: MacRobert Theatre, Stirling
The Cosmonaut's Last Message to the Woman He Once Loved in the Former Soviet Union Paines Plough: Ustinov Studio, Theatre Royal, Bath
Danny 306 + Me (4 Ever) Birmingham Rep & Traverse: Traverse, Edinburgh
The Speculator Traverse: Mercat de la Flors, Barcelona [in Catalan]
The Speculator Traverse: Royal Lyceum, Edinburgh [in English]

2000 *Outside Now* Prada Showroom, Milan
Swansong BBC Radio 4
Candide 2000 Suspect Culture: Old Fruit Market, Glasgow
Oedipus (after Sophocles) Tramway and Theatre Babel: Old Fruitmarket, Glasgow
Victoria RSC: The Pit, London

2001 *Casanova* Suspect Culture: Tron Theatre, Glasgow
Royal Court sponsored visit to Ramallah
Not About Pomegranates with Rufus Norris. Royal Court/Al Kasaba: Ramallah
Dr Korczak's Example TAG Theatre Company: schools tour
The Commuter BBC Radio 3

2002 *Lament* Suspect Culture: Tron Theatre, Glasgow
Outlying Islands Radio 3
Battle of Will Reading National Theatre Studio, London
Outlying Islands Traverse: Traverse Theatre, Edinburgh
M8 documentary Directed and produced Siona McCubbin, BBC Scotland

2003 *San Diego* Tron Theatre Company: Edinburgh International Festival

Being Norwegian Traverse Theatre recording for Radio Scotland 50th Anniversary Celebration
Caligula Donmar Warehouse, London
The Magpie and the Cat Radio 3

2004 Works with British Council/Royal Court writing workshops in Middle East and North Africa. Some projects continue until 2007.
Ramallah Royal Court Theatre, London
8000M Suspect Culture: Tramway, Glasgow
When the Bulbul Stopped Singing (by Raja Shehadeh, adapted for stage by Greig) Traverse Theatre Edinburgh
An Ember in the Straw Radio 4 Friday Play (early version *American Pilot*)

2005 Becomes first Dramaturg of National Theatre of Scotland (until 2007)
The American Pilot Royal Shakespeare Company: The Other Place, Stratford-upon-Avon
Pyrenees Paines Plough with the Tron Theatre Company, Glasgow
Tintin in Tibet Young Vic: Barbican, London
King Ubu Dundee Rep: Dundee
At the End of the Sentence Directed and produced Marisa Zanotti, Oxygen Films

2006 *Yellow Moon: The Ballad of Leila and Lee* TAG: Citizens Theatre, Glasgow
Gobbo National Theatre Scotland Touring Ensemble: North Edinburgh Arts Centre
Joins board of Traverse Theatre

2007 *Damascus* Traverse Theatre: Edinburgh International Festival
Being Norwegian A Play, A Pie and a Pint/Paines Plough: Òran Mór, Glasgow
The Bacchae Royal Lyceum: Edinburgh International Festival
Futurology: A Global Revue Suspect Culture: National Theatre of Scotland and Brighton Festival

2008 *Midsummer* Traverse Theatre, Edinburgh
Creditors (after Strindberg) Donmar Warehouse, London
Suspect Culture's funding is discontinued and the company becomes dormant

2009 *Kyoto* A Play, A Pie and a Pint/Traverse Theatre: Òran Mór, Glasgow
Brewers Fayre Traverse Theatre, Edinburgh
Miniskirts of Kabul. The Great Game Afghanistan Tricycle Theatre, London
Kyoto Radio Scotland

2010 *Dunsinane* Royal Shakespeare Company: Hampstead Theatre, London
An Imagined Sarha (by Raja Shehadeh, adapted for stage by Greig) Tron Theatre, Glasgow
Welcome to the Hotel Caledonia (collaborative project) Traverse Theatre, Edinburgh
Gordon Brown: A Life in Theatre (collaborative project) Traverse Theatre, Edinburgh
Peter Pan National Theatre Scotland: King's Theatre, Glasgow

2011 *Fragile* Theatre Uncut: The Vault Southwark Playhouse, London
The Monster in the Hall TAG: Kirkland High School and Community College, Fife
The Strange Undoing of Prudencia Hart National Theatre of Scotland: Victoria Bar, Tron Theatre, Glasgow
Dunsinane Radio 3, Drama on 3
Midsummer Radio 4, Friday Play

2012 *The Letter of Last Resort* Tricycle Theatre, London
One Day in Spring (curatorial project) A Play, A Pie and A Pint: Òran Mór, Glasgow
Whatever Gets You Through the Night (collaboration with Cora Bissett and Swimmer One) The Arches, Glasgow
Dalgety Edinburgh Fringe Festival and Theatre Uncut: Young Vic Theatre, London
Glasgow Girls with Cora Bissett Citizens Theatre, Glasgow

NOTES

Page 184

1. I am borrowing the terms 'as is' and 'what if' from Jill Dolan's reading of utopia in performance (2005), where she argues for a re-evaluation of the affective and emotional dimensions of theatre and performance, specifically moments that she names 'utopian performatives', as potential routes towards new ways of identification and belonging that might inform political action in the public realm. For a discussion of Dolan's theory in relation to Greig's dramaturgy, see Zaroulia (2011).

Page 191

2. Due to space limitations, I cannot discuss Jacques Derrida's reading of Europe in his seminal *The Other Heading*, which offers a useful framework for examining Greig's work of the early 90s. Derrida —who Greig quotes at the start of Europe—responding to the sociopolitical shifts as well as the institutional changes that happened in the European Union in the early 90s, suggested that Europe's task was to move away from Eurocentric ideologies of cultural superiority and instead, become an 'other heading', recognising 'the heading of the Other' and welcoming difference. Twenty years later, Derrida's thought on cultural and national identities in Europe is still pertinent, particularly considering anxieties over national sovereignty and independence that the financial crisis has instigated.

FURTHER READING

Plays and Scripts

Stalinland. Typescript, 1992.

Europe (London: Methuen, 1996).

Caledonia Dreaming. Typescript, 1997.

Petra. Typescript, 1998.

Greig, David and Lluisa Cunille, *The Speculator/The Meeting* (London: Methuen, 1999).

Danny 306 + Me 4ever (Edinburgh: Traverse, 1999).

One Way Street, in Philip Howard (ed.), *Scotland Plays* (London: Nick Hern, 1999).

Victoria (London: Methuen, 2000).

Not About Pomegranates. Typescript, 2001.

Dr Korczak's Example (Edinburgh: Capercaillie, 2001).

Plays: 1, Intro. Dan Rebellato (London: Methuen, 2002).

Outlying Islands (London: Faber and Faber, 2002).

San Diego (London: Faber and Faber, 2003).

Pyrenees (London: Faber and Faber, 2005).

The American Pilot (London: Faber and Faber, 2005).

Yellow Moon: The Ballad of Leila and Lee (London: Faber and Faber, 2006).

Damascus (London: Faber, 2007).

Miniskirts of Kabul, in Nicolas Kent (ed.), *The Great Game Afghanistan* (London: Oberon, 2009).

Midsummer (London: Faber and Faber, 2009).

Dunsinane (London: Faber and Faber, 2010).

Ramallah, in Philip Howard (ed.), *Scottish Shorts* (London: Nick Hern, 2010).

Selected Plays 1999–2009 (London: Faber and Faber, 2010).

Fragile, in Hannah Price (ed.), *Theatre Uncut* (London: Oberon, 2011).

The Monster in the Hall (London: Faber and Faber, 2011).

The Strange Undoing of Prudencia Hart (London: Faber and Faber, 2011).

The Letter of Last Resort, in Nicolas Kent (ed.), *The Bomb: A Partial History* (London: Oberon, 2012).

Dalgety Typescript, 2012.

For information on accessing unpublished typescripts contact:

Casarotto Ramsay & Associates

Waverley House

7–12 Noel Street

London

W1F 8GQ

Adaptations

Battle of Will (London: Oberon, 2002).
Caligula (London: Faber and Faber, 2003).
Oedipus the Visionary (Edinburgh: Capercaillie, 2005).
The Bacchae (London: Faber and Faber, 2007).
The Creditors (London: Faber and Faber, 2008).
An Imagined Sarha, David Greig and Raja Shehadeh, *Journal of Arts and Communities* 2, 2 (July 2011): 133–44.

Suspect Culture

One Way Street, in Philip Howard (ed.), *Scotland: Plays* (London: Nick Hern, 1998).
Casanova (London: Faber and Faber, 2001).
Eatough, Graham and Dan Rebellato (eds), *The Suspect Culture Book* (London: Oberon, 2013).

Articles and Other Publications

'Internal Exile'. *Theatre Scotland* 3, 11(1994): 8–10.
'Plays on Politics: Andy de la Tour, Cheryl Martin, David Greig', in David Edgar (ed.), *State of Play: Playwrights on Playwriting* (London: Faber and Faber, 1999), pp. 62–70.
'Reaping the Harvest of Scottish Theatre'. *Independent* (9 August 2002).
'A Tyrant for all Time'. *Guardian* (28 April 2003).
'Theatre and Prostitution', Suspect Culture conference, Strange Behaviour: Theatre and Money, 2004 <http://www.suspectculture.com/content/microsites/strangebehaviour/money_greig.html>.
'Doing a Geographical', Suspect Culture conference, Strange Behaviour: Theatre and Geography, 2005 <http://www.suspectculture.com/content/microsites/strangebehaviour/geog_greig.html>.
'The End of the World Review'. Diary piece on the making of Futurology *Guardian* (11 April 2007).
Lovesongs to the Auld Enemy: Essays on England by Scottish Writers. David Greig (ed.) (Edinburgh: Capercaillie, 2007).
'Rough Theatre', in Rebecca D'Monté and Graham Saunders (eds), *Cool Britannia? British Political Drama in the 1990s* (Houndmills: Palgrave Macmillan, 2008), pp. 208–21.

Greig: General Profiles and Criticism

Billingham, Peter, *At the Sharp End: Uncovering the Work of Five Contemporary Dramatists* (London: Methuen, 2007).

Cramer, Steve, 'The Traverse, 1985–1997: Arnott, Clifford, Hannan, Harrower, Greig and Greenhorn', in Ian Brown (ed.), *The Edinburgh Companion to Scottish Drama* (Edinburgh: Edinburgh University Press, 2011), pp. 165–76.

D'Monté, Rebecca and Graham Saunders (eds), *Cool Britannia? British Political Drama in the 1990s* (Houndmills: Palgrave Macmillan, 2008).

Fisher, Mark, 'Scottish Playwrights: Heggie/Lochhead/Greig', Divadelný ústav Bratislava (2004): <www.theatre.sk/sk/download/Studio12/skotsko/Prednaska-Skotsko.doc>.

Holdsworth, Nadine, 'The Landscape of Contemporary Scottish Drama: Place, Politics and Identity', in Mary Luckhurst and Nadine Holdsworth (eds), *The Concise Companion to Contemporary British and Irish Drama* (Oxford: Blackwell, 2008), pp. 125–45.

—, 'Travelling Across Borders: Re-imagining the Nation and Nationalism in Contemporary Scottish Theatre'. *Contemporary Theatre Review* 13, 2 (2003): 25–39.

—, 'David Greig', in Dan Rebellato (ed.), *Modern British Playwriting: 2000–2009* (London: Methuen, 2013).

Inan, Dilek, *The Sense of Place and Identity in the Work of David Greig* (Istanbul: Roza Yayinevi, 2010).

—, 'Encountering the Middle East: David Greig's *Damascus*'. *Selcuk University Journal of Institute of Social Sciences* 26 (2011): 217–26.

Müller, Anja, '"We are also Europe", Staging Displacement in David Greig's Plays', in Christoph Houswitschka and Anja Müller (eds), *Staging Displacement, Exile and DiasporaCDE* 12 (Trier: Wissenschaftlicher Verlag Trier, 2005), pp. 151–68.

Müller, Anja and Clare Wallace (eds), *Cosmotopia: Transnational Identities in David Greig's Theatre* (Prague: Litteraria Pragensia, 2011).

Nesteruk, Peter, 'Ritual, Sacrifice and Identity in Recent Political Drama—with Reference to the Plays of David Greig'. *Journal of Dramatic Theory and Criticism* 15, 1 (2000): 21–42.

Pattie, David, '"Mapping the territory": Modern Scottish Drama', in Rebecca d'Monté and Graham Saunders (eds), *Cool Britannia? British Political Drama in the 1990s* (Houndmills: Palgrave Macmillan, 2008), pp. 143–57.

Proctor, James, 'Critical Perspective: David Greig', *British Council Literature* <http://literature.britishcouncil.org/writers>.

Rebellato Dan, 'Introduction', in David Greig (ed.), *Plays 1* (London: Methuen, 2002a), pp. ix–xxiii.

—, 'Gestes d'utopie [rest of title of article', *Écriture contemporaines: Dramaturgies britanniques (1980–2000)* 5 (2002b): 125–48.

—, '"And I Will Reach Out my Hand with a Kind of Infinite Slowness and Say the Perfect Thing": The Utopian Theatre of Suspect Culture'. *Contemporary Theatre Review* 13, 1 (2003): 61–80.

Reinelt, Janelle, 'David Greig', in Martin Middeke, Peter Paul Schnierer and Aleks Sierz (eds), *Methuen Guide to Contemporary British Playwrights* (London: Methuen, 2011), pp. 203–22.

—, 'Performing Europe: Identity Formation for a New Europe'. *Drama Review* 53 (2001): 365–87.

Rodríguez, Verónica, 'Intervention of the Sensible in the Globalized Society: David Greig's 'Aesthethics' in *The American Pilot* (2005)', *Activate* 1, 2 (2012): <http://www.thisisactivate.net/thisisac_roeham/wp-content/uploads/2012/06/Rodriguez-Intervention-of-the-sensible.pdf>.

Schoene, Berthold, 'Scottish Theatre as World Theatre: The Plays of David Greig', conference paper ESSE September, 2012.

Scullion, Adrienne, '"And So This Is What Happened": War Stories in New Plays for Children'. *New Theatre Quarterly* 21 (2005): 317–30.

—, 'Devolution and Drama: Imagining the Possible', in Berthold Schoene (ed.), *The Edinburgh Companion to Contemporary Scottish Literature* (Edinburgh: Edinburgh University Press, 2011), pp. 68–77.

—, 'Scottish Theatre the 1990s and Beyond', in Baz Kershaw (ed.), *The Cambridge History of British Theatre Vol 3 Since 1895* (Cambridge: Cambridge University Press, 2004), pp. 470–84.

Stevenson, Randall, 'Dealing in Dreams', *Times* (27 August 1999).

Wallace, Clare, 'David Greig: Time-Space Compressions', in *Suspect Cultures: Narrative, Identity and Citation in 1990s New Drama* (Prague: Litteraria Pragensia, 2006).

Zenzinger, Peter, 'David Greig's Scottish View of the 'New' Europe: A Study of Three Plays', in Christoph Houswitschka, Ines Detmer and Edith Halberg (eds), *Literary Views on Post-Wall Europe: Essays in Honour of Uwe Böker* (Trier: Wissenschaftlicher Verlag Trier, 2005), pp. 261–282.

General Studies of Contemporary British and Scottish Drama

Blandford, Steve, *Film, Drama and the Break-up of Britain* (Bristol: Intellect, 2007).

Brown, Ian (ed.), *The Edinburgh Companion to Scottish Drama* (Edinburgh: Edinburgh University Press, 2011).

Brown, Ian and Alan Riach (eds), *The Edinburgh Companion to Twentieth-Century Scottish Literature* (Edinburgh: Edinburgh University Press, 2009).

Edgar, David (ed.), *State of Play: Playwrights on Playwriting* (London: Faber and Faber, 1999).

Elsom, John, *Post-War British Theatre*, 2nd edn. (London, Boston and Henley: Routledge and Keegan Paul, 1979).

Eyre, Richard and Nicholas Wright, *Changing Stages: A View of British Theatre in the Twentieth Century* (London: Bloomsbury, 2000).

Gottlieb, Vera and Colin Chambers (eds), *Theatre in a Cool Climate* (Oxford: Amber Lane, 1999).

Holdsworth, Nadine and Mary Luckhurst (eds), *The Concise Companion to Contemporary British and Irish Drama* (Oxford: Blackwell, 2008).

Innes, Christopher, *Modern British Drama: The Twentieth Century* (Cambridge: Cambridge University Press, 2002).

Kershaw, Baz (ed.), *The Cambridge History of British Theatre Vol 3 Since 1895* (Cambridge: Cambridge University Press, 2004).

Kritzer, Amelia Howe, *Political Theatre in Post-Thatcher Britain: New Writing 1995–2005* (Houndsmills: Palgrave, 2008).

Lane, David, *Contemporary British Drama* (Edinburgh: Edinburgh University Press, 2010).

Leach, Robert, 'The Short, Astonishing History of the National Theatre of Scotland'. *New Theatre Quarterly* 23, 2 (May 2007): 171–83.

Luckhurst, Mary (ed.), *A Companion to Modern British and Irish Drama 1880–2005* (Oxford: Blackwell, 2006).

Middeke, Martin, Peter Paul Schnierer and Aleks Sierz (eds), *The Methuen Drama Guide to Contemporary British Playwrights* (London: Methuen, 2011).

Poggi, Valentina and Margaret Rose (eds), *A Theatre that Matters: Twentieth-Century Scottish Drama and Theatre* (Milan: Unicopli, 2001).

Rabey, David Ian, *English Drama since 1940* (London: Longman, 2003).

Rebellato, Dan, 'National Theatre of Scotland: The First Year'. *Contemporary Theatre Review* 17 (2007): 213–8.

— (ed.), *Modern British Playwriting 2000–2009* (London: Methuen, 2013).

Reitz, Bernhard and Mark Berninger (eds), *British Drama of the 1990s* (Heidelberg: Universitätsverlag C. Winter, 2002).

Ridout, Nicholas, *Theatre & Ethics* (Houndmills: Palgrave Macmillan, 2009).

Schoene, Berthold (ed.), *The Edinburgh Companion to Contemporary Scottish Literature* (Edinburgh: Edinburgh University Press, 2007).

Shellard, Dominic, *British Theatre since the War* (New Haven and London: Yale University Press, 2000).

Sierz, Aleks, *In-Yer-Face Theatre: British Drama Today* (London: Faber and Faber, 2001).

—, *Rewriting the Nation: British Theatre Today* (London: Methuen, 2011).

Stevenson, Randall, 'Border Warranty: John McGrath and Scotland'. *International Journal of Scottish Theatre* 3, 2 (2002): <http://www.arts.gla.ac.uk/ScotLit/ASLS/ijost/Volume 3_no2/1_stevenson_r.htm>.

—, 'Home International: The Compass of Scottish Theatre Criticism', *International Journal of Scottish Theatre* 2, 2 (2001): <http://www.arts.gla.ac.uk/ScotLit/ASLS/ijost/ Volume2_no2/3_stevenson_r.htm>.

Stevenson, Randall and Gavin Wallace (eds), *Scottish Theatre since the Seventies* (Edinburgh: Edinburgh University Press, 1996).

Other Texts Cited

Appadurai, Arjun, *Modernity at Large: Cultural Dimensions of Globalization* (Minneapolis: University of Minnesota Press, 1996).

Augé, Marc, *Non-Places: Introduction to an Anthropology of Supermodernity*, trans. John Howe (1992; London: Verso, 1995).

Barker, Howard, *Arguments for a Theatre* (1989; Manchester: Manchester University Press, 1993).

Bauman, Zygmunt, *Modernity and Ambivalence* (Cambridge: Polity, 1991).

—, *Postmodernity and its Discontents* (Cambridge: Polity, 1997).

Bentley, Eric, *The Brecht Commentaries 1943-1986* (New York: Grove, 1987).

Bertens, Hans, *The Idea of the Postmodern*: A History (London and New York: Routledge, 1995).

Billingham, Peter, "'The Bombing Continues. The Gunfire Continues. The End." Themes of American Military-Cultural Globalisation in *The American Pilot*', in Anja Müller and Clare Wallace (eds), *Cosmotopia: Transnational Identities in David Greig's Theatre* (Prague: Litteraria Pragensia, 2011), pp. 166–79.

Brecht, Bertolt, 'A Short Organum for the Theatre', 1948 trans. John Willett, in George W. Brandt (ed.), *Modern Theories of Drama: A Selection of Writings on Drama and Theatre* (Oxford: Clarendon, 1998), pp. 232–46.

British Council, 'Damascus and a Growing interest in the Arab World', *In Touch Magazine: News from the BC Egypt* 20 (March/April 2009): 6–7.

Carlson, Marvin, *Theories of the Theatre* (1984; Ithaca: Cornell University Press, 1993).

Cheah, Pheng and Bruce Robbins (eds), *Cosmopolitics: Thinking and Feeling Beyond the Nation* (Minneapolis: University of Minnesota Press, 1998).

Coverley, Merlin, *Psychogeography* (Harpenden: Pocket, 2006).

Cresswell, Tim, *On the Move: Mobility in the Modern Western World* (London: Routledge, 2006).

—, *Place: A Short Introduction* (Malden: Blackwell, 2004).

Derrida, Jacques, *The Other Heading: Reflections on Today's Europe*, trans. Pascale-Anne Brault and Michael B. Nass (Bloomington and Indianapolis: Indiana University Press, 1992).

Finlay, Richard J., 'Thatcherism and the Union', in T. M. Devine (ed.), *Scotland and the Union 1707-2007* (Edinburgh: Edinburgh University Press, 2008).

Fowler, Dawn, 'David Greig's Conflict Spaces', in Anja Müller and Clare Wallace (eds), *Cosmotopia: Transnational Identities in David Greig's Theatre* (Prague: Litteraria Pragensia, 2011), pp. 136–50.

Fuchs, Elinor, *The Death of Character: Perspectives on Theatre after Modernism* (Bloomington and Indiana: Indiana University Press, 1996).

Graham, W. S., 'Implements in Their Places', in Matthew Francis (ed.), *New Collected Poems* (London: Faber and Faber, 2004).

Harvey, David, *The Condition of Postmodernity: An Enquiry into the Origins of Cultural Change* (Cambridge MA and Oxford: Blackwell, 1990).

Heinen, Sandra, 'The Staging of Intercultural Encounter in *Damascus*', in Anja Müller and Clare Wallace (eds), *Cosmotopia: Transnational Identities in David Greig's Theatre* (Prague: Litteraria Pragensia, 2011), pp. 180–95.

Inchley, Maggie, 'David Greig and the Return of the Native Voice', in Anja Müller and Clare Wallace (eds), *Cosmotopia: Transnational Identities in David Greig's Theatre* (Prague: Litteraria Pragensia, 2011), pp. 66–81.

Jameson, Fredric, *Postmodernism, or the Cultural Logic of Late Capitalism* (Durham: Duke University Press, 1990).

Kaldor, Mary, *New and Old Wars: Organized Violence in a Global Era*, 2nd edn. (London: Polity, 2006).

Kearney, Richard, *On Stories* (London and New York: Routledge, 2001).

Kent, Nicolas, 'Introduction', in Nicolas Kent (ed.), *The Bomb: A Partial History* (London: Oberon, 2012), pp. 6–7.

—, 'Introduction', in Nicolas Kent (ed.), *The Great Game: Afghanistan* (London: Oberon, 2009), pp. 7–8.

Further Reading

Lehmann, Hans-Thies, *Postdramatic Theatre*, trans. Karen Jürs-Munby (London and New York: Routledge, 2006).

Lízardo, Omar and Michael Strand, 'Postmodernism and Globalization'. *ProtoSociology* 26 (2009): 38–72.

Lonergan, Patrick, *Irish Theatre and Globalization* (Houndsmills: Palgrave, 2009).

Massey, Doreen, *Space, Place and Gender* (Oxford: Polity, 2004).

McAuley, Gay, *Space in Performance: Making Meaning in the Theatre* (Ann Arbor: University of Michigan Press, 1999).

McCrone, David, 'Cultural Capital in an Understated Nation: The Case of Scotland'. *The British Journal of Sociology* 56, 1 (2005): 65–82.

Müller Anja, 'Cosmopolitan Stage Conversations—David Greig's Adapted Transnational Characters and the Ethics of Identity', in Anja Müller and Clare Wallace (eds), *Cosmotopia: Transnational Identities in David Greig's Theatre* (Prague: Litteraria Pragensia, 2011), pp. 82–102.

Müller Anja and Clare Wallace, 'Neutral Spaces and Transnational Encounters', in Anja Müller and Clare Wallace (eds), *Cosmotopia: Transnational Identities in David Greig's Theatre* (Prague: Litteraria Pragensia, 2011), pp. 1–13.

Müller, Heiner, 'Hamlet-Machine', in Marc von Henning (ed.), *Theatremachine*, trans. Marc von Henning (Boston and London: Faber and Faber, 1995).

Murphy, Antoin, 'John Law and the Scottish Enlightenment', in Alexander Dow and Sheila Dow (eds), *A History of Scottish Economic Thought* (London: Routledge, 2009), pp. 9–26.

—, *John Law: Economic Theorist and Policy-Maker* (London: Clarendon, 1997).

Nelson, Robin, '*The Cheviot, the Stag and the Black, Black Oil*: Political Theatre and the Case Against Television Naturalism'. *International Journal of Scottish Theatre* 3, 2 (2002): <http//www..arts.gla.ac.uk/ScotLit/ASLS/ijost/Volume3_no2/5_nelson_r.htm>.

Passerini, Luisa, *Memory and Utopia: The Primacy of Intersubjectivity* (London: Equinox, 2007).

Pattie, David, 'Scotland and Anywhere: The Theatre of David Greig', in Anja Müller and Clare Wallace (eds), *Cosmotopia: Transnational Identities in David Greig's Theatre* (Prague: Litteraria Pragensia, 2011), pp. 50–65.

Pratt, Mary Louise, 'Arts of the Contact Zone'. *Profession* 91 (New York: MLA, 1991): 33–40.

Read, Alan, *Theatre and Everyday Life: An Ethics of Performance* (Houndmills: Palgrave, 1993).

Rebellato, Dan, 'From State of the Nation to Globalization: Shifting Political Agendas in Contemporary British Playwriting', in Mary Luckhurst and Nadine Holdsworth (eds), *The Concise Companion to Contemporary British and Irish Drama* (Oxford: Blackwell, 2008), pp. 245–62.

—, *Theatre & Globalization* (Houndmills: Palgrave Macmillan, 2009).

—, 'Playwriting and Globalisation: Towards a Site-Unspecific Theatre'. *Contemporary Theatre Review* 16, 1 (2006): 97–113.

Reinelt, Janelle, *After Brecht: British Epic Theater* (Ann Arbor: University of Michigan Press, 1996).

Robichaud, Paul, 'MacDiarmid and Muir: Scottish Modernism and the Nation as Anthropological Site'. *Journal of Modern Literature* 28, 4 (2005): 135–51.

'Staging the Nation: The Scottish Play', National Theatre of Scotland Round Table discussion, 28 October 2011 http://www.youtube.com/watch?v=NPCfrn9q-5I.

Steinweg, Reiner, *Lehrstrück und episches Theater: Brechts Theorie und die theaterpädagogische Praxis* (Frankfurt/M: Brandes & Apsel, 1995). "Two Chapters from *Learning Play and Epic Theatre* trans. Sruti Bala <www.bgxmag.com/steinweg2chapters.aspx>.

Taylor, Paul, 'Courting Disaster'. *Independent* (20 January 1995): 27.

Thompson, Charlotte, 'Beyond Borders: David Greig's Transpersonal Dramaturgy', in Anja Müller and Clare Wallace (eds), *Cosmotopia: Transnational Identities in David Greig's Theatre* (Prague: Litteraria Pragensia, 2011), pp. 103–17.

Wallace, Clare, 'Unfinished Business—Allegories of Otherness in *Dunsinane*', in Anja Müller and Clare Wallace (eds), *Cosmotopia: Transnational Identities in David Greig's Theatre* (Prague: Litteraria Pragensia, 2011), pp. 196–213.

Wilkie, Fiona, '"What's There to be Scared of in a Train?": Transport and Travel in *Europe*', in Anja Müller and Clare Wallace (eds), *Cosmotopia: Transnational Identities in David Greig's Theatre* (Prague: Litteraria Pragensia, 2011), pp. 151–65.

Zaroulia, Marilena, '"What's Missing is My Place in the World": The Utopian Dramaturgy of David Greig', in Anja Müller and Clare Wallace (eds), *Cosmotopia: Transnational Identities in David Greig's Theatre* (Prague: Litteraria Pragensia, 2011), pp. 32–49.

—, 'Travellers in Globalization: From Here to Elsewhere and Back Again', in Werner Huber, Margarete Rubik, Julia Novak (eds), *Staging InterculturalityCDE* 17 (Trier: Wissenschaftlicher Verlag Trier, 2010), pp. 263–78.

Zimmermann, Heiner, 'Howard Barker's Theatre of Moral Speculation', in Mark Berninger and Bernard Reitz (eds), *Ethical Debates in Contemporary Theatre and Drama,* vol. 19 (2012), pp. 65–78.

Useful Websites

David Greig: www.front-step.co.uk.
Suspect Culture: www.suspectculture.com.
National Theatre of Scotland: www.nationaltheatrescotland.com/content.
Traverse Theatre: www.traverse.co.uk.
A Play, A Pie and A Pint: playpiepint.com.
Theatre Uncut: www.theatreuncut.com.

Newspaper Profiles, Reviews and Interviews

Benedictus, Leo, '"I really, really, really, really . . . hate jobs"'. *Guardian* (12 April 2005).

Billingham, Peter, *At The Sharp End: Uncovering the Work of Five Leading Dramatists* (London: Methuen, 2007): pp. 73–93.

Billington, Michael, 'In Search of Utopia and Hell', *Guardian* (18 August 1999).

—, 'Review of *Pyrenees*', *Guardian* (1 April 2005).

—, 'Review of *The American Pilot*', *Guardian* (7 May 2005).

—, 'Review of *The Bomb*,' *Guardian* (21 February 2012).

Blake, Elissa, 'Love and Harmonies', *Sydney Morning Herald* (27 January 2012).

Brantley, Ben, 'The Curtain Rises: Enter, Reality', *New York Times* (7 December 2010).

Brown, Mark, 'Feature: *One Day in Spring*, interview with David Greig', *Sunday Herald* (20 May 2012).

Butler, Robert, 'Edinburgh Fringe Review', *Independent* (6 September 1992).

Cavendish, Dominic, 'Edinburgh Festival: Homecoming of the God of Parties', *Telegraph* (14 August 2007).

—, 'Playwright David Greig on his Damascus', *Theatre Voice* (30 July 2007).

Clapp, Susannah, 'The Great Game: From Kabul to Kilburn the Hard Way', *Observer* (26 April 2009).

Collins-Hughes, Laura, 'Translations, and Mistranslations, in *Damascus*', *The New York Sun* (15 May 2008).

Cramer, Steve, 'Review of *Kyoto*', *The List* Issue 624 (5 March 2009).

Cull, Nicholas J. 'Staging Catastrophe: The Tricycle Theatre's *The Great Game: Afghanistan* and Its Diplomatic Journey from London to the Pentagon 2010-11'. *Theatre Topics* 21, 2 (2011): 125–37.

Fahim, Joseph, 'In Damascus, Change Is the Norm', *The Daily News Egypt* (2 April 2009).

Farrell, Joseph, 'From Neverland to Wasteland—Playwright David Greig', *Scottish Review of Books* 6, 6 (2010): <http://wwwscottishreviewofbooks.org/index.php/back-issues/volume-six-2010/volume-six-issue-three/353-from-neverland-to-wasteland-playwright-david-greigs-journey-joseph-farrell>.

Ferris, Lesley, '*The Great Game: Afghanistan* (review)'. *Theatre Journal* 62, 2 (2010): 267–71.

Fisher, Mark, 'David Greig and Gordon McIntyre Interview', *Scotland on Sunday* (13 October 2008).

—, 'David Greig Interview (*Monster in the Hall*)', *Theatre Scotland* (14 September 2011).

—, 'Monster in the Hall – Review', *Guardian* (5 November 2010).

—, 'Playwrights David Greig and David Harrower Share a Bill at the Edinburgh Fringe', *Edinburgh Festival Guide* (11 July 2012).

—, 'Review of *Damascus*', *Variety* (6 August 2007).

—, 'Review of *Kyoto*', *Guardian* (11 March 2009).

—, 'Review of *The Strange Undoing of Prudencia Hart*', *Guardian* (12 February 2011).

—, 'Suspect Cultures and Home Truths', in Anja Müller and Clare Wallace (eds), *Cosmotopia: Transnational Identities in David Greig's Theatre* (Prague: Litteraria Pragensia, 2011), pp. 14–31.

Fisher, Philip, 'David Greig', *British Theatre Guide* (2009).

—, 'Philip Fisher meets David Greig, writer and co-director of *San Diego* at the Edinburgh International Festival', *British Theatre Guide* (2003).

—, 'Review of *Midsummer (a play with songs)* at Soho Theatre 2010', *The British Theatre Guide* (2010).

—, 'Review of *The Great Game: Afghanistan*', *The British Theatre Guide* (2009).

Fordham, Alice, 'Damascus Distorted in British Play. Clumsy Arab Stereotypes Mar Beirut Staging of UK Hit Show', *NOW Lebanon* (18 March 2009).

Fricker, Karen, 'Colonialism in Theatre is Alive and Well', *Guardian Theatre Blog* (7 May 2009).

Gardner, Lyn. 'Damascus', *The Guardian* (6 August 2007).

Good, Thelma, 'Review of the Premiere Performance of *San Diego*', *Edinburgh Guide* (16 August 2003).

Greig, David, 'Interview for BBC Religion', <http://www.bbc.co.uk/religion/programmes/belief/scripts/david_greig.html>.

—, 'Working in Partnership: David Greig in Conversation with Isabel Wright', in Caridad Svich (ed.), *Trans-global Readings: Crossing Theatrical Boundaries* (Manchester: Manchester University Press, 2003), pp. 157–61.

Greig, David and Caridad Svich. 'Physical Poetry: David Greig in conversation with Caridad Svich'. *Performing Arts Journal* 86 (2007): 51–8.

Higgins, Charlotte, 'Road to Damascus', *Guardian* (16 February 2009).

Isherwood, Charles, 'A Soldier's Plane Crashes, and Then the Real Danger Begins', *New York Times* (22 November 2006).

Jackson, Kate, 'David Greig On . . . The Middle East, Scotland and Belonging', *What's on Stage* (12 February 2009).

Lawson, Mark, 'Boy Wonder', *Guardian* (7 December 2005).

McMillan, Joyce, 'David Greig Interview', *Scotsman Festival Magazine* (August 2007).

—, 'Review of *Outlying Islands, Betrayal, Mums and Lovers*', *Scotsman Arts Online* (4 September 2008).

—, 'To Damascus: David Greig's *Damascus* in Syria and Lebanon', *Scotsman Arts Online* (19 March 2009).

Memis, Sharon, 'War, Culture and "the Great Game"', *Foreign Policy* (14 September 2010).

Millar, Anna, 'Big Bang Theory Put into Practice', *Scotland on Sunday* (30 October 2005).

Rodosthenous, George, '"I Let the Language Lead the Dance": Politics, Musicality, and Voyeurism, Interview with David Greig'. *New Theatre Quarterly* 27, 1 (2011): 3–13.

'Scotland and England: What Future for the Union?', *Observer* (28 August 2011).

Sommer, Elyse, 'Review of *The American Pilot*', *CurtainUp* (22 November 2006).

Stasio, Marilyn, '*The American Pilot* Review', *Variety* (21 November 2006).

Taylor, Paul, 'Money Matters: Review of *The Speculator*', *Independent* (18 August 1999).

—, 'There's No Place like Home', *Independent* (28 April 1999): 11.

Whitney, Hilary, 'The Arts Desk Q & A: Playwright David Greig', *The Arts Desk* (6 Feb. 2010).

Williams, Jennifer, '"Talking in Verse" Interview with David Greig', TravCast (24 August 2011): <soundcloud.com/traverse-theatre/travcast-david-greig>.

Wrench, Nigel, 'Writing Macbeth after Shakespeare', *BBC News* (10 February 2010).

NOTES ON CONTRIBUTORS

Vicky Featherstone was the founding artistic director of The National Theatre of Scotland. Under her leadership NTS grew into an internationally renowned company touring extensively round the world, with a commitment to making work which is innovative and breaks the boundariesof what theatre can be. In April 2013 she became the new artistic director of The Royal Court Theatre.

Guy Hollands is currently associate director (Citizens Learning) and has overall responsibility for the extensive education and participation programme that emanates from the Citizens Theatre in Glasgow. Previously he was joint artistic director of the Citizens Theatre and artistic director of TAG Theatre Company after having been a freelance director and community drama facilitator in Scotland since the early 1990s.

Philip Howard is a theatre director and dramaturg, and teaches playwriting and dramaturgy at the University of Glasgow. He is a former artistic director of the Traverse Theatre, Edinburgh and, from 2013, Chief Executive and joint artistic director of Dundee Rep Theatre. He is the editor of *Scotland Plays* (Nick Hern, 1999) and *Scottish Shorts* (Nick Hern, 2010).

David Pattie is a professor of Drama at the University of Chester. He is the author of *The Complete Critical Guide to Samuel Beckett* (Routledge, 2001); *Rock Music in Performance* (Palgrave, 2007); *Modern British Playwriting: The 50s* (Methuen, 2012); and he co-edited *Kraftwerk: Music Non-Stop* (Continuum, 2010) with Sean Albiez. He has published extensively on modern British drama, Samuel Beckett, popular music, and popular culture.

Wils Wilson is a freelance theatre-maker and director. She was co-founder and co-artistic director of wilson + wilson (1997–2007), making innovative site-specific theatre, installation and art in diverse locations across the United Kingdom. Her award-winning work continues to explore the boundaries between audience, story, site and performance, through collaborations with theatre-makers, writers, musicians, artists, academics and inspiring people of all ages and from all walks of life.

Marilena Zaroulia is a lecturer in Drama and Programme Leader of MA Popular Performances at the University of Winchester. Her research focuses on contemporary performance and cultural politics and post-1989 British and European theatre. Recent publications include: '"What is missing is my place in the world": The Utopian Dramaturgy of David Greig' in *Cosmotopia: Transnational Identities in the Work of David Greig*, Wallace and Müller (eds); 'Sharing the Moment: Europe, Affect and Utopian Performatives in the ESC' in *Performing the New Europe*, Fricker and Gluhovic (eds) and 'Members of a Chorus of a Certain Tragedy: Euripides' Orestes, National Theatre of Greece' in *Theatre and National Identity*, Holdsworth (ed). She is one of the convenors of TaPRA Performance, Identity, Community Working Group.

INDEX